A Tradition of
ENGLISH WINE

150 YEARS AGO

It has long been a prevailing Opinion that the raising of Vines to any tolerable Perfection in England was altogether Impracticable; and that all Attempts of that Nature would prove Fruitless, tho' their Opinions were founded upon no better Reason than Want of Experience, it being a common Argument with many People that such and such Things are altogether Impossible, because had they been Practicable they would before have been attempted. But the Absurdity of such Reasoning is too trifling to need any Confutation, unless the Objectors can shew from several repeated Experiments that all Attempts of that Tendency have prov'd Ineffectual.

> The Vineyard, being a treatise . . . .
> Observations made by a Gentleman
> on his Travels [S.J.] *1727.*

A Tradition of

ENGLISH WINE

*The Story of Two Thousand Years of
English Wine Made from
English Grapes*

Hugh Barty-King

OXFORD ILLUSTRATED PRESS

To Jenny

© 1977 Hugh Barty-King and Oxford Illustrated Press

Set by Filmtype Services Limited, Scarborough
Printed by Butler and Tanner Ltd, Frome

ISBN 0 902280 47 3

Oxford Illustrated Press Limited, Shelley Close, Headington, Oxford

Contents

Part V The Grape Rush

Acknowledgements

I am greatly indebted to many who found time to talk to me about aspects of the subject on which they had specialized knowledge, particularly Mr J. L. Ward, chairman of the English Vineyards Association; Miss Carole Pottinger, Grape Wine Division, Merrydown Wine Company; Mr Ray Barrington Brock; Mr A. G. D. Heath, Horticultural Advisory Officer (Fruit and Hops), Ministry of Agriculture, Fisheries and Food, Winchester; Dr Francis W. Steer, archivist and librarian to the Duke of Norfolk; W. Linnard, Information Retrieval Officer, Welsh Folk Museum, St Fagans, Cardiff; Allan M. Harland, Personnel Manager, Angel Hotel, Cardiff; Major General Sir Guy Salisbury-Jones, and his vineyard manager, Mr Bill Carcary, Hambledon; Mr Graham Barrett, Felsted; the late Mrs A. M. Gore-Browne, Beaulieu; Mr Ian Paget, Singleton; Mr Anton Massel; Miss Betty Masters, Deputy Keeper of Records, Corporation of London; Miss G. M. A. Beck, Guildford Muniment Room, Surrey Record Office; Mr Norman Kitz, chairman, Friends of Painshill; Miss Jacobs, matron of the Meath Home, Godalming (Westbrook Place); Mrs Mavis Batey, Hon Sec, Garden History Society; Mrs Richard Flowitt, Godalming; Mr P. F. Steadman, RHS Library, Vincent Square; Mr Thomas Shaw, Keeper of Printed Books, Guildhall Library, including the books belonging to the Institute of Masters of Wine deposited in 1972.

I am grateful too for the considerable amount of written information which I have received in reply to my enquiries, particularly from Mr John L. Lovegrove, Custodian North Leigh Roman Villa; Mr Peter S. F. Noble, chairman of the Wine Development Board; Mrs Mary Hyams; Mr George Ordish; Miss P. Pemberton, archivist, Pilkington Brothers; Hon. Ralph Mansfield; Miss E. J. Wilson; Mr R. H. Harcourt Williams, Librarian and archivist to the Marquess of Salisbury; Rev. Stanley C. Dedman; Mrs Alison Hodges; Mr David Harmsworth; Mr C. D. Walker, National Fruit Adviser, East Malling Research Station, MAFF; Mr A. J. Perrins and Mr F. Sippings MAFF, Whitehall; Mr R. F. Farrar, Wye College, Ashford University of London; Mr M. R. Pollock, Deputy Director, Efford Experimental Horticulture Station, MAFF; Dr F. W. Beech, Head, Cider & Fruit Juices Section, Long Ashton Research Station, University of Bristol; Mr J. Cochrane, Meteorological Office, Bracknell; Monsieur J. Gourdon, Directorate General for Agriculture, Commission of European Communities, Brussels; Mr H. A. Baker, Fruit Officer, the RHS Garden,

Wisley; Miss Dorothy Owen, Curator in Ecclesiastical Archives, Cambridge University Library; the National Library of Wales; Miss Patricia Drummond, Royal Commission on Historical Monuments; the Historical MSS Commission, Register of Archives, Quality Court; Department of MSS, British Museum; the staff of the British Library where the majority of the historical information was found; and the county archivists and staffs of the County Record Offices of East Sussex, West Sussex, Bucks, Surrey, Oxfordshire, Kent, Hampshire, Essex, Dorset, Berkshire, Devon, Cornwall, East Suffolk, West Suffolk, Somerset, Cambridgeshire, Gloucestershire, Wiltshire, Glamorgan, Monmouth, Worcestershire and Herefordshire, Lincolnshire, Greater London.

My thanks are due to the following for permission to reproduce extracts from copyright material: The Royal Society of Arts, *Wine Growing in Great Britain*, the paper read to the Society by Major-General Sir Guy Salisbury-Jones on March 14, 1973; Amateur Winemaker, *Growing Grapes in Britain* by Gillian Pearkes; Wine & Spirit Publications, *The Diary of An English Vineyard* by Alan Rook; Mills & Boon, *Let's Plant a Vineyard* by Margaret Gore-Browne; the publishers of *About Wine*, J. L. Ward's, article of February 1973; and the publishers of *Old Men Forget* by A. Duff Cooper.

Illustrations

The publishers gratefully acknowledge permission to reproduce the following illustrations: *pp.3, 4, 19, 27, 57, 80, 117, 146, 183, 206–7, 212*, Miller, Craig and Cocking; *p.6*, Reading Museum; *p.10*, J. Lovegrove; *p.11*, Royal Commission on National Monuments–NMR Air Photograph, Crown Copyright; *p.12*, The Society for Lincolnshire History and Archaeology; *pp.14, 21, 35, 99, 115 (bottom)*, Radio Times Hulton Picture Library; *p.16*, Vale of Evesham Historical Society; *pp.22, 38, 71, 113 (top)*, The Guildhall Library; *p.26*, Ann Rown Picture Library; *pp.28, 29*, reproduced by gracious permission of Her Majesty the Queen; *pp.30, 34*, E. Smith; *pp.32–3*, Trinity College Library, Cambridge; *pp.42, 52, 58, 61*, The Bodleian Library, Oxford; *pp.62, 69*, Mary Evans Picture Library; *p.63*, Essex Record Office; *p.72*, Public Record Office; *pp.75, 76, 86, 93*, The British Library; *pp.88, 96*, The Surrey Archaeological Society; *p.92*, R. Flowitt; *p.94*, Lady Teresa Agnew; *p.97*, The trustees of the will of the late J. H. C. Evelyn; *p.108*, His Grace the Duke of Norfolk; *pp.120, 121*, Seismograph Service (England) Ltd; *pp.116, 125, 128–30, 132–3, 135–6, 138–40*, National Museum of Wales (Welsh Folk Museum); *pp.153–5*, R. Barrington Brock; *pp.160–3, 165 (left)*, Keystone Press Agency; *pp.164, 215*, Daily Telegraph Colour Library; *pp.165 (right), 173, 189, 196*, Syndication International; *pp.167, 188 (left), 190–1, 193, 197, 203, 211*, MerrydownWine Company Ltd; *pp.174–5, 185, 204–5, 235*, British Tourist Authority.

Colour
Facing *p. 118 (all)*, The Bodleian Library, Oxford; *overleaf (left and right), facing p. 119 (bottom right)*, John Topham Picture Library; *facing p. 119 (top)*, Daily Telegraph Colour Library; *facing p. 119 (bottom left)*, Merrydown Wine Company Ltd.

Foreword

by J. L. Ward
Chairman, English Vineyards Association

Although there is plenty of evidence to show that vineyards have existed in Britain for periods that extend over several centuries, no one, except perhaps the late Edward Hyams, has taken pains to find out much about them. Where were they planted? How many acres were under cultivation? Who owned them? Did they really make a substantial contribution to the agriculture of mediaeval England?

This book sets out to provide the answers and to trace the history of English viticulture up to and including the twentieth century, the second half of which has witnessed a remarkable revival of this ancient husbandry. The saga of England's participation in what has been regarded too often as the exclusive prerogative of our European neighbours makes fascinating reading.

England has been producing wine for a very long time. If production dwindled during the last five centuries, the cultivation of vines never really ceased, except perhaps during the period between the two World Wars. Certainly the mediaeval vineyards were more numerous and much larger than history has hitherto led us to believe. The author dismisses the theory of a radical change in climatic conditions as being the main cause of England's viticultural decline, and modern thinking, based on experience gained in twenty short years of vine-cultivation, tends to support this contention. On examination it has been learned that the weather can be equally troublesome to production areas that lie across the Channel.

Not only is the reader regaled with factual reports of the vineyards which existed in the past, the author also gives a very full account of the present revival of English viticulture, which has taken place, quite unaccountably, during a period of economic uncertainty, galloping inflation and a tax burden of quite unprecedented proportions. A 'blow by blow' account of this curious renaissance is given with perspicacity and sympathetic understanding, providing the reader with an accurate picture of what has so far been achieved. It is perhaps significant that our viticultural revival should coincide with Britain's entry into Europe.

Hugh Barty-King is to be congratulated on presenting the story of this agricultural and industrial enterprise so accurately. Time alone, however, can show that what extent the United Kingdom will be able to gain a legitimate place among the wine-producing countries of the world.

J. L. Ward
Horam, East Sussex
June 1977

Introduction

It will take a long time to demolish the belief that the growing of wine-grapes in the open air vineyard-fashion is 'unsuited' to Britain. The first purpose of this book is to entertain; the second is to contribute to the removal of a scapegoat which for long served those who repudiated the breeding of silk worms and the growing of tobacco in Britain. Lady Hart Dyke confounded the former at Lullingstone at the end of the last century, and my wife's Uncle Frank (among others) disproved the latter at Sevenoaks at the beginning of this. If *anyone* manages to make projects like these succeed, everyone can. I have more sympathy with those who boiled the ashes of vine leaves in water and poured the mixture over their heads to cure their baldness, which could *never* have worked, than the experts who, in the face of centuries of evidence to the contrary, continued to insist (by their neglect of it) that drinkable wine could not be made from English grapes. But the stubbornness of both is equally to be deplored.

Arbitrarily to establish a fixed target, based on the full-blooded drink made from grapes ripened in the hot southern sun, and call it *Wine*, which you either hit or miss, and insist that what is made in England misses, is one way of mentally rejecting the possibility that English wine could ever exist. Such an attitude is still widely held. But between what is palatable and what does not need an 'expert' to pronounce is unpalatable, there is a wide spectrum of different wine which can be produced anywhere in the temperate hemispheres of the world with the correct combination of the natural factors at a chosen site and viticultural expertise knowledgeably applied by the individual vigneron.

The natural factors include the speed and direction of the prevailing wind, the incidence of mist, frost, rain, sunshine, birds, wasps, the nature of the soil, the orientation of the site, the declivity of the slope, the proximity of water to reflect the sun, and of trees to give protection from the wind. Viticultural expertise includes knowing the direction in which to plant the rows of vines, the space the vigneron allows between the rows and between the individual plants, the height to which he allows his vines to grow, the depth to which he plants them in the ground, the way he prunes them, scares away birds and wasps, prevents disease, promotes growth, and encourages ripening.

It is a question of reviewing the natural pros and cons of the chosen site, and applying the known manoeuvres open to the vigneron to modify, nullify or amplify them. It is a question of working out the permutations and combinations and devising a scheme which makes the best of all available factors. Those who wrote on the subject in the seventeenth and eighteenth centuries saw that viticulture was an activity which demanded the attention of what they called 'Ingenious Gentlemen'. To-day it is still ingenuity more than anything else which will win the day.

The most important decision which the vigneron has to make is of course the variety of vine he is going to plant. There was a time when there was little scientific knowledge to guide him in his choice. To-day, however, thanks to the researches of Ray Barrington Brock and his successors, no one need be ignorant of what vines to plant in England and Wales, which grapes, if the vigneron has got everything else reasonably right, are *certain* to grow and ripen.

The argument about whether English viticulture works is over. It does. In the year 1977, with the Media instantly communicating information on everything under the sun to every home in the country, there is no longer any excuse for being unaware of the English wine revival.

It was different, however, before the advent of the Media. Means of communication were limited. The number of people who read the account of the orchard at Penshurst, written by that great Elizabethan poet, Ben Jonson, must have been exceedingly few.

> Then hath thy orchard fruit, thy garden flowers,
> Fresh as the air, and new as are the hours.
> Fig, grape and quince, each in his time doth come;
> The blushing apricot, and woolly peach
> Hang on thy walls, that every child may reach.

The 'warm' Middle Ages were over by Ben Jonson's time, but foreign fruit such as grapes, apricots and peaches still found enough warmth to grow and ripen in the sixteenth-century Garden of England. But not many people knew, and ignorance bred myths. It was easy for people to believe that such fruit was 'unsuited' to current conditions; that the lack of it was due to a climate which had declined, when it was in fact more probably due to *people* being misinformed and becoming disinclined to attempt what they believed to be impossible. Attitudes cooled, more than the climate. The passing of monastic life, which fostered ingenuity and provided the time for experimentation, contributed to the comparative neglect of an activity the potential of which remained constant.

The making of wine from pressed wine-grapes which have achieved the suitable sugar content—vinification—presents a whole host of problems of a more exacting nature than vine-growing. It is a stage to which most viticulturists to-day come gradually. The process is mostly natural, but wine-chemistry plays its part—and it has to be right. Knowledge can only be acquired by tuition followed by experience. In England an efficient co-operative scheme helped many viticulturists over the vinification hump of the early years of the revival of the nineteen-seventies; but more of them are now having a go themselves, and finding to their satisfaction that it too works.

This book is not a manual on vine-growing or wine-making. There are now plenty of books about the techniques of growing wine-grapes and wine-making: Anton Massel's *Applied Wine Chemistry and Technology* (Heidelberg Publishers) is perhaps the most comprehensive book available in Britain on the latter.

I am merely a cheer-leader on the touchline. With this book I try to show that those who seek a place for English wine in the world wine charts should do so without reticence or undue modesty, insofar as their claim is supported by a tradition which I suspect the majority will read about here for the first time. The art of viticulture and wine-making was introduced by the Romans who occupied Britain in the first century AD and planted vines brought over from the continent: the *vitis vinifera* was not a native of these islands. The tradition, once established, was never extinguished, though there were times when it was strong and times when it was weak; and the 'common vicissitude of things' caused a quarter of a century of suspended animation between 1920 and 1945. Vinification processes differed widely, and the taste of English wine down the centuries, both red and white, which writers tried unsuccessfully to capture in words (mostly by comparison with known Rhenish and Gascon wine) must have differed as widely. But all of it was drinkable; the part of the mix which never made the grade remained verjuice, non-fermented, non-alcoholic, non-wine.

Much of what has been written about the history of English viticulture and the making of English wine has been guesswork; it is not a subject which has been highly documented or given serious consideration by social historians. Moreover, the meticulous account-keeping of the religious communities, so much of which has survived, has given a prominence to the viticulture of the Middle Ages at the expense of the less well recorded earlier and later periods, and this has given the picture a false perspective. My research has only scraped the surface, and much evidence, which will give the tradition a firmer outline, still remains to be uncovered. But my digging seems to have gone deeper than most. I came across few references of any substance to the vineyard at Painshill for instance, and none to the vineyard at Westbrook. Other authors have drawn weighty conclusions from much less evidence. My guesses, I feel therefore, are as good as theirs, and on occasions better. It is this which emboldens me to fly this kite in the hope that some may be spurred to shoot it down (with more convincing evidence), or better, send it soaring higher—and give the boost to the morale of our present-day viticulturists which they so greatly deserve.

H. B-K
Ticehurst, East Sussex
April 1977

Part I   The First Thousand Years

ONE

Romans Bring Vines from Gaul and Britons Acquire a New Skill

The Roman Occupation

When Alexander the Great invaded Bactria (modern Uzbekistan in the USSR) in the fourth century BC, he found grape vines (*vitis silvestris*) growing wild in the countryside. When, around AD 1000, Leif Ericson of *Greenland Saga* fame landed on the North American coast and one of his crew found vines (*vitis labrusca*) in the interior, they decided to call the place Vinland. The ancient Greeks made wine (*oinos*) from the wine-grapes which grew all over Attica, Thessaly and other parts of the peninsular; and to Italy, where they found vines growing with equal profusion, they gave the name Oenotria. But France and Britain it seems had no native vine. When Julius Caesar invaded Britain in 55 BC, he saw no sign of the plant which was a commonplace back home. Not that *wine* made from grapes was unknown in Britannia; the Belgae who lived in the south of the island had been importing wine from Italy for a century before Caesar landed, in the same way as the natives of Gaul had done well before the Roman Occupation, first from Greece and then from Latium.

After Caesar's punitive raid into Britain in 55 BC the island enjoyed almost a century of freedom from further molestation. For it was not until AD 43 that the emperor Claudius sent an army to Britain in the hope of finally taming the wild inhabitants of that reputedly extra-barbarous region.

Though unconquered, commerce and trade must have given the people of Britain acquaintance with Roman civilization in the years following the departure of Caesar's army in 54 BC. But they were still far from civilized themselves, and military conquest proved no easy task. It was the

Roman general, Julius Agricola, who subdued the country and penetrated as far north as the rivers Forth and Clyde. In AD 84, when Agricola left Britain after six years of campaigning, the legions remained in occupation.

Wine-drinking had high priority in the lives of Roman soldiers and officials. Where there was none to be had locally, the army caterers arranged for supplies to be sent from the nearest depot; and when the Romans found that there was no vine native to the land in which they settled, they sent for cuttings and plants from the vineyards and nurseries of Latium and Greece. In Gaul, they planted vines in the valley of the Rhône, in Aquitania, in Burgundy, on the Loire and, before they abandoned Gaul in the fifth

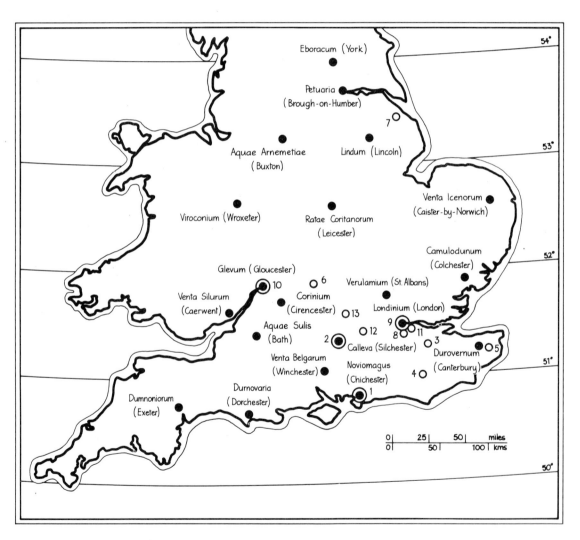

century, they had planted vines around Paris, in Champagne, beside the Moselle and the Rhine, in Languedoc and in Auvergne. The encouragement of vine-growing and wine-making was part of the process of Romanization which included persuading the locals to wear Roman clothes, speak Latin and live in towns. The flow of wine had to be maintained—Falerna for the patricians and officers, Posca for the plebs and other ranks.

Throughout the first two centuries of the Roman occupation the British climate was as hot and dry as 1975 and 1976, and the Romans lived a Mediterranean-style life with daily business conducted in the open air in the forum. When Roman officials intermingled with the subject race across the Channel a new Romano-British community arose. Settlement among the native Britons meant civil administration and a horde of administrators as well as soldiers. They *all* wanted their wine ration, so it became important to supplement the supplies of imported wine by the encouragement of local viticulture.

Though there is little evidence that they did so, it would seem strange if between the last years of Agricola's administration and the year 90, none of the Roman officers and officials who found themselves uprooted from the Mediterranean attempted to establish vineyards in the area of their new posting, and made no effort to create opportunities to practise the techniques of wine-making which played so large a part in Roman life. Indeed by remarking that there were no olive trees or vines in Britain in Agricola's time, the naturalist Pliny would seem to be explaining why the Romans found it necessary to repair Nature's omission and plant some. The wine-grape plants would have been brought over from Gaul where they had been growing and ripening in conditions similar to those prevailing in the latest extension of the Roman Empire, where the army of occupation were doing their best, in difficult circumstances, to make a home from home.

The grape vine is not native to Britain; it was first planted by the Romans. It is likely that there were vineyards at most of the main civil settlements shown on this map, but, after two thousand years, traces of Roman vineyards remain only at the following places:

1 *East Dean*
2 *Silchester*
3 *Ightham*
4 *Cissbury Ring*
5 *Wingham*
6 *North Leigh*
7 *North Thoresby*
8 *Bermondsey*
9 *Londinium*
10 *Gloucester*
11 *Southwark*
12 *Boxmoor*
13 *Hambleden*

AD 90: the Edict of Domitian: Vine-planting is Forbidden in Roman Provinces

There was nothing to stop Roman citizens planting as many vineyards as they wished from the moment the conquest of Britain was over and the occupation began; but in the year 90 the Emperor Domitian put a curb on the *native* inhabitants of conquered territories. He issued an edict forbidding the natives of all Roman provinces to plant new vineyards on land they themselves owned. No copy of this edict has survived and the principal evidence of its existence is a statement by the writer Suetonius, which has been interpreted in a number of conflicting ways. Some have read into it a ban on the planting of new vineyards even in Italy; some talk of the 'displanting' of vineyards in the provinces so that only half of them were left; others assert that vineyards could be planted but only by permission of the emperor. One reason for the ban may have been a circumstance which was to be repeated two thousand years later: the accumulation of a 'wine lake', caused by over-production and under-consumption, the level of which it was necessary to reduce. Other suggested reasons have included the scarcity of grain, the neglect of the arts of agriculture and the need to put every acre of land to corn-growing. Yet another theory has been that there was a need to check the drunkenness which caused the natives to plot sedition. Domitian is known to have relaxed the edict in Asia however, and nowhere to have insisted on its observation very rigorously.

The natives of Gaul certainly soon found a way round the ban by bribing Roman officers and administrators who were 'citizens' and thus untouched by it, to buy a parcel of land which then became Roman soil. It was legal to plant a vineyard on Roman soil, and after three or four years, when the vineyard started to bear fruit, the land was re-sold to the cunning native. If the ancient French conceived and worked such a dodge, there is no reason to think the ancient Britons could not have done the same. In any event it is unlikely that this edict would have caused a decline in vine-growing in Britain, or anywhere else, as it does not seem to have required the destruction of existing vineyards, only that new vineyards should not be planted on land owned by natives. It does not look as if it was ever intended

Before the Roman occupation Britons did not grow wine-grapes or make wine. The Belgae tribe imported wine from Aquitania in Gaul, which they stored in wooden barrels: these laths were found lining a well at Silchester.

to include Roman citizens who were free to plant new vineyards anywhere in the empire they chose.

Vine-growing must have been widespread outside Italy for Columella to have thought it worth his while in AD 66, or thereabouts, to write the detailed textbook *De Re Rustica* in which he gave practical advice to vine-growers. He came not from the centre of the empire, but from its southern outpost in Spain, the area around Cadiz which later became associated with the fortified wine called Sherry.

Doubtless many a Roman who had settled himself into a villa beside the river Darenth in southern Britain would have pored over *De Re Rustica* to see how far Columella's advice applied to Rome's most northerly province. It is possible that many vines brought over from Gaul would have been planted in what are now our southern counties where to-day it is known they can grow and ripen; and that many gallons of wine would have been made from their grapes and stored in a *seria* or jar of the kind discovered in the land of the Belgae at Devizes, or in a wooden wine barrel of the kind whose laths were found lining a well at Silchester and which is now in Reading Museum.

AD280: Domitian's Ban is Lifted

A hundred and fifty years after Domitian's death in 96, his ban on natives in Roman provinces planting new vineyards was still in force—on papyrus at least; although by the year 200 those to whom it could apply had been reduced, because from that year all town dwellers became Roman citizens and so outside the ban.

In the year 276 the emperor Marcus Aurelius Probus came to power. For the first six years of his reign he had difficulty in holding the empire together. He needed all the support he could muster from his provincial subjects in suppressing the claims of rival emperors. One of the ways he used to gain support was to lift all former restrictions on the planting of vines and on the making of wine: it seems he announced that Domitian's ban was at an end.

In every account of English viticulture the repealing by Probus of Domitian's edict of AD 90 is made a major milestone, and most assert that before it there was no viticulture in Britain. As with Domitian's original 'ban', the text of any announcement by Probus has not come down to us, only a statement by his biographer Vopiscus in his *Vita Probi: Gallis omnibus et Hispanis ac Britannis, hinc permissit ut vites haberent vinumque conficerent*— he allowed the natives of Gaul, Spain and Britain (though some believe that

he was referring to the people of Britanny) to have vines and make wine. Most wine historians over the centuries have reckoned that there were no vines grown in Britain before the year 280, the supposed date of Probus' repealing the ban of Domitian.

It seems to me extremely unlikely that there were no wine-grape vines grown in Britain before 280. There is no denying however that the lifting of the ban will have given vine-growing new impetus in Britain, as it was meant to do. The level of the 'wine lake' needed raising not lowering; the Roman suppliers could no longer cope from their side of the Alps. The barbarians were at the frontiers, and if Roman civilization was to survive every aspect of it, including wine-making and wine-drinking, needed to be encouraged. Probus took the initiative by having Roman soldiers plant vineyards on Mount Almus near Sirmium and on Mount Aureus in Upper Moesia; and there was an outbreak of planting activity in Gaul and Spain.

The Religious Incentive

By the second century there was another incentive for the making and consumption of wine, though in terms of volume it played a minor part in this story. Because the sight of red wine reminded people of blood, the essence of life—*sanguis uvae*—it had long had symbolic significance for those who sought to explain the mysteries of life and death, and to demonstrate findings which could not be expressed in words by forms of worship and ritual. The cult of Mithras striving to pinpoint the struggle between the animal and human in Man—Good and Evil—devised rites in which wine was drunk mixed with blood. The founder of the new Christian worship instituted the sacred meal with the breaking and eating of bread, and the drinking of wine, as a perpetual commemoration of his sacrificial death on the cross; and it became, as the Eucharist, the central rite of *every* form of Christianity.

Britons first heard of Christian worship from Gaulish merchants, and from Roman soldiers and officials, in the first century. It made slow headway in competition with other religions throughout the second and third centuries, but Christianity ceased to be an underground cult when the Emperor Constantine made it the official religion of the empire in 312. In the civilized Britain of the fourth century it became the dominant faith. The arrival of Christianity had only a small effect on English viticulture, but it did give a cultural reason for Christian communities to continue cultivating their vineyards after the departure of the Romans with their wine-orientated culture and the arrival of the beer-swilling Anglo-Saxons.

Evidence of Roman Vine-Growing

The evidence of English viticulture in Roman Britain is sparse but not entirely lacking. Sir Harry Godwin in his *History of the British Flora* (1956) gives Silchester as one of the four Roman sites where grape seeds have been found. The other three are in the City of London, at Bermondsey and in Gloucester. Grape seeds have also been found on a Roman site in Southwark, and vine plants have been found near a Roman villa at Boxmoor. The finding of grape seeds at Silchester supports the tradition that this was the part of the country in which the Romans planted England's first vines.

In the second century the emperor Antoninus Pius (138–61) had a 'guidebook' made listing all the military roads which the Romans built in Britain. It gave the name and position of the 'stations' on each of them. On the road between Venta Belgarum and Calleva Atrebatum there was a station named 'Vindomis', twenty-one Roman miles from the former and fifteen Roman miles from the latter. Taking Venta Belgarum as Winchester and Calleva Atrebatum as Reading (though some think it was Silchester), and translating the Roman measure into English miles, this would put Vindomis on the site of the house which to-day is known as 'The Vyne'. It is close to the village of Sherborne St John to the north of Basingstoke, and some three and a half miles south of Silchester. The Latin name 'Vindomis' would seem to mean 'home of the vine' and this is what most have taken it to be in spite of some who claim 'vin' means 'white', and not 'wine' or 'vine', and that Vindomis or Vindonum was a place of refuge (dunum) on white chalk, like Vindogladia between Wimborne and Blandford in Dorset.

The station of Vindomis was a four-square entrenched camp with a villa, which was the residence of the officer commanding the troops who manned it. It is thought that this villa and its garden stood where The Vyne does now. There is evidence of the camp, and Roman remains have been found at The Vyne. However there is, as yet, no evidence of the Roman commander ever having planted a vineyard here to provide him with the wine to which he was accustomed. The house, still on the site to-day, was originally known as Sherborne Coudray and was not called The Vyne until the sixteenth century—so the name has no connection with any possible Roman vineyard.

There were signs that perhaps there had been a vineyard at the Roman villa at Wingham in Kent when excavations were carried out there in 1882. It was reported that 'Roman tiles lie scattered over a large portion of the field called The Vineyard even as far as the highway from Wingham to

Adisham.' (*Archaeologia Cantiana*, vol XV). There is also a tradition that there was a Roman vineyard on the Sussex downs near Chichester at East Dean (Charlton); and locals will tell you that there was a Roman vineyard at Ightham in Kent—where the A25 runs to-day.

However, the Romans certainly planted a vineyard at North Leigh near Witney in Oxfordshire, for on the hillside to the north east of an excavated villa the terracing can still be seen in the morning sun. The field is some 500 yards from the villa and covers more than three acres—not up to Columella's recommendation, but still quite sizable. Little is known about the inhabitants of the villa whose livelihood probably depended on farming. They are more likely to have been Romanized Britons, people of some importance in the native tribe of the Dobunni, than true Romans.

'The siting of a vineyard in this area would make sense' John Lovegrove, today's Custodian at North Leigh, tells me, 'by virtue of the fact that there were at least two other villas within a mile of the North Leigh site. . . . The vineyard, if such it is—and the general appearance of the site would tend to confirm it—would not in all probability have been planted before the middle of the third century. . . . This dating of the vineyard at North Leigh coincides with the enlarging of the first- and second-century buildings into a courtyard villa.'

Evidence of a Roman vineyard has survived at North Leigh in Oxfordshire where this terracing covers more than three acres some five hundred yards from an excavated Roman villa.

Three quarters of an acre of ground on the south slope of Cissbury Ring in Sussex (shown here from the air: the south side of the hill is at the top of the photograph) may have been a Roman vineyard. (NMR Air Photograph—Crown Copyright)

Evidence from the ground is similarly given by Rev Edward Turner in a paper read to the Sussex Archaeological Society in 1849 on the Roman occupation of Cissbury. 'To this evidence of the Roman occupation of Cissbury' he stated, 'the remarkable circumstance of about three-quarters of an acre of land, sloping immediately from about the centre of the south side of the fosse and sheltered on the east and west sides by rising hills, being called within the memory of persons now living "the Vineyard", a spot which must strike everyone visiting this interesting locality as peculiarly well adapted to the culture of the vine which the Romans are supposed to have first introduced into this country.'

'This connected with Cissbury' continues Mr Turner, 'is, I believe, the only instance of the name [the Vineyard] being retained in Sussex. In Worcestershire it is by no means uncommon for fields in the immediate vicinity of Roman stations to be called "Vines" or "the Vineyards".' (*Sussex Archaeological Collections*, vol 3). The Latin name for the variegated vine *Cissus heterophyllus variegatus* should have relevance, but I cannot suggest how.

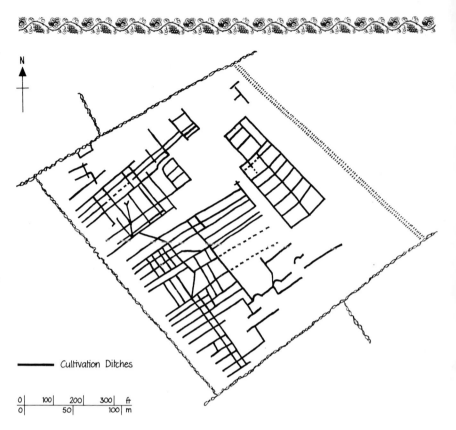

The archaeologists who made this sketch of the system of trenches at North Thoresby in Lincolnshire suggested that the site was an unsuccessful experimental vineyard established around AD 277.

——— Cultivation Ditches

0	100	200	300	ft
0		50		100	m

There are signs of Roman vineyards further north than Worcester-shire. In 1955 Romano-British pottery was found during the ploughing of a field at North Thoresby in Lincolnshire. Examination of the site revealed that the whole field was covered by dark bands of soil, close to which were remains of Romano-British pottery together with animal bones and large stones. Air photographs showed the whole area formed a definite grid which turned out to be ditches dug into the natural clay (see the plan reproduced here). It covered twelve acres on an easterly slope. The ditches which were twenty-five feet apart, ran with this slope. There was a theory that they were field boundaries,* but the archaeologists' report suggests 'a much more likely explanation for these ditches is that they were dug for the cultivation of a crop whose character may be conjectured, although no conclusive evidence was recovered.'

---

* An even more exhaustive investigation was made in 1929 by E. Cecil Curwen into the terraced land and grassy ridges in Sussex which he called 'lynchets', of which he wrote in *Prehistoric Sussex* (London: The Homeland Association, 1929). They were unconnected with vine-growing, he thought.

The system at North Thoresby was elaborate and could only be justified by a crop of considerable value. The Romans planted fruit trees in individual planting holes not trenches, though as the distances between the ditches at North Thoresby were appropriate for a fruit orchard, this possibility could not be ruled out. 'However the most obvious purpose for an elaborate system such as has been described would seem to be for the cultivation of grape vines, and these would provide a crop of sufficient value to justify the amount of preparation involved' stated the archaeologists' report. 'It is tentatively proposed therefore that the site at North Thoresby was an unsuccessful experimental vineyard, established in all probability soon after the edict of Probus of *c.*277, presumably by a land-owner of some substance who could afford to experiment with new crops in this way. The attempt did not last long apparently, due to the choice of unsuitable soil and aspect, lack of expertise and possibly also to the development of unsuitable weather conditions.' (*Lincolnshire History and Archaeology*, vol 2).'

The Tradition Survives in Celtic Britain and Anglo-Saxon England

In 397 the Roman legions began to withdraw from Britain leaving the civilization they had built so painstakingly over the previous 350 years to the mercies of heathen and barbarous tribes, the Jutes and Angles and Saxons who poured in between 449 and 590. Those Christian Britons who managed to escape being slaughtered retreated to Wales, and to the far west of the Britain which was now fast becoming 'England', taking with them their wine-drinking and vine-growing tradition.

When England became virtually heathen again during the Dark Ages, Christian beliefs and rites were kept alive in monastic communities on Lindisfarne, on the island of Iona and other remote locations; but in 597 Pope Gregory sought to stop England becoming too firmly entrenched in her own form of Celtic Christian worship and sent Augustine to Britain to 'convert' the English to the Roman version of Christianity which was shared by the rest of western civilization.

Adoption of the Roman rite did not herald the introduction of wine in church services as an innovation, since the Gallican Rite, which the Celtic Church used, also had the Eucharist with its ritual bread and wine as its central feature; but under the influence of the Roman Catholic Church the monastic ideal took new root in England. Self-supporting religious orders, mainly under the rule of St Benedict, were formed in large numbers, each growing their own fruit and vegetables, breeding fish and making

The Anglo-Saxons continued the wine-making tradition; among the many laws made by King Alfred was one concerning the keeping of vines. This illustration is from a tenth-century manuscript.

their own wine for use at the Mass, for their refreshment after it, and for entertaining distinguished visitors and itinerant preachers. This gave a new fillip to English viticulture which, after its Roman birth and prolonged infancy, acquired the distinctive pedigree and separate tradition which enabled it to take its part in the everyday life of the kingdom.

The growing of wine-grapes and the making of wine was a commonplace not many historians would have bothered to note. But in 731, in his *Ecclesiastical History of the English People*, the Venerable Bede (672–735), who spent his life in a monastery founded by Irish monks at Jarrow, saw fit to record *'opima frugibus atque arboribus insula, et alendis apta pecoribus et jumentis Vineas etiam quibusdam in locis germinant'*—'apart from fruit and trees, horses and sheep, vines grew in many places.' Bede also asserted that Ireland was not without vines in his time.

King Alfred, who rallied a national army to defeat the Danes in 871, was more than a warrior. He tried to maintain and protect English traditions in an effort to make a nation of the families and hamlets which lay scattered across the south of Britain. He was a lawmaker, and one of his laws made it imperative that anyone who damaged another man's vine should compensate him with the amount the aggrieved man estimated to be the cost— *'si quis damnum intulerit alterius vineae vel agro vel alicui ejus terrae, compenset sicut quis illud aestimet.'*

King Alfred's near contemporary, Charlemagne King of the Franks, was equally concerned to encourage viticulture. He gave German viticulture, neglected since the withdrawal of the Romans in the fifth century, a new lease of life by ordering the planting of vines on the north bank of the Rhine. Alfred did not go as far as that, though from the point of view of weather and climate wine-grapes had just as much chance of growing and ripening in a vineyard beside the Mole as on the banks of the Rhine.

King Alfred's grandson, King Edwy, who came to the throne in 955, made what many regard as the earliest written reference to a vineyard in England to survive. This was a grant he made of a vineyard in Pattensburg in Mere in Somerset to Glastonbury Abbey.

One who must have known and loved the vineyard in Mere was Dunstan who was Abbot of Glastonbury in 940. He became Archbishop of Canterbury and was spiritual adviser to Edwy's successor, King Edgar the Peaceful (957–75), one of whose grants has also survived. This gave away a vineyard at Wecet (Watchet in Somerset) together with the vine-dresser. Like Alfred, Edgar made laws concerning the vineyards, which were now a common feature of Anglo-Saxon life, not only in the growing monastic communities—there were forty Benedictine monasteries in England in the reign of Edgar—but on the great family estates of the nobility. For this there is plenty of evidence.

In the twelfth century William of Malmesbury, who lived most of his life in Gloucestershire, looked back on the Anglo-Saxon scene in his Latin *Chronicle of the Kings of England (De Gestis Pontificum Anglorum)*. 'The Vale of Gloucester' he wrote (in William Camden's translation),

> yields plenty of corn and fruit. . . . Here you may behold highways and publick roads full of fruit trees not planted but growing naturally. The earth bears fruit of its own accord, much exceeding others both in taste and beauty, many sorts of which continue fresh the year round, and serve the owner till he is supply'd by a new increase. No county in England has so many or so good vineyards as this; either for fertility or for sweetness of the grape. The wine has in it no unpleasant tartness or eagerness, and is little inferior to the French in its sweetness.

Another Gloucestershire vineyard described by William of Malmesbury was one at North Hamlets* which was part of the garden of the Abbot of Gloucester's house just outside the city. He also described a vineyard at Thorney in the Fens near Peterborough: 'There not even the smallest piece of ground is unproductive; the land is covered with vines which spread over the ground and grow up high on supporting posts'—'*nulla ibi vel exigua terrae se subigit; hic praetexitur ager vineis quae vel per terram repunt vel per bajulos palos in celsum surgunt*'.

---

* Was this the hamlet called 'the Vineyard' which the historian Sir Robert Atkyns described in 1712 as lying on the rising ground near the site of the large mansion built in 1381 for the Abbot of St Peters? The house had been burnt down by the eighteenth century, but the rest of the property had continued as domestic land until the Dissolution when both vineyard and park were granted to the Bishop of Gloucester.

The Norman Conquest

Although Anglo-Saxon viticulture had only a tenuous relationship with the Church, it was to its advantage that Canute, the Dane who usurped the throne of England in 1017, was nonetheless a good Christian, and that the end of paganism came with the accession of the pious but weak Edward the Confessor in 1042, the last of King Alfred's house. The Normans were Christians and the conquest of England did not involve the destruction of monastery vineyards and castle wineries. When they pushed as far north as Ely they saw so many vines they called the area L'Isle des Vignes, and left them to grow and ripen, as they had already done for so long, for the benefit of present and future generations.

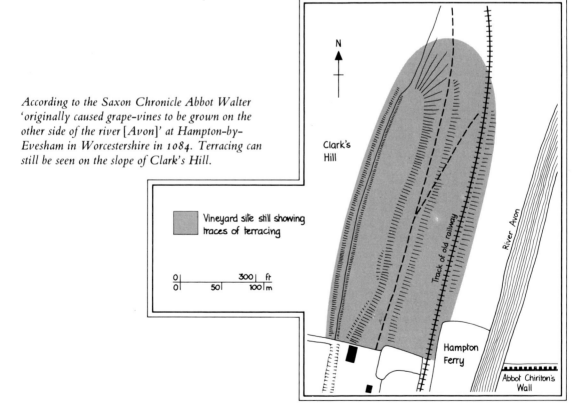

According to the Saxon Chronicle Abbot Walter 'originally caused grape-vines to be grown on the other side of the river [Avon]' at Hampton-by-Evesham in Worcestershire in 1084. Terracing can still be seen on the slope of Clark's Hill.

N

Clark's Hill

Vineyard site still showing traces of terracing

0   300 ft
0   50   100 m

Track of old railway

River Avon

Hampton Ferry

Abbot Chiriton's Wall

The arrival of the Normans from across the English Channel signalled the planting of wine-grapes by nobles, farmers and monks more intensively than ever. During the reign of William the Conqueror churches, monasteries and convents were built all over England, each with a corner of land set apart for the culture of vines and wine-grapes from which to make sacramental wine. They were endowed by the Norman barons, anxious to curry favour with their king, to demonstrate their piety and allegiance, and to make sure that by saving their souls they won the coveted place in the Christian heaven.

The Normans, who became the ruling class of England, introduced French viticultural traditions to the conquered country. One of the earliest Anglo-Norman vineyards seems to have been on the site where the army of Harold, the last Anglo-Saxon king, was defeated. William Lambarde wrote in *A Perambulation of Kent* (1570) 'History hath mention that there was about that tyme [the Norman invasion] great store of Vines at Santlac (near to Battel in Sussex)'. It will have been one of many vineyards inspired by the new regime which began in 1066.

A typical post-Conquest plantation was the vineyard which monks established in 1084 at Hampton-by-Evesham in Worcestershire. The Saxon Chronicle relates it was Abbot Walter 'who originally caused grape-vines to be grown on the other side of the river [Avon]' at Hampton. The traditional site is north of Great Hampton on the slope of Clarks Hill overlooking the river at Hampton Ferry which leads to Abbot Chiriton's Wall. To-day the lower parts of this slope have been obscured by a farm track, a railway line and a caravan site, yet traces of terracing can still be seen. Towards the top of the rise they are still more noticeable. Use of the land for growing vines, leaving the pattern on the ground which has survived to to-day, continued for over a century. It is known that in 1216 officials of the abbey included a Warden of the Garden and Vineyard; though it had been put down to grass by 1535 when the *Valor ecclesiasticus* recorded 'rent of pasture called le Wynyarde . . . 23s 4d'.

Terraces of course do not guarantee vineyards; and there is also the hazard that someone has misread the Latin word 'vivaria' for 'vinaria', and in translation put 'vineyards' where he should have written 'fishponds'. The reference to vineyards at Chaddesley Corbet in north Worcestershire in John West's book *Village Records* is quite certainly such a misreading, for, as C. J. Bond of Oxfordshire County Museum points out to me, the fishponds are still clearly visible on the ground in 1977. It may be, too, that some of the vineyards listed in Buchanan's Worcestershire volume in *The Land of Britain*, published by the Land Utilization Survey, derive from a similar misapprehension.

The Domesday Record

A good, though probably not a full, picture of the extent of the vineyards being cultivated in England at the end of the eleventh century was given in the Domesday Survey which King William ordered to be made in 1080 and 1086—when the population of Britain was about three million. If one excludes Holborn, which is mentioned in association with a vineyard without actually stating whether there was one in that locality, there were forty-two entries recording vineyards, comprising forty-five place names in fourteen counties (regarding Middlesex and Greater London as one):

1 : Somerset
    1 : Glastonbury
    2 : Meare
    3 : Panborough
    4 : North Curry
    5 : ⎧ Muchelney
    6 : ⎨ Midelney
    7 : ⎩ Thorney

2 : Gloucestershire
    8 : Stonehouse

3 : Wiltshire
    9 : Lacock
    10 : Wilcot
    11 : Tollard Royal
    12 : Bradford-on-Avon

4 : Dorset
    13 : Wootton
    14 : Durweston

5 : Worcestershire
    15 : Hampton-by-Evesham

6 : Bedfordshire
    16 : Eaton Socon

7 : Cambridgeshire
    17 : Ely

8 : Suffolk
    18 : Clare
    19 : Ixworth
    20 : Barking
    21 : Lavenham

9 : Essex
    22 : Rayleigh
    23 : Hedingham
    24 : Belchamp
    25 : Waltham
    26 : Mundon
    27 : Ashdon
    28 : ⎰ Stambourne
    29 : ⎱ Toppesfield
    30 : Stebbing
    31 : Debden

10 : Buckinghamshire
    32 : Iver

11 : Berkshire
    33 : Bisham

12 : Kent
    34 : Chart Sutton
    35 : Chislet
    36 : Leeds

13: *Hertfordshire*
  37: Standon
  38: Ware
  39: Berkhamsted

14: *Middlesex (Greater London)*
  40: Colham
  41: Harmondsworth

42: Kempton
43: Kensington
44: Staines
45: Westminster (Chenetone)
(46: Holborn)

When they made their survey in 1086, the Domesday Commissioners recorded vineyards at forty-six places in England. The place-names are listed in the text.

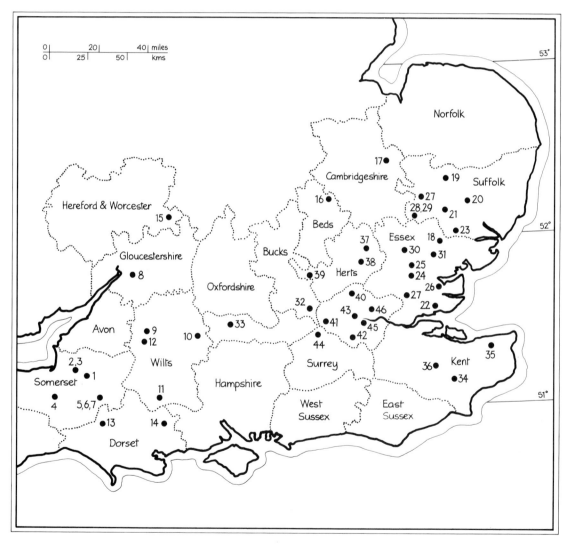

The two entries which name more than one vineyard are bracketed together. These are the three island sites which were the fief of the abbey of Muchelney in Somerset, namely Muchelney itself, Midelney and Thorney; and Stambourne and Toppesfield in Essex. The leading authority on the survey, Sir Henry Ellis, who wrote *A General Introduction to Domesday Book* in 1833 was of the opinion that:

> From the entries in the Survey and from other authorities we gather that in the Norman times few of the great monasteries were without their vineyards. . . . Other proofs beside those which Domesday affords might readily be brought that wine of native growth was formerly used in England. The quantity, however, produced never could have been sufficient for consumption of the inhabitants; and its inferiority is probably a better reason for having been supplanted by foreign produce than any stipulated destruction of the vines by treaty [he was refuting the suggestion that England had made a treaty with France agreeing to do this]. The encouragement of the vine as a fruit has continued in England at all periods.

Ellis was quite sure in his own mind that there was a distinction between orchards and vineyards in ancient documents.

The Domesday surveyors put the size of the vineyard on four occasions in acres, but in every other case in the measure on which no one can agree its modern equivalent: *arpenni*, translated into English variously as 'arpents' 'arpends' and 'arpennies'. It was probably equivalent to 100 perches square.

Often the French arpent was used to measure the vineyard and the English acre the pasture. At Leeds in Kent—Ledani Castrum—which William the Conqueror gave to his half-brother Odo, Bishop of Baieux, the survey recorded two arpents of vineyard and eight acres of meadow. Among the possessions of the Church of Glastonbury in Somerset there were three arpents of vineyard at Glastonbury itself (on Weary-All Hill and still retaining its designation as a vineyard as late as 1894); and in the manor adjoining an island called Meare there were sixty acres of land and two arpents of vineyard. The old ruined wall of this vineyard still stood in 1894 together with some of the stone projections to which the vines had been fastened. 'Another island belongs thereto' stated the Domesday Survey 'which is called Padenebene; there are six acres of land and three arpents of vineyard.' These two places, Meare and Pamborough, are close to Glastonbury, and they must be the vineyards given by King Edwy in the tenth century. Both belonged to the abbey.

The four vineyards measured in acres were at Durweston in Dorset, belonging to Aiulf the Chamberlain who became Sheriff of Dorset and who owned another vineyard at Tollard Royal; Lacock run by Edward the Sheriff of Wiltshire; the royal manor of North Curry in Somerset; and at

The people of Anglo-Saxon and Norman England made wine from wine-grapes grown on south-facing hillsides and wine was drunk by everyone in the kingdom except the very poor.

East Socon in Bedfordshire. The largest in the survey was the one which formed part of the possessions of Henry de Ferrers at Bisham Manor in Berkshire. This was twelve arpents, and that at Belchamp in Essex was eleven, at Waltham ten, at Kempton eight. Most of the vineyards measured two to three arpents. Only one had its yield recorded, that at Rayleigh in Essex: 'twenty muids (*modios*) if it does well (*si bene procedit*)'. A modio was thirty-six gallons. The vineyard at Wilcot in Wiltshire however was described as 'good'—*vinea bona*. The surveyors made a point of indicating which vineyards were new: the one at Hampton-by-Evesham was *vinea novella* for instance, being planted by the monks of Evesham in 1084, two years before the Survey. Those at Kempton, at Chenetone in the village of Westminster, and the one on Hugh de Grentmaisent's manor at Ware were *noviter plantatae* (newly planted).

It is unlikely that the only vineyards in existence at the time of the Domesday Survey were those which rated a mention. It is reckoned for instance that there was a small vineyard within the precincts of the Tower of London, and it is odd that only one, Stonehouse, was recorded in the famous vine-growing county of Gloucestershire. It is probable that in fact the county had many vineyards in the eleventh century both enclosed and unenclosed; Stonehouse would have been well known in the district, for before the Conquest it had belonged to a big landowner called Tovi, though by 1086 it had been acquired by one William de Ow. It was interestingly near to the Roman settlements of Frocester and Woodchester. 'There could be few warmer spots in the county' remarked Canon Henry Nicholson Ellacombe, vicar and gardener at Bitton in Gloucestershire who made a study of English vineyards in the 1890s, 'than the south-western slope of the hill above Stonehouse. . . . About a mile and half north of Stonehouse is a farm which bears [in 1890] the name of Vinegar Hill Farm; it is now and probably always has been, in the Parish of Standish, but the name is interesting as testimony to the cultivation of the wine in the immediate neighbourhood of the spot where the Domesday Commissioners found it.'

Domesday made no mention of any vines in Staffordshire or, more surprisingly, in Hampshire. But it did record that one Alward, the holder of an estate at Lomer in the latter county, was paying ten sesters of wine in 1066, but did not state whether it was his own produce. It was presumably some kind of feudal tax. There was no mention in Domesday of a vineyard in Surrey, but a certain Walter, a sub-tenant at Wandsworth was described as *vinitor*, a vine-dresser or vineyard keeper. An entry regarding William Camerarius did not make it clear whether he was actually running a vineyard in Holborn, but in 1833 Sir Henry Ellis gave him the benefit of the doubt.

Essex had the largest number of vineyards in the survey, covering at least forty-two and a half arpents, a fifth of the total. I make it nine vineyards, though Miller Christy who wrote a piece on 'Essex as a Wine-

The high-walled garden at Castle Hedingham may be the site of one of the many Domesday Book vineyards in Essex. This is a later engraving of Castle Hedingham where, in the eleventh century, Aubrey de Vere owned a vineyard.

Producing County' in *The Essex Naturalist* (vol XI, 1899) made it eight. He excluded Ashdon. Most of the Essex vineyards seem to have been planted since the days of Edward the Confessor, and thirteen arpents had not yet begun to bear when the Domesday commissioners paid their visit nineteen years after the Conquest. Ranulf Peverel's vineyards at Debden and Stebbing were recent plantations as only half the area was producing fruit. The whereabouts of 'Belcamp' is not entirely clear, but it was probably either Belchamp Walter or Hatfield Broad Oak (Down Hall).

Horace Round, who made a study of the Essex vineyards in the Domesday Survey at the beginning of this century, considered Suain's vineyard at Rayleigh the most interesting of all those mentioned because of the reference to the yield. Both the park and the vineyard, he pointed out, were new—as new as the castle which Suain had built there.

It was the story of the Roman Occupation all over again—except that between the Roman and Norman invasions there had never been a time when England had not had its vines and its wine. Apart from anything else, once planted it was difficult to get rid of them. Horace Round said that in the middle of the eighteenth century wild vines bearing red grapes were still visible on the site of the Domesday vineyard at Castle Hedingham, Aubrey de Vere's seat—'the still lingering descendants of the vineyard of its Domesday lord'. The Domesday vineyard at Chislet in Kent, which was given by King Ethelbert to the Prior of the Monastery of St Augustine on its foundation in 605, had an even longer life, for there is mention of it still flourishing in 1434.

Vineyards were a good long-term investment in the Middle Ages as they are now; and particularly if undertaken on a big scale. Once planted, the life of a plant on its own root—no grafting nonsense then—was a century or more. The expertise was passed on by a pluralist landlord, attracted by the ease and reward of vine-growing, from an estate in one part of England to an estate in another. The monasteries and convents were fixtures; but the barons were given manors all over the kingdom. If it was possible successfully to grow wine-grapes vineyard-fashion in Somerset it could be done equally successfully in Kent. The vineyard of the manor of Standon in Hertfordshire belonged to Rohais wife of Richard Fitzgilbert de Tonbridge, lord of Clare. Besides his vineyard at Castle Hedingham, it is thought that Aubrey de Vere planted another larger one of eleven arpents some four miles away on his manor of Belchamp Walter; he had a third vineyard across the Suffolk border at Lavenham, and a fourth on his Middlesex manor of Kensington.

The picture of vineyard ownership revealed by the Domesday Surveys of 1080 and 1086 is very much more aristocratic than monastic. The pace was being set by the new nobility rather than the clergy, though of

course the priors and abbots in areas like Glastonbury and Canterbury continued to cultivate the vine and make wine for the Mass—and the convivialities which followed. But eleventh-century English wine was essentially royal and noble—as it had been for a thousand years.

Part II   Mediaeval Commonplace

1086 to 1485

TWO

Every Abbey, Monastery and Mansion has Its Vineyard

Vineyards Abound in the Twelfth Century

The royal tradition of viticulture was maintained throughout the four centuries that followed the Norman conquest. Wine fit for a king was made at Windsor Castle from vines grown in the Little Park from at least 1155. In the reign of Henry II (1154–89) the pay of the vintager or vineyard keeper and the expense of gathering the grapes were among the regular charges on the Pipe Rolls at Windsor from the beginning of the series in 1155. The Abbot of Waltham, who was parson both of old and new Windsor, received his tithe in wine pressed from the grapes which grew in Little Park. The wine-making at Windsor Castle was a commercial operation. It was primarily for the royal household to drink, but what was left over was sold 'to the king's profit'. The fame of it was still a talking point in the sixteenth century when William Lambarde said he had read that even if a tenth of the Windsor vines yielded there was 'great plenty' of wine, which made him think 'that wine had been made long since within the realm, although in our memory it is accounted a great dainty to hear of'.

The vines were grown on a small plot 250 feet by 85 feet in what was the Castle Ditch east of Henry VIII's Gateway and under the high wall of the Military Knight's Lodgings. It was certainly still there two hundred years later when King Edward IV entertained Louis de Bruges, Governor of Holland, at the castle, and after hunting in the West Park 'showed him his garden and vineyard of Pleasour'. The site marked 'vineyard' on the plan in Tighe and Davis's *Annals of Windsor* (1858) has never been built on. It appears in seventeenth- and eighteenth-century engravings with various

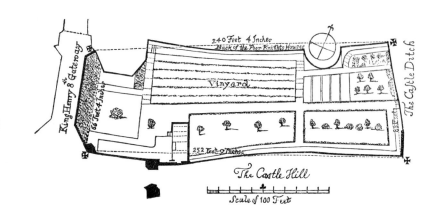

Tighe and Davis, in their Annals of Windsor *(1858), indicate that this piece of ground beside Henry VIII's Gateway at Windsor Castle was the site of the mediaeval royal vineyard. (Reproduced by gracious permission of Her Majesty the Queen)*

degrees of vegetation. To-day the site is a grassy stretch on the left of Castle Hill in the part of the grounds open to the public. Apart from the plantation at Windsor, Henry II had royal vineyards at Purley, Stoke, Cistelet, and in Herefordshire and Huntingdonshire.

Away from the seat of power, down in the west country and in Wales, the great religious houses had managed to retain a comparatively calm continuity denied to other parts of the island which were, in the twelfth century engulfed in political and military intrigue. Here monks and abbots had tended their vines with skill and devotion in the same way as they had guarded the light of learning and culture throughout the Dark Ages. Giraldus Cambrensis, Gerald the Welshman, writing some hundred years after the Norman irruption, remembered tranquil days spent as a boy in the vineyard at Maenor Byr (Manorbier Castle), his birthplace, in what was Pembrokeshire and is now part of Dyfed. It had under its walls, he wrote, 'besides a fishpond, a beautiful garden enclosed on one side by a vineyard and on the other by a wood'. In the same paragraph he told of vineyards in Glamorgan and Gwent. 'The vine is held up with poles and frames of wood' he said, 'and by that means it spreadeth all about and climbeth aloft.'

A similar description was given by Alexander Neckham, master of Dunstable School and later (1213–17) Abbot of Cirencester, in his book *De Naturis Rerum*. Written in 1175, it was probably the best book on natural history of that date, though he was keener to moralize on the facts than state them. His 167th chapter was 'about Vines' (*de Vinea*) in which presumably he was describing the vineyards he had himself seen in England, perhaps in Gloucestershire. Vine branches supported by stakes and intertwined formed decorative arbours, he said (*thalamos aspectu decoros vites proebent*); furthermore they had a practical use if grown against houses

28

because *'pampinus latitudine tua excipit aeris insultus, cum res ita desiderat et fenestra clementiam coloris solaris admittit'*—they made good sun blinds. This continued to be a favourite use of vines on houses until the fifteenth century at least.

However, vines were not grown in the open air in twelfth-century England just to provide shade or decoration but in order to make wine. It was the sole purpose of the 'vintners' of Tewkesbury who in 1195 were employed to make wine on their press from grapes grown in the demesne vineyard, as accounts for the honor of Gloucester show. In July 1176 Pope Alexander III issued a papal bull to Richard Dean of Wells confirming the grant of tithes 'and cherset of the produce and wine of the whole parish of Wells and the cherset of Herpetru'. The parish included a village called Winesham.

Viticulture was part of the common round, its activities important landmarks in the calendar. On a miserere seat in the parish church of the Worcestershire town of Ripple the symbol for February was the pruning of the vines. Those who took part acquired the names of the trade—such as Elwinus at Mear, and Alan Vinetarius who sold a plot of land at Parva Dartford in Kent in 1195. The vineyard keeper was the *vinitor*—there was no Anglo-Saxon word for vine. In the reign of Henry II (1154–89) there

An earlier vineyard may have been part of a much bigger garden later covered by Nell Gwynn's House and now by the Royal Mews. Both sites can be seen on this Hollar print (1660). (Reproduced by gracious permission of Her Majesty the Queen)

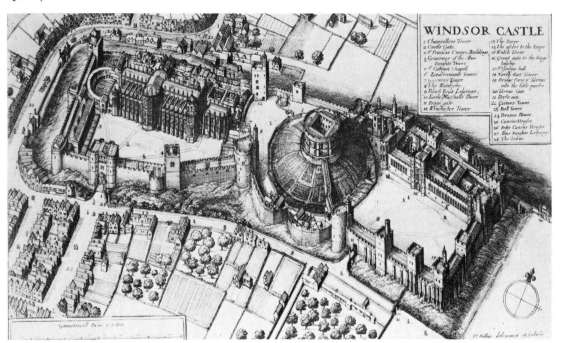

30

is a reference to an allowance being made to a sheriff 'for money delivered to his vine-dresser at Rockingham and for necessaries for the vineyard'; and there is a note in the Annals of Dunstable about the Prior pleading with the abbey paymaster to have pity on Stephan and Peter who were both described as '*vinitors*', and who would have been skilled labourers.

Unskilled labour was supplied by the tenants as part of their feudal service to the lord of the manor. References have survived from the twelfth century of tenants doing their stints of vineyard duty at Reading Abbey, Ramsey Abbey in Cambridgeshire, Whitley Abbey in Berkshire (1158), Sherborne Castle in Dorset (1160), and Margam Abbey in Glamorgan (1186). Inevitably part of the work of the tenants at the manor of Glaston was to cultivate the vineyard—'*fodit in Vinea*'—and the tenant who had the principal charge of them was '*Elwinus Custos Vinee*'. Canon Henry Ellacombe could still see signs of the Glastonbury Abbey vineyard at Meare in 1890. 'There is a ruined wall which formerly served as the back wall to the vines and some of the stone projections are there to which the vines were fastened. The field itself is still called the Vineyards.'

But the vineyards of twelfth-century England were by no means confined to the west country. There is an entry in a Roll of 1130 which mentions the making of two vineyards on Ranulf Peverell's land at Maldon (Mealdona) in Essex. It gives particulars of the pay and clothing of the vineyard keeper and speaks of sixteen barrels of wine having been sent up to London from Maldon in 1130:

> And in making two vineyards of Maldon, and in clothing
> and wages of the vineyard keeper: 52 shillings.

> And in buying 16 tuns and conveying them to Maldon,
> and from Maldon to London: 10 shillings.

There is evidence of other mediaeval vineyards in Essex, at Great Hallingbury, North Ockendon, Havering, Tendring, Roydon, West Bergholt, Great Horkesley, Stapleford Abbots, Chelmsford, Great Baddow, Great Coggeshall (the Abbey of Coggeshall) and Saffron Walden (the Abbey of Walden).

Vineyards to maintain Ely's reputation as the Isle des Vignes were known to be flourishing between 1109 and 1131, and there are accounts of tenants digging in the vineyard of the Bishop of Ely. Martin, Abbot of Peterborough planted a large vineyard for his abbey community in Northamptonshire during the reign of King Stephen (1135–54). In 1143 Stephen ordered the restoration to Holy Trinity Priory, London, of its land in Smithfield which Geoffrey, Earl of Essex had seized and converted into a vineyard. In 1151 Robert de Sigillo, Bishop of London, and many others

Previous page: the grape-harvest is illustrated on a misericord in Gloucester Cathedral. Vine-growing and wine-making were part of the common round of mediaeval life in England and were a favourite subject for decoration in places of worship.

This plan of the Canterbury Cathedral Chapter lands from a psalter of 1150 shows (top left) a vineyard (vinea) next to an orchard (pomarium).

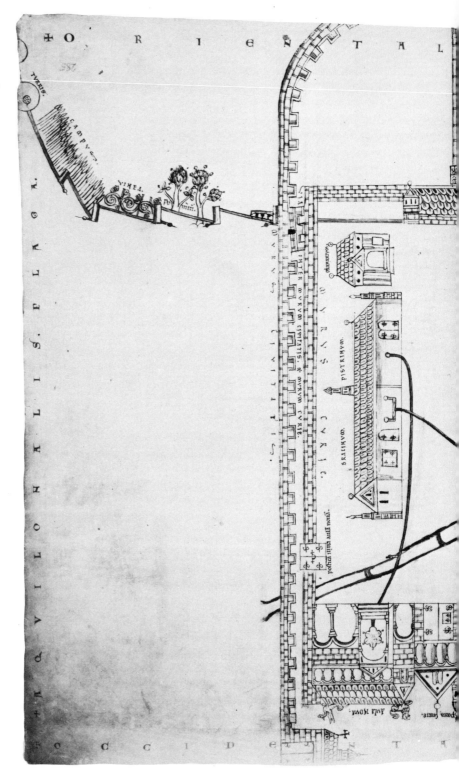

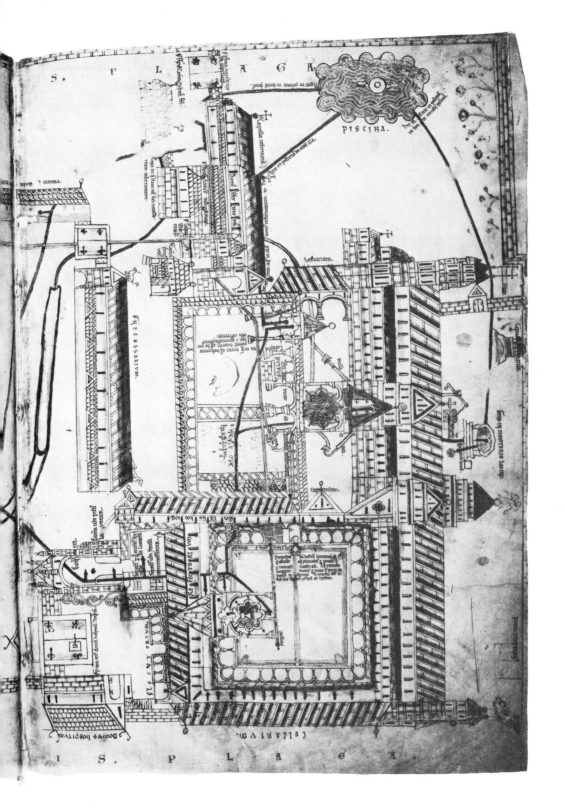

A decoration of Vine leaves and grapes from the Abbot's parlour at Muchelney Abbey, Somerset, one of the Domesday Book vineyard sites.

with him, were poisoned by eating grapes from his own vineyard—he would have done better to have made wine from them. In Worcestershire there were vineyards at Allesborough Hill (Pershore Abbey), Brushley, Leigh Abberton, Severn Stoke, Sedgebarrow, Ripple, Elmley Castle; two at Chaddesley Manor and four at Cotteridge. There were vineyards as far north as Lincolnshire; the twelfth-century *Registrum Antiquissimum* contains many references to them; and Vine Street in Lincoln marks the site of one of them. The register of Spalding Abbey tells how John the Almoner planted a vineyard and orchards. Open air wine-grapes were grown as far north as Durham and Edinburgh.

1154: Aquitaine Becomes an English Realm

Henry II, the first Plantagenet, inherited from his father the demesnes of Normandy, Maine and Anjou to which, when he married the divorced Queen of France, were added Poictou and Guienne which Eleanor brought as her dowry. Thus, when Henry ascended the throne of England in 1154, the kingdom he ruled embraced not only England, Anjou, Maine and Poictou, but also the great vine-growing area, famous for its wine since the days of ancient Rome under the name of Aquitania, and known in the twelfth century as Aquitaine or Guienne, and to-day as Bordeaux.

The effect this had on English viticulture was probably much less than writers who felt obliged to account for a 'decline' have traditionally pre-

34

sumed. Wine from Bordeaux had been coming to England, and had been drunk by the English for a thousand years or more. It was no great novelty; the inclusion of Aquitaine in Henry II's empire would not have changed drinking habits overnight, but the 'wines of Gascony' will have become very much cheaper. The quantity of English wine was never great and its quality was altogether different; French and English wine had never competed and were never to compete. The Benedictines at Glastonbury continued to cultivate English vines unaffected by the new political arrangement with the territory of their brother Benedictines at Saint Emilion and elsewhere in Guienne. The scale of English, as compared with French, viticulture was small, but that was immaterial.

As Samuel Pegge (1763) pointed out, 'it is not to be supposed that *at any time* since the first introduction of the vine here the inhabitants of the island produced wine enough for their own consumption, but rather that in all seasons they imported a great deal from abroad'. It should be remembered that wine was a universal drink in twelfth-century England when, at a penny a gallon, it was drunk by all but the poorest. This was still the case, though to a slightly less degree, in the thirteenth century when the average price of Gascon wine never exceeded 2d a gallon (a vine-keeper earned 2d a day.) But of course the biggest wine consumers were those rich enough to afford large quantities.

Aquitaine (the Roman Aquitania and today's Bordeaux region) became an English realm in 1154, but the English continued to make their own wine on winepresses such as this one depicted in a twelfth-century manuscript.

There is no reason to think that those who kept the English vineyards were ever positively discouraged by the large-scale drinking of imported wine. What would have discouraged them was wine drinking going out of general fashion—as it did in the twentieth century. As it was, they continued to make their modest contribution to the total amount consumed, unwilling to abandon a tradition which had been part of English life for more than a millennium—for certainly as long as it had been of *la vie Bordelaise*.

The Tradition Subsists in Spite of Cheap Gascon Wine

The arrival of large quantities of French wine on the quays of London did not deter those with property in the capital from planting open-air vines as part of the normal amenities.

The year 1292 is the date on a grant of a house and vinery in the parish of All Saints, Fenchurch in London; and in 1295 the Earl of Lincoln is known to have had a vineyard in Holborn. It was at the end of the thirteenth century too that the bishop of Ely acquired property in the parish of St Andrew, Holborn, for a 'hostell' in which to stay when he visited London. John de Hotham who was Bishop of Ely in the reign of Edward III (1327–77) added to this town house a kitchen garden, an orchard and, as befitted someone whose seat was in the centre of the Isle des Vignes, a vineyard. It would appear that this was a newly planted vineyard and separate from any which William Camerarius, as recorded in the Domesday Survey, may have run in the eleventh century; this had probably long since been scrubbed. John de Hotham may have heard of the earlier vineyard in Holborn and, encouraged by the knowledge that vines would grow in that part of London, determined to bring the Ely tradition of viticulture to the metropolis.

This town house of the bishops of Ely in Holborn was known as Ely House (Ely Place survives, together with a row of houses of a later age, which are one of the great architectural treasures of London). Its vineyard thrived for many a year, though the fame of its grapes was overshadowed by that of the strawberries from the Ely House kitchen garden. The site is marked by what the eighteenth-century mapmaker Rocque called Vine Street, now called Vinehill and approached by Vine Street Bridge.

Though there was little of it, or perhaps *because* there was so little of it, English wine, to those who made it, was something rare and worth the cossetting—and the hard work. If the soil was too rich the end-product was less fine. The thirteenth-century writer Bartholme thought perhaps that

36

this could be said of Somerset. 'A good deal of Somerset must be land too fat and moist in which the vine outrageth and beareth too many, too great and long leaves, bows and branches, and little fruit.' In spite of this, he said, 'the abbots of Glastonbury who doubtless believed in the passing nobility of wine, than which nothing is more profitable if it be taken in due measure and manner, had vineyards on the sunny slopes of Pilton'. It was in a county where Husbandmen's Calendars still marked March as the month for pruning vines and December for brewing both ale and wine. (The Pilton vineyard was revived by Nigel Godden seven hundred years later, as was the vineyard at Beaulieu Abbey, planted by Cistercian monks in 1269, and revived in the twentieth century by Margaret Gore-Brown.) Also down in the west country it is recorded that in 1203 Sir David Blount of Mangotsfield gave '42 acres of pasture, 147 acres of underwood and a moiety of a vineyard to Lawrence and Sybile de Maur for their lives'. It is not known who inherited the other half. Tradition has it that there was a vineyard at Moorend, and perhaps Sir David's was part of it.

There were mediaeval vineyards in Gloucestershire, at Winchcombe Abbey (there is still a Vineyard Street in the town); at the monastery at Hailes near Winchcombe where in 1315 there was a Vineyard Bridge; at Upton St Leonards, Over, Cold Ashton, Badgeworth, and Henbury near Bristol where to-day stands Vine House, the site of what was once known as the Bishop's Vineyard, which was attached to a palace of the Bishop of Worcester. This vineyard was not in the garden of Vine House but in the garden of the Old Vicarage across the Hazel brook. Over is about a mile west of Gloucester and the site was beside what was known as The Bridge of the Vineyard. I do not know when the monks of Bath Abbey planted vines at Cold Ashton in the Hamswell Valley but the Manor Court records of 1476 assure us 'the homage there done fully; they [the tenants] give to the Lord for certain this day 6s 8d and for the works of the vineyard 11d'. Bath Abbey also owned the vineyard at St Catherine's, Batheaston, which is now the vegetable garden across the road from the grey stone mansion. There was once a vineyard too between Olveston and Thornbury. Canon Ellacombe saw the remains of the terracing in 1890. 'It is well situated, both as to soil and aspect, for the growth of vines, but it is supposed that vines have not been growing there for the last 300 or 400 years.'

In 1252 there must have been a vineyard at Great Maplestead in Essex. For in that year John de Hoding granted to Sarah de Martnall and Isabella, her daughter, all his lands at Mapletrested which included a mill and a vineyard. This was probably on the slope of the hill above Hull's Mill in Great Maplestead. The neighbouring parish of Little Maplestead also had a vineyard, for an undated deed of the time of Edward I (1272–1307) shows that Robert de Harlow of Little Maplestead 'quit-claimed' to the Hos-

pitallers of St John of Jerusalem living at Little Maplestead Hall, then known as 'le Hopitâl', the annual rent of twelve pence arising from a parcel of land in Hokholt, 'near their vineyard.'

    A thirteenth-century Latin deed refers to the leasehold sale of a house garden, shop and vineyard at Colchester. According to a deed of 1242 there was a piece of land adjoining the town known as 'Wynescroft' which would seem to indicate vine-growing. Miller Christy (*The Essex Naturalist*, 1899) said there was still a 'Vineyard Lane' in Colchester in 1899 running parallel with the outer side of the old town hall on the southern aspect. 'This suggests that vines were formerly grown here, trained against the sunny side of the town wall; but whether this was done by the Romans or (as is more prob-

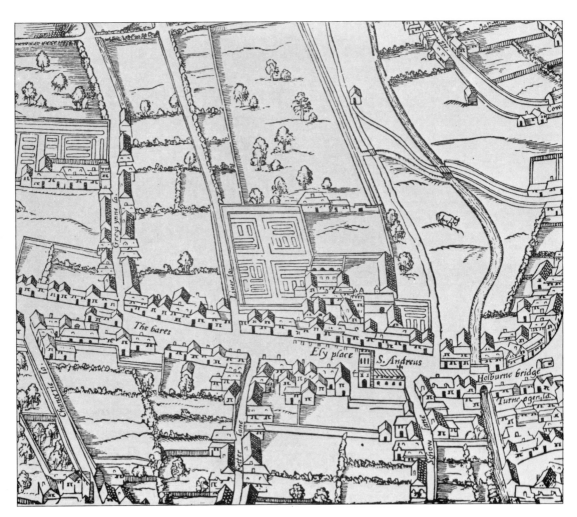

able) in later times, by the monks of St John's Abbey, only a few hundred years distant, must here be left in doubt.'

There is little reason to think that there were fewer vineyards and wineries in England and Wales because Aquitaine was ruled by the King of England. As André Simon, doyen of wine historians has written, (*English Wines and Cordials*, 1946)

> Having a staff of skilled vine-dressers and many vines to which much labour and money had been devoted for some years, Churchmen were loth to give up this culture; at the same time being able to obtain much better wines from the Continent at lower cost they did not feel bound to drink

Left: modern Holborn in central London was once open country as this old map shows. It was here that the Bishop of Ely built a 'hostell', to which was added, in the fourteenth century, a vineyard, as befitted one whose diocese covered 'L'Isle des Vignes'.

Right: when John Rocque drew this map in 1746, Holborn had been built over, but the site of the Ely House vineyard was still marked by 'Vine Street' and 'Vine Court'.

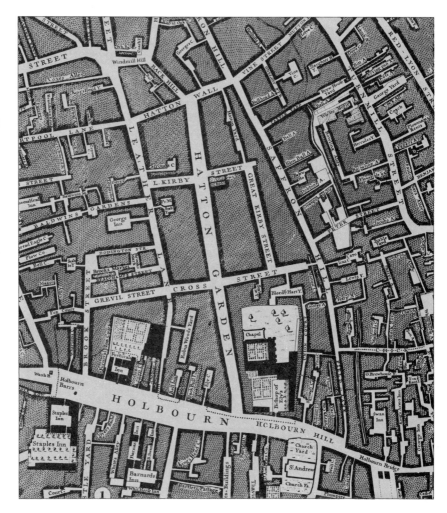

the produce of their own vineyards, and they attempted to sell at any rate some of it. The archives of the Church of Ely have preserved an account of such transactions, which shows how little saleable home-grown wine was made, and that the grapes often failed to ripen properly, verjuice being all that could be made.

Vine-growing and wine-making continued all over the King's English realm as well as in his French realm, and the chance references which have survived can reveal only a small proportion of the real total. Not all English wine was to everyone's liking. The story is told of the visit by King John (1199–1216) to Beaulieu Abbey to which the Cistercian monks had been moved from Faringdon in 1204. He took one taste of the wine made from the grapes of Beaulieu vineyard which the monks proudly set before their king and called for his steward. 'Send ships forthwith to fetch some good French wine for the abbot!'

Certainly wine was not being made commercially in England. It could not be said that anyone attempted to create in England a *wine industry* as there was in France and Italy.

The Thirteenth-Century Church Invests in English Wine

How many of the Domesday vineyards were still operating a hundred years after the survey was taken is not known for certain, but probably most of them. Certainly those at Meare and Panborough in Somerset were still there in the twelfth century, and there was one too at Minehead; and there were now many more than the forty-two noted by the Domesday commissioners. A vineyard at Timberscombe near Dunster was granted by the prior of Bath to Richard Le Tort in 1245: 'one furlong at the vineyard which we and our monks of Dunster have of the house of Henry of the vineyard in the manor of Timberscombe'. Jocelin Bishop of Wells owned a vineyard; an Inspeximus and confirmation of his referred to a gift made by Peter Dean of Wells and the Chapter to Robert Gyfarde, Chaplain, of all tithes of the Church of St Cuthbert Wells except sheaves of all manner of corn in garden or field, tithes of the bishop's vineyard and of the mills of the parish, of the white monks and of hay. This document can be dated to around 1265. The vineyard was still in existence a hundred years later, for it was mentioned in a lawsuit concerning the vicarage of St Cuthbert Wells in 1357; and an ordinance of Robert, minister of the church of Bath, of 1393 again referred to a tithe of this Wells wine.

In 1259 vineyards were being cultivated at Gear and Halnoweth in St Martin in Meneage, Cornwall.

There was a vineyard at Three Bridges in Sussex which is now buried under a shunting yard; at Buxted not far from West Hoathly there were the remains, in 1870, of what were perhaps mediaeval vines in a sheltered position surrounded by high rocks. In Gough's *Topographical Collections* in the Bodleian Library, Oxford, there is a drawing of Dr Saunder's charity farm at Buxted hewn out of the rock. It is dated May 28, 1785 and written on the back in pencil is 'Rocks in Buxted in Sussex called "The Vineyard" there being formerly a plantation of vines here which throve well, being sheltered from the winds and open to the meridian sun.' Traces of the site having been a vineyard remained in 1859 at least. There were vineyards at Ewhurst in Sussex, probably planted by the monks of Robertsbridge Abbey; at Buston the former seat of the Fane family where remains of The Old Vineyard are still to be traced in the outline of three terraces; and at Ticehurst on the site of Ticehurst House.

In the time of Henry de Eastry, Prior of Canterbury in 1285, the Cathedral Church and the Abbey of St Augustine's were 'plentifully furnished with vineyards' according to William Somner (1640) who also mentioned vineyards at Cólton, Berton, St Martin's Chertham, Brook and Hollingbourn. A map of 1230–74 showed a vineyard just outside Canterbury city wall. The Domesday vineyard at Chislet was still flourishing in the thirteenth century, and in the reign of Edward III (1327–77).

In the thirteenth century the Archbishop of Canterbury, who was both a temporal and a spiritual leader, owned thirty manors. One of the biggest English wine-making operations of the Middle Ages, and the nearest to being 'commercial', was that undertaken to supply wine for His Grace's cellars. Vineyards for this purpose had been planted at two of these manors, a big one at Teynham and a smaller one at Northfleet. Both had been in the possession of the archbishops of Canterbury at the time of the Domesday survey.

The fertile soil of Teynham made it famous in later years for fruit other than grapes; but there is evidence of a vineyard having been there as early as the twelfth century. Among the charters of the priory of St Gregory at Canterbury there is one, of Archbishop Hubert Walter, which confirms to St Gregory's a tithe of the wine of Teynham. In his *History of Kent* (1797) Edward Hasted remarked that this was 'a kind of donation which appears by others of the like to other religious houses to have been esteemed of no small value.' Twelfth-century accounts showed details of the outgoings and the income at the Teynham vineyard. The latter included sixpence from the wood cuttings (*chasonis*) of the vine. Expenditure included the cost of 20,013 props (*scarettis*) made for the vineyard and two new palisadoes (*bachiis*); and the cost of peeling and manuring the vines (*compostandis*).

de inte superflua demo

temp do gratum.

consta propri

epo

In the wages of one cultivator from the Sunday following St Valentine's Day to Michaelmas for 224 days: 37s 4d [2d a day]

In Payments to same: 16s 8d

To same for his clothes: 8s

Between 1292 and 1294 Teynham wine appeared as an item on receipts of the bailiwick of Maidstone and showed that some of it was *sold* to the king: 'XVI doleis (casks) 1 pipa vini in manerio de Thegnham venditi domino Regi.' The receipt also showed verjuice (*viridi succo*) and cider (*cicera*).

The earliest record of the Northfleet vineyard is in a rent roll of archiepiscopal manors for 1235, the second year of the primacy of Archbishop Edmund Rich:

In peeling (*discalcianda*) the vine, layering (*provignianda*), digging, hoeing and propping it up with trellises (*scalettanda*), and in payment of the cultivator (*vineatoris*), and in vine tools to be mended: 44s 5d

In mending six casks for wine (*doleis ad vineam*) and in wine measures, and in repairs of casks, and in gathering the grapes and in tallow and soap for the wine press (*et in sepo et sapone ad torculum*) and in a small hogshead (*et in caudela*), and other expenses of the vintage time (*et aliis custis vindemiandi*): 17s 3d

In three gallons of must (*musti*, i.e. sweet wine) for filling up a cask: 6d

Sales of Northfleet wine in 1273, after the Archbishop's household had consumed what they wanted, were entered in the manorial accounts as:

20s for one cask of wine
11s 6d for ½ cask
42s for 2 casks
4d for sale of herbage in the vineyard

Under 'Expenses' appeared:

Purchase of five casks and a measure for wine, and cleaning and binding these, and in tallow and soap bought for the shaft (*fusillum*) [of the wine press]: 6s 1d

Gathering grapes: 8s 3d

Pruning, digging, hoeing and binding up (*liganda*): 34s

To cultivator of the vine and to the reeve (*preposito*) a year: 20s

The most familiar 'Occupations of the Month' were continually being illustrated on calendars; these illustrations were made in Canterbury around 1280 and show (above) the pruning in March, the planting in April, and (below) the treading of the grapes in September, and Janus feasting in January.

43

The bailiff's and reeve's account for Northfleet in 1299 included:

In getting trellises from Bexley: 18d
Purchase of 8 wine casks and carriage: 16s
In taking a cask to Lambeth: 15½d
Payment to cultivator per annum: 10s

As well as sending Northfleet wine to the Archbishop's palace at Otford in the Darenth Valley (of which the ruins can still be seen) and to his London residence at Lambeth, it was also sent to Wrotham.

In 1278/9 the sale of the wine from Northfleet and Teynham together brought in £57 13s. Costs were fairly high but wages were steady—between 1273 and 1296 they only went up a halfpenny. Total outgoings at the Teynham vineyard in 1270/1 were £5 10s 4d and in 1273/4 £11 2s 8d. In the earliest account for the smaller vineyard at Northfleet expenses were £3 2s 2d; £2 18s 4d in 1273 and £4 10s 5½d in 1298.

One of the reasons for the 'decline' of wine-making in England is always given as the cheapness of Aquitaine wine. Yet in 1260 a dolium or cask of the best French wine cost between twenty and forty shillings; whereas in 1278, when a large amount was sold, the highest price for a cask of Northfleet or Teynham wine was 23s. In 1270 it fetched only 13s 4d a cask, though in 1273 Northfleet wine was sold at 20s a cask.

The Bishop of Rochester also possessed vineyards: at Halling and Snodland. On the other side of the Thames in Berkshire, there had been a vineyard at Reading Abbey since the twelfth century; there was a vineyard at Tidmarsh in 1239 and a 'vinarium' at Wallingford in 1281. The vineyard at Abingdon Abbey gave its name to a street which still exists—at its northern end Stert Street turns into a road running north-east called The Vineyard which finally becomes Oxford Road. The monks cultivated their vines on the land to the south of the street. Abingdon Vinnal is said to derive its name from the Celtic word Gwinllan meaning a vineyard.

Vineyards were not, however, confined to the Home Counties; there were flourishing vineyards further north in Herefordshire, Worcestershire, Cambridgeshire and Suffolk. There was certainly a vineyard in the city of Hereford in 1229, and the household roll of Bishop Swinfield shows that there were many on the estates belonging to the Bishops of Hereford. In 1276 Bishop Cantilupe, Swinfield's predecessor at Hereford, renewed the vineyard at Ledbury which still flourished in Swinfield's day. In 1289 Cantilupe made seven casks (*dolia*) of white wine at Ledbury. It was transferred to Bosbury, another of the Bishop of Hereford's estates, and drunk there the following summer. Since, in the thirteenth century, there were

no glass bottles and no corks, wine was usually drunk within twelve months of its manufacture. Any kept for more than a year was known as 'old wine'.

Worcester Priory had a vineyard at Fladbury in the reign of Henry III (1216–72). According to Dr T. Nash the ground was still called The Vineyard in 1781, the year he published his *History and Antiquities of Worcestershire*, and it still belonged to the rector of Fladbury. Until 1240 at least there were also vineyards in Worcestershire at Grimley, Bushley and Droitwich, where there is still an area called The Vines on the south-facing slope below Dodderhill Church, north of the river Salwarpe and west of Chapel Bridge on the Worcester–Birmingham road. An enclosure map of Middle Littleton names a field south of the church 'Vineyard'; and at South Littleton the name 'Vineyard Orchard' is given on a tithe map; but there is no evidence to show that these were mediaeval. Similarly a tithe map for Ombersley shows 'Wyneyards' and 'Vineyard Close' east of Suddington, though there is no mention of these on any other document to indicate their age. To-day there is still a farm named Winyards between Winnall and Lineholt in the north-western part of Ombersley.

There is evidence of thirteenth-century vines in East Anglia to be found in deeds concerning lands described as adjoining a vinery at Wherstead in Suffolk in 1280 and 1290. At his death in 1289 Roger de Trumpington held a chief messuage (parcel of land) in Trumpington, the village just to the south of Cambridge, which included a little vineyard; and monks were certainly cultivating vines at St Edmundsbury, or Bury St Edmunds —the abbey vineyard was still marked on an eighteenth-century map.

If in the thirteenth-century viticultural scene it would appear that the clerics were hugging the centre of the stage, it is only because they were the subject of the few references which have survived. What I have managed to dredge up from county archives and elsewhere is not even the 'fair sample' of the modern market research survey, for the way it is constituted is due entirely to chance. But fair or unfair it needs multiplying up, and only then can one get some idea of the extent of the activity throughout mediaeval England and Wales.

Once planted, the vines which took so long to mature, remained on the same site from one generation to another. From a very early time Winchester and its environs were famous for their wines. John Twyne thought the city acquired its name through that connection. *'Urbs vini vel vinifera quasi dicas munitio vel fortificatio ubi crevit optimum vinum in Britannia'* —it was called the city of wine and a wine-growing stronghold and fortress, where the best wine in Britain grew. The poet Robert of Gloucester wrote:

Testis est London ratibus, Wintonia Baccho
(London is known for its shipping, Winchester for its wine.)

Not everyone has subscribed to this theory of the origin of Winchester's name. Just as there are many to oppose those who seek to explain the meaning of Vindomis (see page 9), there are many who say, as I have pointed out in Chapter One, that 'win' means white and has nothing to do with wine. Certainly the town was Caer Gwent before the Romans came, and the Belgae called it Venta Belgarum; but there is no doubt that Winchester was reputed for its vineyards. In their *Historic Winchester* (1882) A. R. Bramston and A. C. Leroy assert 'Winchester was doubtless one of the foremost in this as its wine was very famous'. A church at the north end and east side of Kingsgate Street was once known as All Saints in the Vineyards. That Winchester's vineyards were not mentioned in the Domesday Survey must mean that they were planted after it; but the city still played a leading role in English viticulture at the beginning of the fourteenth century; this is demonstrated by the fact that in 1303 Winchester refused to consent to an increase in the duty on wine suggested by Edward I in that year.

Many vineyards which had featured in the Domesday Survey were also being worked far into the fourteenth century. The three-acre vineyard at Ely was certainly still very productive in 1368 according to a chronicle of the Monastery—'*multum dans vinea vinium*'. The Tewkesbury vineyard owned by the Earl of Gloucester was still flourishing in 1185, and is known to have been yielding a crop between 1327 and 1359, with tenants working in it throughout the year. The Black Death will have unmercifully picked off the pickers but left the vines unaffected. The Tewkesbury vineyard was still in existence in the mid-sixteenth century.

It was not the only vineyard in the district. In the thirteenth century wine-grapes were grown at nearby Twyning and, by 1238, the Tewkesbury Wine made from them had attained more than a local reputation, for in that year a tun of it was bought for the king's household. The evidence for a vineyard at Twyning comes from a document of almost a hundred years later (1335) which states: 'A messuage and land in Twyning near Tewkesbury are held of William de la Zouche by the service of carrying the letters of the lord of Tewkesbury . . . and finding one man for 16 days to make hay and for another 16 days of hand-labour in digging the vines and collecting grapes for vines for 3 days.'

There was a vineyard at the beginning of the fourteenth century on the Island of Lundy off the North Devon coast. In Devon too there was a vineyard at a place with the same name as the Roman one in Oxfordshire North Leigh (or Northlegh). John la Forestere of Tiverton rented lands

there in 1359 for five silver marks 'saving the advowson and the fisher and the vineyard'.

The Mohuns had vineyards at Dunster and Minehead in Somerset; but they stopped cultivating the one at Dunster during the reign of Henry IV (1399–1413) and added it to the Park. In 1890 Canon Ellacombe described a small plot of ground at Dunster which was less than an acre in extent, on the south side of the hill and called The Vineyards 'in a very sunny and sheltered situation'. The ground was in terraces but he was not sure whether they were made for vine growing or for the later Dunster industry of clothmaking.

A document refers to a vineyard at Hadley in Essex in 1303:

Free tenants: John Franceys holds one messuage, and the aforesaid John and all the other tenants carry hay in the Lord's meadow and they have twelve flagons of ale or 12d and shall dig in the vineyard one dole [*fodiet in vineis 1 dolam*] which contains in length 4 feet and in width 3 perches. Also he shall gather grapes for one day, either himself or another man, and then he shall have food and drink from the Lord.

Roger de Brumf' holds one messuage . . . and he shall dig also in the vineyard of the domain two doles at the price of a penny each dole.

And the same accounts for the hire of one man for twenty days, for tending and repairing the vineyard—4s.

The tenth year [1317]: of the issue of the vineyard, he gives no account *because there were no grapes this year*, and of 5d of herbage sold in the vineyard as contained in the same.

The final item is interesting evidence that there were good and bad years, good crops, bad crops and no crops as much in the 'warm' Middle Ages as in later years.

The Vineyards of Fourteenth-Century London

It seems that the Westminster vineyard in Domesday was not the one within the twelve and a half acres over which Edward the Confessor's Palace of Westminster spread itself. Its location is a mystery, though its existence is undoubted. Quoting as his authority George Gilbert Scott's *Gleanings* of 1863, Dr Arthur Stanley in his *Historical Memorials of Westminster Abbey* (John Murray, 1882), states, 'in the adjacent fields were the Orchard, the Vineyard and the Bowling Alley which have left their traces in Orchard Street, Vine Street and Bowling Street'. Vine Street, which ran between

the Church of St John the Evangelist in Smith Square and Horseferry Road was renamed 'Romney Street' in 1869—after the wine of that name or the painter? The vineyard whose site it marks will have been the 'Vine-garden within the Mill-ditch of Westminster' mentioned in a privy seal granted by Charles II to Edward Billing.

The mediaeval City of London abounded in vineyards. 'The street now denominated *the Vineyard* within the walls of the city of London' stated Samuel Pegge (1763), 'might produce formerly, we think, very passable grapes; since in London, as it seems, they had vines very commonly in their gardens in the reign of Edward III (1327–77).' He was probably referring to the sheltered spot along the old City Wall once tended by the Minoresses of St Clare which to-day goes by the name of Vine Street off the Minories. Aldersgate Street was once named Vine Yard according to

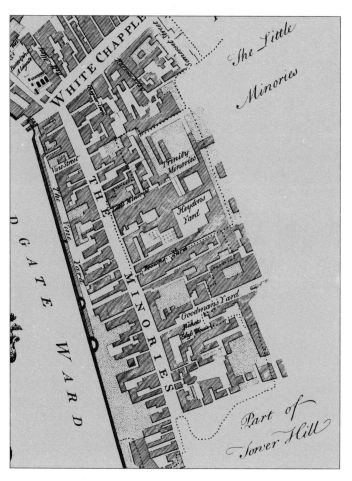

This eighteenth-century map of Portsoken Ward in the City of London shows 'The Vine Yard' and 'Vine Street' which recall the mediaeval vine-growing activities of the Minoresses of St Clare in a sheltered spot along the old City Wall. Today there is still a Vine Street—off the Minories.

London County Council list of 1955, but what this signifies I am not sure.

Account rolls in the Corporation of London Records Office from the late fourteenth century refer to the open air vines growing in the Bridge House Garden at the south end of London Bridge at Southwark. The bridge-master's accounts for 1382 have an item of expense for the Saturday next before the feast of the Purification of the Blessed Mary: 'also paid to a certain man hired for *four days* to cut the vines in the Bridge House Garden, 16d'. The vineyard must have been of some size if it took him all that time. In the following year there was 'also paid to a certain man for the repair of the vines of the Bridge House Garden and for the purchase of rods and stakes, 2s 10d'. The weekly payments for 1404–21 recorded the pruning, tying and splaying of the vines, and, in 1468, Thomas Maners was paid 'for trenching a ditch and planting of the same with vines in a close belonging to the bridge in the field of Greenwich'—presumably a second site. Two names recur; John Arnold repeatedly paid twelve pence for pruning the vines, and Michael Bonar sixteen pence for cutting them. But none of the accounts contain any reference to the making of wine.

Until 1955 there was a Vine Yard off Sanctuary Street, Southwark which probably marked the Bridge House Garden vineyard. On the south bank of the river, in Bermondsey, is Vine Lane (Vine Yard in earlier maps) which runs from Tooley Street to the Thames and marks the site of a vineyard attached to the wealthy riverside palace belonging either to the Abbot of Battle or to the Prior of Lewes; or it may have been part of Bermondsey Abbey itself. There is also a Vinegar Yard off St Thomas Street, Bermondsey.

Back again on the other side of the river, what of the Vineyard Walk off Farringdon Road, Finsbury? Accounting for this in his *History* of the parish of Clerkenwell in 1881, William Pinks was of the view that there had been a vineyard here 'in monastic times' for the Priory of St John of Jerusalem. (Though, with the aid of more recent research Gilliam Bebbington in her *London Street Names* (1972) considers it was part of the precinct of Clerkenwell Nunnery.) In 1306, said Pinks, there was mention of a tenement called Le Vyne. The ground was once very much higher and called The Mount 'against whose western slope vines grew untrained row above row until they reached the Summit where stood a small cottage belonging to the cultivator'. Both the vineyard and the keeper's house, he said, were depicted in *The North Prospect of London* by Bowles in 1752. In 1859 The Old Vineyard public house stood on the site and displayed a sign which read: 'After the City Clerks partook of the water of the Clerks' Well from which the parish derives its name, they repaired hither to partake of the fruit of the finest English grapery.' Pinks however denounced this as erroneous and absurd. He could not believe, presumably, they could ever have ripened

enough to be *eatable*. The Mount on which the vines grew was flattened soon after Bowles published his *The North Prospect of London*, and Vineyard Walk was built. The rich soil which had fed the grapes was sold for an immense sum.

Clerkeshagh was the name of a 'curtilage' or garden which together with a field called La Vyne—a vineyard's gender seems to be at will—was conceded to Robert de Aylynchagh and Walter Atte Welle by Sir John Dabernon in 1335. This was at Aylynchagh in Great Bookham, Surrey. It is thought to have been the messuage and lands called 'Vines' mentioned as forming part of the manor of Eastwick in 1571 (Phenice Farm).

Fourteenth-Century Vineyards in Kent

In his *Vine-Growing in England* (1911), H. M. Tod FRHS remarked 'it scarcely seems too much to say that the Kent vineyards extended from Thame to London and southward by Tonbridge and Sevenoaks to Tenterden district and the marshes not much less thickly than the hop grounds do now'.

On September 24, 1326 Edward II, who was returning to London from a visit to the south coast, came through the Weald of Kent and stayed the night at Bockinfield. Hamo of Hythe, Bishop of Rochester, took the opportunity of ingratiating himself with his monarch by sending him a present both of grapes from his vineyard at Halling and wine made from them. The story is related by the Kent historian William Lambarde who lived in Halling; by his day (1570) the Halling vineyard had become 'a good plaine meadowe'. William de Dene, historian of the See of Rochester who also lived near Halling, said that Bishop Hamo had renewed the vineyard four years before he made this gift to King Edward. 'This place seems to have been peculiarly adapted to the culture of vines; and indeed it is a warm and promising situation; for the abbess of Malling had also a vineyard here, the bishops of Rochester receiving from her, as we read in another author, a boar and a portion of wax *pro decimis vinearum de Hallynge*.'

The Register Book of the Temporalities of the Bishop of Rochester recorded the services due to the Bishop from his tenants at Snodland and Halling in the time of Edward III (1327–77) and these included the picking of blackberries to mix with the grapes for wine making, presumably to give richness to its red colour and a bit more body.

Besides the vineyards at Halling and Snodland the Bishop of Rochester had a vineyard in Rochester itself. This was very extensive and produced great quantities of grapes from which excellent wine was made. The Benedictine monks in the Priory of St Andrew at Rochester also had a large

plantation of vines in their enclosure, still called The Vinesfield in the twentieth century.

In the fourteenth century, at Sevenoaks, there was an estate known as the Farm on the Vine. It was later called Bethelham Farm and is now known as Bligh's Farm. This was almost certainly the home farm of the Archbishop of Canterbury's holding so far as Sevenoaks was concerned. On old style maps the name 'sevenoke Vine' covered quite a large area to the north of the farm. The name commemorated the small vineyard cultivated for the Archbishop's table by his bailiff in Sevenoaks, and is kept alive to-day by the famous Vine Cricket Club, formed in 1734—or perhaps earlier.

There was a famous Kentish vineyard at Langley just south of Maidstone and the abbots of St Augustine's at Canterbury owned three—at Northolme, at Fishpoole near Littlebourne and at Coningbrook in the parish of Sellinge (between Willesborough and Kennington).

Edward Hasted tells a colourful story in his *History of Kent* (1797) of how the Northolme vineyard came to be planted, probably about 1325, by Ralph Bourn who was elected Abbot in 1309.

> At this time the abbot caused vines to be planted near the Northolmes, then called Nordhome, which was before a hiding place for thieves and a resort for every kind of wickedness to which there was a common way by Le Kenile by the subterfuges of which the iniquity was the more easily carried forward. To remove this scandal the abbot by the King's licence and authority levelled their dark holes and hiding places, grubbed up the thorns and bushes, cut down the trees, surrounded the whole with a wall and planted a choice vineyard in it, as above-mentioned, much to his honour and the advantage of the monastery.

At the bottom of Fishpool Hill at Littlebourne were the Ponds which were supplied from a spring called Arrianes Well (Adrian's Well?). They were reservoirs in which the monks reared fish for the refectory of the convent of St Augustine. 'The sides of the ponds, now equally thick with coppice wood', stated Hasted 'were antiently a vineyard . . . The lands in this parish are in general very poor and gravelly'—which of course is what a vine likes.

The cost of running the vineyards of St Augustine's Abbey, Canterbury, in the fourteenth century was considerable. The vine-keeper at Northolme received 52s a year, and 43s 1d was paid to the workers who did the digging and pruning. Ladders cost 33s 11d including carriage; spades, hoes, and other tools 5s 2d.

A town charter of Faversham, dated 14 November 1302, by which Edward I confirmed privileges conferred by Henry III, also granted 'that on their own wines which they should sell they should be quit of the royal duty in respect of one barrel of wine before and another behind the mast'. In the ninth century Coenwulf King of Mercia had had a royal villa at Faversham, and perhaps the siting of a vineyard there and this 'royal' privilege derived from that fact. Kent wine had a reputation for quality. William Thorn, Abbot of Northolme Abbey, declared in his *Chronicles* that their wine was '*ad commodum et magnum honorem.*'

The man who bought the wine and was in charge of the cellar where it was stored was the cellarer, whose responsibilities however extended to the kitchen and refectory and managing everything to do with the supply of meat and drink for the establishment which employed him. The accounts of the cellarer of Battle Abbey in Sussex for 1385 showed he bought two pipes of wine at the Canterbury Winchepe and one pipe in London. These will have been red wine, probably from Gascony, to supplement the white wine from Battle Abbey's own vineyards which were extensive. But this cellarer also bought English wine from neighbouring vineyards. Battle Abbey records of 1365 include a receipt of money from 'the Wyneyarde of the Rectory of Hawkherste'—the village just across the border in Kent. Selling wine across county borders was in order, but in 1335 Edward III passed a statute which restrained foreigners from exporting wine out of the country, though whether this was directed at protecting English wine is debatable. Samuel Pegge, writing in 1763, thought not. 'For we do not find in our histories that the preceding years had been particularly unfavourable, so as to occasion a scarcity of that commodity. Wines of foreign growth were probably intended; and indeed I am not aware that any person has ever drawn an inference from that statute in favour of the English vineyards.'

Vine-growing and wine-making flourished in fourteenth-century Flanders, on the same latitude as southern England, as this illustration of Flemish vintners from the Romance of Alexander *(1339 to 1344) demonstrates.*

Kent will have had close relations with neighbouring Sussex, but it also seems to have had viticultural ties with Gloucestershire. At Tonbridge there was a vineyard in the grounds of the castle which was owned, in Edward III's day, by Gilbert Earl of Gloucester who also had a vineyard in Tewkesbury. On the Kent coast there had been a vineyard at the Priory of Folkestone for centuries, and it is likely there had been one within the oblong fort, known as a Vespasian Camp, at Folkestone during the Roman Occupation. There was still a vineyard in the town in the fifteenth century: one John Cowper bequeathed his wife an acre and half of land 'in le Wyneyerd'. In the same part of Kent the name 'Vineyard' is still attached to land at Tong, indicating a planting of ancient ancestry.

In other counties fifteenth-century documents show evidence of vineyards at Great Baddow and Copford in Essex, at Deerhurst in Gloucestershire, at Astwick near Biggleswade in Bedfordshire. Fifty years ago traces of the latter were to be found in the Vine Farm which occupied an isolated position at the extreme corner of Langford abutting on Astwick.

Apart from the vineyards there will have been the wineries, but references to them are rare. However it is known that in the courtyard of Thaxted manor house in Essex in 1348, along with the great stable, the grange, the smithy, the granary, the bakery, the pundfold and the pigsty there was an out-building called 'la Pressourhous' where wine was pressed. It must have been one of many.

1453: the French Regain Aquitaine

English wine made from grapes grown in the vineyards bordering the Rother, the Medway and the Itchen never acquired that degree of potency or equalled the fullness of the *vino clareto* from the banks of the rivers which emptied into the Bay of Biscay, but it continued to be a rare and distinctive drink for men of taste, and in a class of its own—*'magnum honorem'*. This status was unaffected by the sequence of events which led to the Land of Claret being recovered by its former owners. In 1449 Charles VII, king of France, invaded Normandy and, within twelve months, expelled the English. Encouraged by this success he turned his attention to Guienne, and after three centuries of English rule the whole province, including the towns of Bayonne and Bordeaux, were 'finally swallowed up in the French monarchy'.

Throughout the fourteenth century Gascon wine had constituted some eighty per cent of England's total wine imports (three million gallons)

at an average price of 3½d a gallon, compared with German wine from the Rhine at 1s 2d a gallon, Italian wine at 2s and Cretan wine at 4s.

English viticulture and wine-making were probably as little affected by the loss of Aquitaine as they were by its acquisition three hundred years before. The easy flow of cheap Gascon wine which became known as 'Claret' had sustained the English taste for wine-drinking, and, when Aquitaine was regained by France and the price of Gascon wines inevitably rose, the predilection remained—and the urge to make as much as possible of the fine, flinty English wine whose delicate flavour had always suited the palates of the Establishment from the King downwards. Only two years before his defeat at Bosworth King Richard III appointed John Piers 'Master of our Vyneyarde nigh unto our Castell of Wyndesore' for the term of his life with wages and fees of sixpence a day. Some say that vines were no longer growing in Little Park as late as that and the name Vineyard was just being maintained out of tradition, but I like to think otherwise. Tighe and Davis (1858) say the vineyard was still in existence in the reign of George III (1760–1820).

That the Kingdom of England had a 'classic' vineyard in its back garden on the banks of the Gironde and Garonne for three centuries may have discouraged the island population from exerting themselves to the full extent they might otherwise have done in the cultivation of their own vines and the making of English wine; but the picture I have been able to paint of continued viticultural activity, surely disposes of the assumption, which I have met with wherever I have turned, that Eleanor of Aquitaine, by bringing Henry II the lands of Bordeaux as her dowry, delivered a wounding blow from which English vineyards and English wine never recovered. It would seem in fact that English viticulture, healthy before 1154 and as healthy, if not healthier, throughout the remainder of the Middle Ages, was as much a mediaeval commonplace as fishing for eels and minstrelsy.

Part III   A Great Dainty

A SEVENTEENTH-CENTURY VIEW
OF THE ENGLISH CLIMATE

The air of England is temperate but thick, cloudy and misty, and Caesar witnesseth that the cold is not so piercing in England as in France. For the sun draweth up the vapours of the sea which compasseth the island, and distills them upon the earth in frequent showers of rain so that frosts are somewhat rare; and howsoever snow may often in the winter time, yet in the southern parts (especially) it seldom lies long on the ground. Also the cool blasts of sea winds mitigate the heat of summer. . . .

The English are so naturally inclined to pleasure, as there is no country wherein the gentlemen and lords have so many and large parks only reserved for the pleasure of hunting, or where all sorts of men allot so much ground about their houses for pleasure of gardens and of orchards. The very grapes, especially towards the south and west, are of a pleasant taste, and I have said, that in some counties, as in Gloucestershire, they made wine of old which no doubt many parts would yield at this day, but that the inhabitants forbear to plant vines as well because they are served plentifully and at a good rate with French vines, as for that the hills most fit to bear grapes yield more commodity by feeding of sheep and cattle.

Fynes Moryson, *Itinerary* 1617

1485 to 1700

THREE
Post-Mediaeval Decline: An Exaggeration

The succession to the English throne in 1485 of Henry VII signalled the end of what is now called the 'Middle Ages': the end of a way of life overawed by religion and dominated by the Church. Society was beginning to turn its attention to more worldly matters, to commerce, manufacture, navigation, industry and the arts. If, so far, viticulture had been undisciplined and unscientific, there was now the opportunity for a different approach. Always more attuned to a secular ambience than to the monastic rule of duty, it would seem that English viticulture had never been healthier—in spite of comments of the kind made by the anonymous Italian traveller who noticed the grapes growing everywhere as he went about the English countryside of 1501. 'Wine might be made from them in the southern parts but would probably be harsh' he jotted in his journal.

He assumed that the grapes were being grown in order to be made into wine, and that was the principal purpose of every vineyard. The cultivation of fine eating-grapes would not be possible until glass became available which admitted light and contained heat (generated from 'pine stoves' and the like). A vine planted against a wall which reflected and increased the heat of the sun, or was heated by the fire behind it—a 'flued wall'—would produce passable dessert grapes; but grown in well-spaced rows 'vineyard fashion' a vine produced wine-grapes destined only for the wine-press and unsuitable for the table.

When Henry VIII succeeded to the throne in 1509 it is reckoned that there were 139 sizable vineyards in England and Wales, of which eleven were owned by the Crown, sixty-seven by noble families, and fifty-two by the Church. Writing at the end of the sixteenth century, William Harrison believed the country to be producing between two and three thousand tuns of wine a year, or 630,000 gallons. The best English wine, he said, was called

'Theologicum' because 'it was from the clergy and religious men, unto whose houses many of the laity would often send for bottles to be filled with the same'.

An English 'Herbal and Bestiary' from the early sixteenth century shows 'Sorbus', the White Rose, and the Vine with a serpent curled around the trunk.

58

The Problem of Climate

In spite of these facts it is usually supposed that at the end of the Middle Ages viticulture declined in England due to changes in the climate. Evidence of viticultural activity in England has always been hard to find, and it is true that there seems to be even less evidence of viticulture after the fifteenth century. Less ground and less people, producing less grapes and less wine, may characterize the period following the accession of the Tudors, but I find it difficult to believe that the sole cause was a change in climate. Whatever climatic change may have occurred, Europe and its vineyards shared the effect with England and its vineyards. If it was sufficient to affect England's viticulture, it affected Europe's too; though of course a small change for the worse would have a more telling effect on vines growing in a more northerly latitude—more on the edge, so to speak, of incompatibility—than those to the south which enjoyed a greater degree of tolerance.

A growth threshold of 10°C for vines means that the growing season usually starts between mid-April and mid-May. A fall in temperature of only one degree centigrade during these months will delay the start of growth by about ten days one year in two, with a three in twenty chance of at least twenty day's delay. As the climate cools, cloud cover and rainfall increases, and the earlier appearance of autumn rain and frost would have shortened the ripening and harvest period in a country where every additional day of sunshine must be critical. Due to this the frequency of successive vintage failures would gradually have become apparent.

Low temperatures in winter, so long as they are not extreme, have little effect on dormant vines in whatever part of Europe they grow. Severe frosts affected the northern limit of vineyards in France and Germany in a few of the historic winters, and cultivation was never resumed in some parts of France after 1709. The winters of the 1430–1440 decade might have had a similar outcome both in France and Germany. It is the summer warmth which matters. Professor Hubert Lamb, in *The Earlier Mediaeval Warm Epoch and Its Sequel* (1965), gives the prevailing temperatures in central England from 800 to 1950. In the high summer (July and August) of 1500–1550 the prevailing temperature was 15.9°C, the same as it had been in 1350–1400, and higher than in 1400–1450 (15.8°C) and 1450–1500 (15.6°C). Between 1150 and 1300 it had been a consistently high 16.7°C; but between 1550 and 1600 it fell to 15.3°C.

To a layman these variations seem miniscule. Indeed Professor Lamb,

was prompted to make his investigations by the controversy over whether they were large enough to be significant in upsetting the balance of Nature. His conclusion was that the range of alteration of the average temperature level had significant implications for agriculture and the human economy. The changes in the south 'are thought to account for the history of the vineyards'. His statistics showed that it was 'cool springs, May frosts and to a less degree lack of summer warmth that in the end told against the vine in England'.

In his *Britannia* published in Latin in 1586, a book which came nearest to being a sixteenth-century Domesday Book, William Camden recalled William of Malmesbury's eulogy of Gloucestershire's fine vintage. Camden saw a certain decline from that time, though he did not believe that it was due to any inexorable cause, dictated by Nature, from which Man had no escape. 'Neither do I believe with the idle and discontented husbandmen whom Columella reprehends, that the soil worn out by excessive fruitfulness in former ages, is now become barren. But from hence (to pass to other Arguments) we are not to wonder that so many places in this country from their vines are called Vineyards because they formerly afforded plenty of wine; and that they yield none now is rather to be imputed to the sloth of the inhabitants than the indisposition of the climate.'

To me that seems the most sensible observation ever made on English Viticulture: it remained as true throughout the following centuries as it was when it was made. Both the sloth of the inhabitants and the indisposition of the climate have always made it difficult to grow wine-grapes in England. The volume of grapes required for wine-making means they have to cover a large area of ground. In hotter climates average results will come with a minimum of effort; in more temperate, borderline climates closer attention, more hours of work and a greater degree of technical knowledge, are needed, and the latter must be more precisely applied. Nature does not work so hard for vine-growers in the north as she does for those further south. In England, it has always been a question of planting the right variety of vine: one which would grow and ripen in a less benevolent climate.

Opposite: it seems that outsize bunches of grapes were picked at Bruges in the sixteenth century on the same latitude as Somerset in England. This illustration is from a 'Book of Hours' of 1525.

1536: the Dissolution of the Monasteries

The abbots and monks, living, as they did, in close, regimented communities which grew their own food and drink, had undoubtedly brought English vine-growing and wine-making to the state of an 'industry'.

In its last session of 1536 the Reformation Parliament dissolved two

In spite of the Dissolution of the Monasteries in 1536 which many people believe put an end to English viticulture, the pruning of vines and the treading of grapes continued to be featured in sixteenth-century prayer book calendars reflecting everyday occupations.

hundred monasteries and one hundred nunneries each of whose annual revenues amounted to less than £200. During the next three years Henry managed to bribe or browbeat the remainder into submission, and had all the monastic houses vested in the Crown.

An element of the English viticultural scene which placed the activity in the centre of English life was removed for ever. The knowledge, enthusiasm and energy of the monks who worked the vineyards and winepresses were never to be replaced in quite the same way. However although all religious orders were abolished, many expelled monks were appointed to benefices, and new bishoprics were created at Bristol, Chester, Gloucester, Oxford and Peterborough. An abbot who had been used to drinking wine from his own vineyard was unlikely on becoming a bishop, to have lost his taste for so pleasant a part of his way of life. The king issued many royal injunctions on such matters as the removal of superstitious images and the deportment of the clergy, but there was no dread ban on the clergy keeping a vineyard or on the drinking of wine made from their own grapes. Those who had mismanaged the more disreputable monasteries and abbeys which were scrubbed entirely off the map may have been the worst and laziest vineyard-keepers; though of course it is equally possible that many of them might have been unacceptable for the very reason that they knew how to keep immaculate vineyards but neglected the care of souls.

What was the fate, for instance, of the vineyard at Barking Abbey of which a terrier (property register) of 1540 contained the following entry:

Item: a vineyard, empaled with elmes, well stored with vines, by estimacon 5 acres—[rent] 20 shillings.

The map, by Ralph Agas, of Tilty in Essex, shows that the vineyard was still a going concern at the end of the century. When properties such as Pershore Abbey and Battle Abbey became noblemen's country estates there is little reason to doubt that the new owners prized the bonus acquisition of a well-maintained vineyard and winepress, and ensured that the standards were kept up and, where low, raised. When Pershore Abbey was dissolved, 'le Wynward' was assigned to Conan Richardson for an annual rent, and in 1554 it passed with the abbey to William and Francis Sheldon. The site of the Pershore Abbey vineyard is just outside the north west end of the town on well-drained, sloping ground facing south and east, and is to-day filled with a new housing estate which commemorates it in its name.

Vine-growing and wine-making did not disappear from England after the dissolution of the monasteries in the middle of the sixteenth century even though this coincided with the coming of what has been called the 'Little Ice Age'. The vineyard of Darley Abbey in Derbyshire, for instance, which must have been one of the most northerly in the kingdom, was still functioning in 1557 in the reign of Mary Tudor according to Samuel Pegge (1763) who added 'And if I be not mistaken the several villages there of

This rather fuzzy image is a section of the four-hundred-year-old map, drawn by Ralph Agas in 1593, of Tilty Abbey in Essex. It seems to indicate the survival of the vineyard after the suppression of the abbeys and monasteries in 1536.

South Winfield, North Winfield, and Wingerworth all take their names from the vineyards formerly flourishing at those places'. The same can be said for the Vineyard Fields of Fobbing (1539) and The Vineyard at West Thurrock (1547), both in Essex.

In Kent, records of 1580 tell of vineyards in the manors of Wardens and Fyll in Egerton, Boughton Malherbe and Hool Mill in Harrietsham. The noblemen of Elizabethan England were proud to fill their cellars not only with Rhenish and Gascon wine but with the fresh, *wine of the country* as distinctively English as Colchester oysters, Stilton cheese, downland honey, Cox's orange pippins and the intoxicating poetry of William Shakespeare.

The actor-poet who was writing between 1590 and 1610 knew from Geraldus Cambrensis's description how open-air vines were grown in Wales in the eleventh century. In *The Tempest* (Act 4, scene 1) Iris talks of the 'pole-clipt vineyards'. When Shakespeare was writing *Henry VIII* he referred to what would have been common knowledge at the end of the sixteenth century. He gave these lines to Archbishop Cranmer who had known the vines of Westwell Priory in Kent, given to him by Henry VIII:

> In her days every man shall eat in safety
> Under his own vine what he plants, and sing
> The merry songs of peace to all his neighbours.

In writing the speech of the Duke of Richmond on the Plain of Tamworth before the Battle of Bosworth in the second scene of the fifth act of *Richard III* Shakespeare drew on what he himself had seen all over England and knew was familiar to his audiences:

> The wretched, bloody and usurping boar
> That spoil'd your summer fields and fruitful vines
> Swills your warm blood like wash and makes his trough.

Vines under Glass

The vines of England, set in rows in the open-air ambience of a vineyard, had always grown and ripened naturally under the summer sun. The existence of a vineyard signified wine-making; the two went together because, for the most part, the vines of England produced the small wine-grapes for pressing, not eating. However, at the end of the sixteenth century, English

gardeners started intensifying the sun's heat by leaning glass sashes against the wall on which the vines grew. Glass became more readily available in the fifteen-sixties when there was an influx of glass-makers from Lorraine, who made broad glass, or 'cylinder' glass for glazing; there was also a revival of the English glass industry at Chiddingfold in the Weald. To keep the glass sashes in position a framework came to be built around them, and these developed into the glass 'houses' which entirely enclosed the vine. This led to a specialized form of viticulture, concentrating on the production of single vines within the confined space of the glasshouse which produced larger, sweeter, more palatable grapes for eating at the table as 'dessert'. Glass also allowed a vine to be grown in an enclosed space which could be heated by a stove yet admit light, which had not been possible before. In order to get light, vines had been grown against heated walls without any covering, but obviously walls and glasshouses prohibited the quantities of vines required for wine-making. Those who sought to produce their own *vin de pays* continued to grow wine-grapes in open-air vineyards.

The Seventeenth Century: an Age of Science and Ingenuity

Curiosity was the new motive power of seventeenth-century England, and it was directed as much at what one might loosely call 'gardening' as anything else. The feudal aristocracy had followed the example of the monks but the unsettled political conditions of the Middle Ages and recurrent local wars discouraged expenditure of time and money on cultivating plants and trees which were so easy to destroy; but by the fifteenth century every manor house had its garden, and the rise of prices and growth of population in the sixteenth and seventeenth centuries further stimulated interest in horticulture and market gardening, particularly around London. The skill and attention being given to the successful cultivation of fruit such as apricots and strawberries was also applied to the cultivation of grapes. There were many men of vision and energy eager to explore, exhort and advise. Typical was 'that learned and great Observer' Sir Hugh Plat who, in his Author's Epistle to *The Garden of Eden* (of which more later) addressed to all Gentlemen, Ladies and all others delighting in God's Vegetable Creatures, explained that his purpose was 'the pleasuring of others who delight to see rarity spring out of their own labours, and provoke Nature to play, and shew some of her pleasing varieties when she hath met with a stirring Workman'.

Another compiler of practical information on how to make the earth yield her produce was Sir Thomas Hanmer who devoted a whole section

of his *Garden Book* of 1633 to viticulture. But he was one of the few who felt obliged to discourage it.

Ignorance was born of vagueness, knowledge of precision. The educators of the seventeenth century believed that the way to enlightenment was through classification which they applied to horticulture along with everything else. The pleasing varieties of vine which Nature was prepared to offer a stirring workman, though not purporting to be those necessarily suited to England, were listed by John Parkinson for the guidance of other apothecaries like himself in making up preparations—such as using the ashes of burnt grape leaves as a 'lye' for the relief of stone and gravel in the kidneys. He listed twenty-three in his *Theater of Plants* (1640) including The Blacke Grape of Orleance, the Frontignacke or Muske Grape, The Damasco White Grape, The Raisin of the Sun Grape. Was the *Vitis Sylvestris trifolia Canadensis* which constituted number five of his main classification of Tribe 16, The Vine, a relation of the Canada-grape which Samuel Hartlib recommended for England (see page 68)? Or was that the *Vitis laciniatis-foliis* which he sub-titled Parsely Vine?

Parkinson like Hanmer was patronizing about growing vines in the open air.

> Many have adventured to make vineyards in England, not only in these later days but in ancient times . . . For although divers both nobles and gentlemen have in these later times endeavoured to plant and make vineyards and to that purpose have caused Frenchmen, being skillfull in keeping and dressing Vines, to be brought over to perform it, yet either their skill faileth them or their Vines were not good, or (most likely) the soil was not fitting, for they could never make any wine that was worth the drinking, being so small and heartlesse, that they soon gave over their practice.

King James I (1603–25), had a vineyard on his estate at Oatlands Park in Surrey. There is no record however of whether the wine produced from its grapes was worth the drinking and to what extent, to disprove Parkinson's theory, it was great and full of heart. The King's interest in viticulture extended his commanding a Frenchman called Bonavil to write a short treatise on Vines and Silkworms for the instruction of the plantations of Virginia. Besides the royal vineyard at Oatlands, the King had a Physic and Vine Garden near St James's Palace. At a later date, close to Rosamond's Pond not far from the site of this garden, stood The Vineyard tavern, sometimes called The Royal Vineyard.

King James's vineyard was not the only one in Surrey. Charte Park near Dorking was called The Vineyard when it belonged to the Sondes family. Beresford Hope bought it and added it to the grounds of Deepdene which was built in 1652. 'Vine Row' in Richmond marked the site of a

vineyard—to-day there is still a road called 'The Vineyard' running from Richmond Hill to Church Road, and a 'Vineyard Path' parallel to Mortlake High Street which may mark the site of Sir William Temple's Sheen vineyard.

Wine-grapes would have filled the vineyard in the walled garden of the Manor of Quekes or Quex on the East Kent coast near Birchington. In London numerous 'Vine Courts' appeared, though they probably only signified single vines on a wall. In 1620 there is first mention in Middle Temple records of the Vine Court off Inner Temple Lane; and in 1630 there was known to be another off Shoe Lane by Currier's Alley (now St Brides Street). Harry Harben lists eleven Vine Courts in his 1918 *Dictionary of London.*

Whether the fields named 'Vineyard' still grew grapes, any more than the many 'Bullrings' still housed bulls, is not clear. What of the Vineyard Field at Saffron Walden (1605), and the field still being called The Vineyard on the site of the Domesday vinery at Great Waltham in 1616? Both of these are in Essex. Certainly the Domesday vineyard of Ely in the grounds of the abbey, which had been laid out by the first abbot in 970–81, was still being cultivated in 1684, though the last recorded sale of wine seems to have taken place in 1469. In the 1607 edition of *Britannia* William Camden says it was decayed. Place Name Lists of counties are of course full of 'Vine Halls' and 'Vine Farms'—in my own county of Sussex I know for instance of a seventeenth-century Vine Hall at Mountfield and a Vine Farm at Framfield owned by a John Vine—and anyone looking for ground on which to plant a vineyard to-day could not do better than choose such a site. For if the soil and situation had once been favourable for the growing and ripening of wine-grapes, they will still be to-day.

In the Weald of Kent there was a vineyard planted by one Captain Nicholas Toke who according to H. M. Tod (1910) 'so industriously and elegantly cultivated and improved our English vines that the wine pressed and extracted from their grapes seems not only to parallel but almost to outrival that of France'. After all, 'the Commune of Beaune grows at least three classes of wine and there is nothing to prevent Sussex growing wine equal to the second of these as well as the ordinary'.

Edward Hasted writing in 1797 confirmed this. 'There was a vineyard at Godinton in Captain Nicholas Toke's time from which was made wine of an extraordinary fine sort and flavour.' Nicholas Toke had five wives and died aged 93 in 1680 which meant he only just missed the great earthquake of May 1580' which frightened the inhabitants so much they rose from their beds.'

In the sixteen-twenties Sir Peter Ricard was also having a notable success with a vineyard and winepress at Great Charte in the Weald of

Kent, where every year he produced six or eight hogsheads of English wine. I have already quoted from *The Compleat Husband-man; or A Discourse of the whole Art of Husbandry both Forraign and Domestick. Wherein many rare and most hidden secrets and experiments are laid open to the view of all for the enriching of these nations,* by Samuel Hartlib, published in 1659. Hartlib instanced Sir Peter Ricard as one of the Ingenious Gentlemen who usually made wine 'very good, long lasting, without extraordinary labour and costs'. His wine was 'very much commended by divers who have tasted it, and it hath been very good'. And this in spite of the Wilde of Kent, as he called it, being 'very moist and cold'. Great Charte was called the Certh in Domesday Book which noted a vineyard there, and to-day is Ashford.

Hartlib recalled other 'experiments' by amateurs who were far removed from earlier generations of professionals who had made wine regularly on monastery winepresses; one was by a Gentle-woman in Surrey who, having stamped on some grapes which she had surplus in order to make verjuice (grape juice) found to her surprise 'after drawing it forth . . . found it very fine brisk *wine*, clear like *Rock-water*.' So

> I desire Ingenious men to endeavour raising of so necessary and pleasant a commodity; especially when French wine is so dear here, and I suppose is likely to be dearer. I question not but that they shall finde good profite and pleasure in so doing and that the State will give all encouragement to them; and if the French wine pay excize and customes* and the Wines here be toll-free they will be able to affoord them far cheaper than the French can theirs, and supply the whole Isle, if they proceed according to these Rules.

The first of Sam Hartlib's rules was to choose the best sorts of grapes *which are most proper to this Isle.* It seems an obvious one, but it is what so many twentieth-century growers ignored. He recommended four sorts: the Parsely Vine or Canada-grape; the Rhenish-grape; the Paris-grape; and the Small Muskadell.

Hartlib had strong views about the relevance of latitude to viticulture.

> Whereas we find at this present day vines flourishing many hundred miles more towards the North both in France, Lorraine and Germany, and that they are crept down even to the latitude of England (for the Rhenish-wines grew within a degree of the west-southern places of this isle, and Paris is not two degrees south of us), yet vines grow threescore miles on this side

---

* A customs duty of fourpence a gallon was introduced in 1671 but the Methuen Treaty of 1701 reduced the duty on port.

of Paris, as Beaumont; yes, the vines of these places are the most delicate; for what wine is preferred before the neat Rhenish for Ladies, and at table; and truly in my opinion, though I have travelled twice through France, yet no wine pleased me like Vin D'Ache and of Paris especially about Rueill which is a very fine brisk wine and not so fuming up to the head and inebriating as other wines. I say therefore that it is very probable that if vines have stept out of Italy into Alsatia, from thence to these places which are even as far north as England and yet the wines there are the most delicate, that they are not limited and bounded there. For a hundred miles more or less can set little alteration in heat or cold, and some advantages which we have will supply that defect.

He recommended that any Gentleman wanting to plant a vineyard should choose a fine, sandy, warm hill open to the south east rather than the south west.

'When the time of grape gathering is come . . .' What to do and how to do it are explained in this manual of 1656. Viticulture still flourished in sixteenth- and seventeenth- century England in spite of the supposed change of climate.

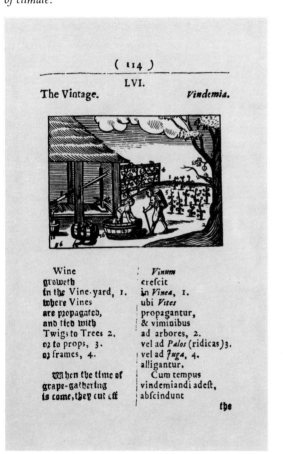

(114)

LVI.

The Vintage.   *Vindemia.*

Wine | *Vinum*
groweth | crefcit
in the Vine-yard, 1. | in *Vinea,* 1.
where Vines | ubi *Vites*
are propagated, | propagantur,
and tied with | & viminibus
Twigs to Trees 2. | ad arbores, 2.
or to props, 3. | vel ad *Palos* (ridicas)3.
or frames, 4. | vel ad *Juga,* 4.
 | alligantur.

When the time of | Cum tempus
grape-gathering | vindemiandi adeft,
is come, they cut off | abfcindunt

the

(115)

the Bunches, | *Botros,*
and carry them in | & comportant
meafures of three |
bufhels 5. | *Trimodiis,* 5.
and throw them | conjiciuntque
into a Vat, 6. | in *Lacum,* 6.
and tread them with | calcant *pedibus,* 7.
their Feet, 7. |
or ftamp them with a | aut tundunt
wooden Peftill, 8. | *ligneo Pilo,* 8.
and fqueefe out the | & exprimunt
juice in the | fuccum .
Wine-prefs, 9. | *Torculari,* 9.
which is called muft,11. | qui dicitur *Muftum,* li.
and being received in | &.*Orcâ* 10.
a great Tub, 10. | exceptum,
it is powred into | *Vafis* (Doliis) 12.
Hogfheads, 12. | infunditur,

it is ftopped up 15. | operculatur, 15.
and being laid clofe in | & in *Cellis*
Cellars upon fettles 14. | fuper *Cantherios* 14.
it becommeth wine. | abditum, in Vinum a-
It is drawn out of | E *dolio*   (bit.
the Hogfhead, | promitur,
with a Cock, 13. | *Siphone,* 13.
or faucer, 16. | aut *Tubulo,* 16.
(in which is | (in quo eft
a Spigot) | *Epiftomium*)
the Weffel being | Vafe relito.
unbunged.

I 2   Zytho-

If any finde such a fine warm hill and do dung and fence it well, he hath a greater advantage of most of the vineyards of France by this conveniency than they have of our Isle by being a hundred miles more South; for most of their vineyards are in larger fields not enclosed, on land that is stony and but indifferently warm. But some will say that wet weather destroys us. It's true that the wet will destroy things: sheep, corn & c. Yet no man will say that therefore England will not produce and nourish these creatures; and if extraordinary wet years come, they spoil even the vines in France; but take ordinary years and our moisture is not so great (though some abuse us and call England *matula Coeli*) but the vines especially those I have mentioned before, will come to such perfection as to make good wine; and if extraordinary raines fall yet we may help the immaturity by Ingenuity as I shall tell you anon, or at worst make vinegar or verjuice which will pay costs.

The advantage of England was that the island was not subject to nipping frosts that could occur during May in France; the island air was 'more grosse' than on the continent, not so piercing and sharp. English winters were not so sharp as in Padua, and England was not so subject to hail storms in the summer. 'We may make an abundance of wine here with profit, the charges of an acre of vineyard not being so great as of the hops ... 2,000 vines an acre at 50s a year is the ordinary rate for the three diggings with their crooked instrument called Sventage, and the yield was usually four tuns an acre.'

Hartlib recommended getting a vigneron from France where there were plenty of them and at cheaper rates than ordinary servants in England. The man could also act as gardener. 'If we here in England plant vines as we do hops, it will do very well; but let them not be packt together too thick as they do in France in many places, least they too much shade the ground and one another.' His recipe for a good compost was brimstone, pigeon dung, lees of wine, blood and lime (with moderation).

Lord Salisbury Plants Thirty Thousand Vines At Hatfield

An Ingenious Nobleman who anticipated Samuel Hartlib's ideas was Robert Cecil, the first Earl of Salisbury, the builder of the new Hatfield House, the magnificent Jacobean mansion which still stands to-day, in the grounds of a very much older building. The earlier building had become an episcopal residence for the bishops of Ely in 1109 when the abbey of Ely

*Between 1607 and 1611
Robert Cecil, first Earl
of Salisbury, built this
mansion at Hatfield.
In the walled area still
known as The
Vineyard he planted
thirty thousand French
vines.*

became a bishopric—and the connection between Hatfield and the Isle des Vignes is interesting though probably not of any great significance.

Whether or not he was inspired by the viticultural tradition of the former owners of the old manor, Lord Salisbury decided that he too would have a vineyard; and there is a document in the archives at Hatfield House which shows that in 1610 he paid the botanist John Tradescant to go to Flanders to buy vines. In February 1611 the French ambassador to the Court of St James's, Antoine de la Boderie, sent Lord Salisbury 20,000 vines, with an assurance that another 10,000 would follow. These were planted in the walled area still known as The Vineyard on both sides of the steep banks of the Broadwater, a stretch of the river Lee.

Accounts, which have survived, show payments made over the next two decades to gardeners for dressing the vines, but by about 1640 other kinds of fruit trees were being planted as well. John Evelyn paid a visit in 1643 and noted in his diary 'the most considerable rarity besides the house were the garden and vineyard, rarely watered and planted'—finely, that is of course, not infrequently. It is known that the vineyard was being well looked after when Charles I was a prisoner at Hatfield in 1647, though probably by the end of the Civil War it had become more of a pleasure garden than a wine-producing vineyard. There are no records among the many early references to the vineyard in the archives at Hatfield of grapes actually being harvested. 'One presumes that some wine was produced,' R. H. Harcourt Williams, the present Lord Salisbury's librarian and archiv-

Vnderstanding by yo lo[rdshi]ps speech yesterday
that yo were about to send some present of
gratificacon to Madame de la Boderye in
regard of yo vynes, lett yo lo[rdshi]ps honnty w[hi]ch
knowes the true limits of honor of itselfe should be
misledd by my dysesteeming the things y[ou]d
a sodayne, wh[i]ch y valaed the but att 4s the
thought good to lett yo lol know that y before it be to late
misredned my selfe; for 20000 att 8 crownes
the thousand, cometh to neer 50 sterling, besyds
the cariage. And besydes the Amb[assado]r sent me word
yesternight by his Maistre d'hostell that ther
are 10000 more a coming, w[hi]ch he hath consigned
to be deliuered heer to me for yo lol vse. w
wilbe heer in 15 dayes. yo lol knowing this only
y need say not more of it // for these w[hi]ch we
shall haue eyther fro him or mr Bell more then
the ground prepared will receyue, we will make
a nurcery of them, sett thick together in some smd
peece of ground adioyning, to supply those still
w[hi]ch we shall fynd dyscayne or dying.

y haue talked w[i]th wryght of the Temple that
made my lord Cooks pypes of irth, who tells me
that ther is neuer a yard but my lo Cook must
pay 12d for, besydes the cariage digging the
trenches and making vp the ground agame w
vpon the point will come to the same redoming
that the other demands of 12s a yard. Wright
him selfe was attending forth me all this forenoone att yo
lol chamber to geue satisfaccon therin. y am
sorry to truble yo lol w[i]th such pore things as thes
but it is necessery we haue a resolucon herin, els those
things will not be reddy by the tyme yo lol woll haue the
done

Brittayns
Burse 5 feb
1610

                    yo lol most bomde seruat

                          Tho: wilson

ist tells me, 'but no accounts of it were kept and we have no idea of what it was like'. It is likely however that the grapes, being grown 'vineyard fashion' were wine-grapes, with those grown against the walls, dessert grapes.

Samuel Pepys found himself in Hatfield on July 22, 1661 and strolled over to see the house and its renowned garden.

> Up by three and going by four on my way to London; but the day proves very cold so that having put on no stockings but thread ones under my boots I was fain at Bigglesworth to buy a pair of coarse woollen ones and put them on. So by degrees till I come to Hatfield before twelve o'clock where I had a very good dinner with my hostess at my Lord of Salisbury's Inn, and after dinner though weary I walked all alone to the Vineyard which is now a very beautiful place again; and coming back I met with Mr Looker my Lord's gardener (a friend of Mr Eglin's) who showed me the house, the chappell with brave pictures and above all the gardens such as I never saw in all my life; nor so good flowers nor so great gooseberries as big as nutmegs.

He paid the vineyard a second visit in 1667. H. B. Wheatley who edited an edition of Samuel Pepys's *Diary* for George Bell & Sons in 1924 stated in a footnote: 'the vineyard is still carefully kept and is one of the last of its age existing'. This seems to infer that a vineyard with vines growing in it, and not just a piece of land called The Vineyard, still existed in 1924; but in 1976 Mr Harcourt Williams was of the opinion that by 1700 'the vines had probably been replaced by fruit trees'. A number of yews were also planted there at this time, he says. Writing in *Notes and Queries* of July 13, 1946 someone signing himself 'H'A.' stated 'a mediaeval vineyard at Hatfield is mentioned by Pepys (22 July 1661) and is still in existence'. That H.A. should think the vineyard at Hatfield was mediaeval does not make him a reliable witness to the existence of the vineyard in 1946—unless he is hinting at some evidence which he alone might have that the Bishops of Ely planted an auxiliary vineyard, as it were, in Hertfordshire in 1109 to supplement the main supply from their Cambridgeshire vines.

Four years after his first visit to Hatfield Pepys had forgotten he had ever made it. 'Thence to the Duke of Albermarle' he wrote in his diary for May 1, 1665,

In this letter Thomas Wilson tells Lord Salisbury that, in his opinion forty thousand vines are likely to be more than the four-acre vineyard at Hatfield can take, so he will make a nursery for the surplus 'sett thick together'.

> where I was sorry to find myself to come a little late and so home, and at noon on going to the 'Change I met Lord Brunkard, Sir Robert Murry, Deane Wilkins, and Mr Hooke going by coach to Colonell Blunt's to dinner. So they stopped and took me with them. Landed at Tower Wharf and thence by water to Greenwich; and there coaches met us; and to his house, a very stately sight for situation and brave plantations; and among others a vineyard, the first that ever I did see.'

Colonel Blunt's house was at Writtlemarsh near Blackheath.

Samuel Pepys is said (by Captain C. A. Knapp in *Notes and Queries* July 13, 1946) to have attended a dinner party at Watford (he thought) at which he drank wine from grapes grown in the host's own garden 'than which all the company declared no wine out of France was more mellow'. I cannot find this entry however. 'Pepys's words' comments Captain Knapp, 'are sometimes taken to prove that French wines of that period could not have been sweet as at present but must have been acid as an English wine would be.'

John Evelyn had been a guest of Colonel Blunt's before Samuel Pepys. In his diary of 1655 he recorded going 'to see Colonel Blount's subterranean warren and drunk of the wine of his vineyard which was good for little'. He also visited a vineyard at Much Hadham in Hertfordshire in 1643. Certainly in 1649 there was a field at Much Hadham called Vineyard Croft which in 1946 had become Vineyard Springs.

In his diary entry of July 17, 1667 Samuel Pepys remarked on the excellence of the wine made by Admiral Sir William Batten from the grapes he grew in the beautiful garden of his house at Walthamstow. Referring to the taking of some prizes by a ship in which he and Sir William had an interest, Pepys wrote: 'I at Sir W. Batten's [where I] did hear the particulars of it; and there, for joy, he did give the company that were there a bottle or two of his own last year's wine, growing at Walthamstow; than which the whole company said they never drank better foreign wine in their lives'.

The English Vineyard Vindicated by John Rose (1666) and Eulogized by William Hughes (1670)

Being one day refreshing myself in the Garden at Essex-house and amongst other things falling into discourse with Mr Rose ... about vines, and particularly the cause of the neglect of vineyards of late in England, he reason'd so pertinently on the subject ... I was persuaded to gratifie his modest and charitable inclinations to have them communicated to the world.

Thus John Evelyn in his Preface to *The English Vineyard Vindicated* by John Rose, Gard'ner to His Majesty [William III] at his Royal Garden in St James's, Formerly Gard'ner to her Grace the Dutchess of Somerset, published in 1666.

'I know Your majesty can have no great opinion of our English Wines' the gardener told his sovereign in his Dedication,

as hitherto they have been order'd [?]. But as I persuade myself it is not altogether from the defect of the climate, at least not in all places alike; nor, I am sure, of the Industry of Your Majesties' subjects, but in some what else which I endeavour to encounter in these few pages; so if by Your Majesties' gracious Acceptance of the Essay, Gentlemen shall be encourag'd to plant these sorts of Vines which I here recommend, and to cultivate them by my directions, that precious liquor may haply once againe recover its just estimation, be the product of Your Majesties Dominions and answer the ambitions of . . . John Rose.

It was a dedication 'To the prince of plants, to the Prince of Planters'.

The title pages of the books by John Rose and William Hughes.

So many planters went, he said, for good soil, but this only contributed to the amplitude of the leaves, the luxury of the branches and the precipitation of the roots, rather than the excellence of the fruit and the just

THE *ENGLISH*

VINEYARD
VINDICATED

BY

JOHN ROSE

Gard'ner to His *MAJESTY*,
at his Royal *GARDEN*
in St. *James's.*

Formerly *Gard'ner* to her *Grace*
the *Dutchess* of *Somerset.*

With an Address,

*Where the best Plants may be had at
easie Rates.*

LONDON,
Printed by *J. Grismond* for *John Crook*,
at the *Ship* in St. *Pauls Church-yard*,
1666.

The Compleat Vineyard:
OR,
An Excellent way
For the
PLANTING
OF
VINES,
According to the
GERMAN & *FRENCH* manner,
and long Practised in *ENGLAND.*

Wherein

Is set forth the ways, and all the circumstances necessary for the Planting a Vineyard ; with the election of the Soil ; the Scituation thereof ; the best way for the Planting of the young Plants ; the best time and manner of Proyning ; the Turning and Translation of the Ground;

With other
NECESSARY OBSERVATIONS.
Also,

The fashion of Wine-presses ; the manner of brusing and pressing Grapes ; and how to advance our English Wines.

Enlarged above half by the Author, *W. Hughes.*
LONDON, Printed by *J. C.* for *Will. Crook*, at
the *Green-dragon* without *Temple-bar.* 1670.

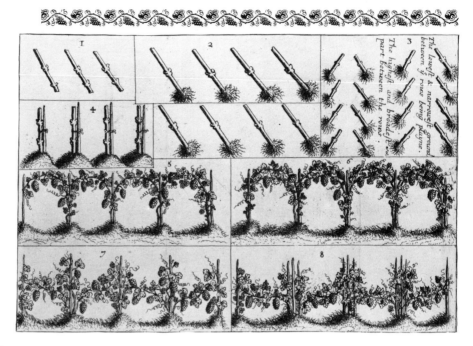

Within the illustration: The lowest & narrowest ground between ye rows being playne. The highest and broadest part between the rows.

A detailed illustration from The Compleat Vineyard *which was published in 1670. The advice given by William Hughes still holds good today.*

stature of the stem. Sandy, loamy soil was what vines needed, and this was obviously the kind of soil in William III's garden at St James's in which he found 'the new white grape with red wood and a dark leaf, the fruit of which ripens as soon in standard as against some walls'.

He deplored 'the strange decay of them [vines] amongst us for these latter Ages' and, as I have already said, put down the cause as 'our own neglect and the common vicissitude of things'. He then offered some words of wisdom of which the English viticulturists of the nineteen-fifties and sixties could well have taken heed.

> Nor are Gentlemen to be therefore deterr'd because this late age has neglected the planting of vineyards, that therefore it is to no purpose now to begin; since the discouragement has only proceeded from their mis-information on this material article of the choyce of soile and situation, whilst giving ear to our forraign Gardners coming here into England, then took up those rules which they saw to be most practical in Countries of so little affinity with ours.

He was one of the first to see that to compare our achievements in the circumstances dictated by English soil, English weather, English topography and England's island locale, with those resulting from the very different conditions of the land mass across the Channel, was meaningless. English wine-grapes and English wine had a character and tradition of their own.

76

One who like Rose also had full confidence in the future of a purely English viticulture was William Hughes who, in *The Compleat Vineyard* of 1670, pointed proudly to 'such vineyards and wall vines as produce a great store of excellent good wine' and that in spite of the fact that 'we are no nearer the pole than well-known German wines'. 'Our English wines are known to us' he said, 'and distinguished most properly by the names of deeper and paler coloured Clarets. White Wines are of two sorts, either sweeter or more sharp or austere, also a small Frantinick Wine—these are the Wines which this Climate most affords.'

As with manual-writers there was no dearth of classifiers. A horticulturist called Ray, in 1688, followed Parkinson's list with one which specified eleven sorts of vine; and the third oldest list is reckoned to have been compiled by a near namesake of his, John Rea, who in 1702 repeated Ray's list but added five of his own. John Rose listed some forty or fifty varieties.

How Good was Seventeenth-Century English Wine?

What of the wine made from all this viticultural activity? Accounts of it are sparse—perhaps because it was so common and unworthy of special remark. According to the county historian, Dr Robert Plot, Dr Ralph Bathurst, president of Trinity College, Oxford (and, significantly, Dean of Wells that traditional vine-growing area) 'made as good Claret here at Oxon AD 1685, which was a very mean year for that purpose, as one could wish to drink. Which is so far from wonder, that we are informed they planted vineyards and made wines antiently all over the kingdom'. The grapes growing on the south east slope of the Oxford Physic Garden were famous at this time, and maybe the doctor's Anglo-Gascon vintage was pressed from these.

Dr Plot had news of an even more North Country Wine than that. In his *Natural History of Staffordshire* (1686) he related:

> The Vine has been improved by the right worshipful Sir Henry Lyttelton to that advantage at Over-Arley which is situate low and warm, being surrounded with hills, that he has made wine so good there that it has been altogether undistinguishable from the best French wines by the most judicious palates; but this, I suppose, was done only in some favourable over-hot summer though, if Vines were placed advantageously, 'tis possible it might be done in an indifferent year.

Only slightly further to the south George Skipp is known to have been making red and white wine at the end of the seventeenth century from the grapes he grew at his vineyard at Upper Hall, Ledbury.

A principal incentive for wine-lovers to make their own liquor was the increasing cost of the imported variety. Since the fifteenth century the government had been fixing an official maximum price or 'assize' price for imported wine in order to control the cost. In 1553 the assize price of Gascon wine or 'clairet' was £5 a tun, or 8d a gallon. But by 1575 it had doubled to £10 a tun (1s 4d a gallon), which was certainly below its market value. By the end of the sixteenth century it had doubled again in London to 2s 8d a gallon. Rising taxation put up the cost even more, so that in the reigns of Charles II, James II and William III it had become prohibitive. William III raised the duty on wine in 1693 and imposed a scale according to the country of origin. The highest was on French wine at £22 2s 10d a tun; Rhenish wine paid £19 15s 3d a tun. In 1697 the duty on French wine was raised to £47 2s 10d.

Thus the inducement to stop drinking costly foreign liquor and turn to 'home-made' wine was very strong. The latter, it must be admitted, included fermented drinks made from fruits and herbs to be found growing wild throughout the English countryside. The fermentation of such herbal wines depended on considerable dosages of cane sugar. Before the discovery of America the only sweetening agent had been honey, which had been used in the making of mead and metheglin and was comparatively scarce. The supply of cane sugar from the West Indies became abundant and inexpensive for the first time in England during the seventeenth century.

It would not appear however that Sir William Temple, essayist and statesman (1628–99), was concerned with making wine from the grapes he grew in his famous Dutch garden at Sheen, in spite of it being on the site of a former Carthusian monastery. In his essay *The Gardens of Epicurus* (1685) he remarked: 'I may truly say that the French who have eaten my peaches and grapes at Shene, in no very ill year, have generally concluded that the last are as good as any they have eaten in France, on this side Fontainbleu.' But in viticulture as such, Sir William showed a very great interest, and was responsible for introducing to England four new varieties of grape: The Arboyse; the Dowager; the Grizelin Frontignac: 'the noblest of all the grapes I ever ate in England but it required the hottest wall and the sharpest gravel and must be favoured by the summer too, to be very good'; and one called the Burgundy, which he grew on an east wall and from which he might have made wine. After the Glorious Revolution of 1688 and the succession of William III, Sir William Temple moved to Moor Park where he established a second and more famous garden, of which no part, however, seems to have been a vineyard.

Sam Hartlib considered wine 'the greatest blessing of God which Hot Countreys especially enjoy, as temperate Countreys do Milk, Butter and Cheese in abundance'. The practice of making wine from English wine-grapes grown in open-air vineyards had not been brought to a full stop by a change in climate or by the transfer of monastic property to lay hands in the middle of the sixteenth century. The extent of the decline has been exaggerated. But there is no escaping the fact that viticulture, a difficult and demanding craft with rewards that varied in extent from year to year, had become less attractive in the years that followed the Dissolution. To seventeenth-century writers the hey-day of English wine-making seemed very remote, which underlines the degree of neglect. Even Sam Hartlib, who spent so much time researching this branch of husbandry, could only muster the weak conclusion that, notwithstanding God of his goodness had distributed peculiar blessings to each country according to whether they were hot, temperate or cold, 'I *dare say* it's *probable* that vineyards have formerly flourished in England, and we are to blame that so little is attempted to revive them again' (my italics).

The conditions which favoured the production of English wine had not changed, only the attitude as to how worthwhile it would be to take advantage of them. Sam Hartlib's use of the word 'revive' assumed suspended animation, not death. He was right. The tradition was still very much alive, though less known about than it might have been because of the lack of communications in those times. To effect complete recovery—though not a return to monastic 'factories'—more Ingenious Gentlemen were needed with the time and inclination to uncover for themselves what the years had obscured, and be inspired to experience, as others had done before them, the unique satisfaction of growing their own grapes and making drinkable wine of reasonable quality and reasonable cost.

1700 to 1800

FOUR

Viticulture Becomes
Scientific and Commercial

1727: 'S.J.' Asks Men of Quality to Discard Their Prejudice

No longer part of the cultural tradition of England as it had been in monastic times, serious commitment to large-scale wine-grape cultivation and wine-making now had to be justified commercially. The Good News spread, albeit slowly, that what stood between the persevering adventurer and success was not unsuitable weather and unsuitable soil but a prejudiced climate of opinion, the *idée fixe* that wine-making was not in the English tradition, and the reluctance to waste energy on anything other than an enterprise with recently demonstrated rewards, either in terms of cheap wine for the master's own table or easy money from the sale of it.

It was a boisterous age, and the drinking of wine was accompanied with little ritual or finesse. The stronger the potion the quicker the intoxication. A finer sort of liquor, such as English wine, would have held little attraction for many wine-drinkers, but those who were prepared to give the matter their consideration and weigh the pros and cons of becoming their own suppliers will have been heartened to read in Dr Hales's *Compleat Treatise on Practical Husbandry* (vol IV):

> This we can say with certainty, that very good wine may be made in England, and that in many parts of the kingdom there are pieces of land which may be turned to some account this way at a small expence . . . I have drank with the distinguished and eminent Dr Shaw wines made under his

own care from a little vineyard behind his garden at Kensington which equalled many of the lighter wines of France; and while due care was taken of the vineyard at Hammersmith, a great deal of very good wine was obtained there *for sale*, yet neither of these were favourable spots.'

Hales, who had a nursery at Teddington, advised would-be viticulturists to use the worst land. Vines, he said, thrived on poor soil. 'But they must be of a proper condition and whether pleasure *or profit* be the intent of the plantation, either will depend in great degree on that first choice.' (The italics are mine.) There were signs, for the first time since the Middle Ages, of commercialism in English viticulture.

Dr Hales of Teddington had the support of William Hanbury who wrote in his *Complete Body of Gardening*: 'I have known good wine made of grapes in England and have drunk our Burgundy no way inferior as my taste could find out to that noted wine which we have constantly imported from that country'. But the morale of any would-be viticulturist hesitating to take the plunge would have been boosted most of all by the writer who, for fear of ridicule or whatever else, preferred to shelter under the anonymity of the initials, S.J. and was the author of *The Vineyard, Observations made by a Gentleman on his Travels*, published in 1727.

'It has long been the prevailing opinion' he told the Courteous Reader in his introduction,

> that the raising of Vines to any tolerable Perfection in England was altogether Impracticable; and that all Attempts of that Nature would prove Fruitless, tho' their Opinions were founded upon no better Reason than Want of Experience; it being a common Argument with many People that such and such Things are altogether Impossible, because had they been Practicable they would have before been attempted. But the Absurdity of such Reasoning is too trifling to need any Confutation, unless the Objectors can shew from several repeated Experiments that all Attempts of that Tendancy have prov'd Ineffectual.

There had been several instances of people drawing wine from grapes of their own growth in England 'which they have found to excel many foreign Wines in their pleasant, brisk and palatable Flavour'. The lack of wine in England 'was not owing to the Unkindness of our Soil or the Want of a benign Climate, but to the Inexperience of our Natives or a Want of Curiosity in such as are capable of convincing themselves by an easy Experiment of the Practicableness thereof'. For long the growing of silk in England was regarded as an impracticable and ridiculous project; and the authors of such a proposition were treated with all the ill nature imaginable 'as silly, idle, chymerical Fellows'. They were told if it was possible it would

long before have been put in practice. Yet Colbert instituted such an experiment in France and a useful and profitable manufactory was established. So it could be in England with the vine, particularly in view of the improvements made in husbandry and gardening.

S.J. pointed out that Pliny in his *History* commended the Wines of England for Goodness and an agreeable Taste, and Relish, peculiar to the growth of this Country; as not being so apt to turn eager and sour as others were.

'Thus Interest originally was the Motive to discontinue the Cultivating of Vines in England, and turning the Vine-yards into arrable Lands; a Practice not much unlike it, we see at this very Time in Kent where Thousands of Acres of Arrable is turn'd into Cherry Gardens and Hop Grounds.' It was not more than a century or two before that the planting of peaches, nectarines, apricots and hops had been thought to be as ridiculous as planting a vineyard was believed to be in 1727, and all attempts to do so had been decried as impracticable. But the perseverance of those who planted hops in spite of the prejudice was crowned with success. 'Why an equal Success may not be expected in Planting of Vine-yards here in England would puzzle the Objectors to shew; And a little Time and Experience convince them that all their Cavils against the Possibility thereof are vain and groundless.'

The very fact that the English climate was not over-warm was an advantage for English viticulture. Grapes when gathered for the Press in these parts must not be so ripe as when gathered for the tooth. Those brought to the markets of London were over-ripe, and so not fit for making wine.

'Tis probable this Observation will be decry'd by those Persons who will not give themselves the Liberty of considering, and resolve to act upon, an implicit Faith, divesting themselves of Reason in favour of any prejudicial Notions they are possess'd of; who, having once obtained some favourite Absurdities, are so bigoted thereunto that the plainest Demonstration and Reason will not be sufficient to dispossess them of this Demon of Obstinacy, and nothing less than a Miracle can be expected to root out their Ignorance.

In his dedication of *The Vineyard* to the Duke of Chandos, S.J. said he hoped that many would put Practicableness of planting and cultivating vines to the test. When they had done so he doubted not 'it will be found upon Experience to answer Expectation' and they would be convinced

vineyards are easily reconcilable to the temper and soil of our climate. The objections of the want of sun is easily confuted when the temperateness of our soil is considered in opposition to the intemperature of France & c. The

wine of the Mosel which lies so northerly that the grapes never come to the maturity which they do in the southern parts of England were yet by the industry of the inhabitants rendered fine, potable, pleasant and preferable to those of many more southern parts.

He told such people to ask the cider makers. whether apples full ripe and mellow were most proper for making that liquor, or those not so ripe. 'The Answer they will receive to this Question might be sufficient to evince that Grapes may be as well too ripe to make Wine of, as not ripe enough.' For S.J.:

> that so Useful and Advantageous a Part of Agriculture has been so long neglected to the Reproach of the Natives of our Island and the Impoverishment of the Nation in General who have annually remitted large sums of Specie to purchase this exhillerating Liquor from Foreigners, which we might as well raise at home with a little Industry, and by a right Application. It seems as if Attempts of this Nature had been neglected not altogether out of a parsimonious Temper but for want of a true Knowledge and some due Encouragement. The Farmers content themselves with their yearly Crop of Grain; and are indeed necessitated so to do, by Reason many times their Circumstances will not permit them to continue several years in Expectation of a Return; which they must do at their first Planting a Vineyard; tho' afterwards the annual Income would make them a very ample Satisfaction, would their Circumstances permit them to wait the Event.

Vines, contended S.J., had once been as much strangers in Italy as in Britain. Cherries were more rare in Italy in Virgil's time than vines were in Britain. That exotic and foreign plants flourished in Britain which until then had been strangers, demonstrated the improvement in agriculture. This was the strongest reason to induce further experiments 'especially in those which, by Nature and Neighbourhood of the Soil and Climate where they thrive so well, seem more adapted to this Country than several others which have been introduced from more distant parts.'

'Would some of our Quality, whose Circumstances will better permit them, try the Experiment for a few Years, till a Vineyard could be brought to Perfection!' he concluded. 'The Success of so generous an Example would cause an Emulation amongst others; and their introducing so beneficial a Piece of Agriculture would render them truly Patriots of their Country, and add a Lustre to their Characters by shewing their Endeavours tend to the Interest and Welfare of their Fellow-Subjects and to remove the Obligations of being beholden to our Neighbours.'

The Eighteenth-Century Dialogue Continues

Twenty years after S.J.'s fulminations, Philip Miller rammed home the message in *The Gardener's Dictionary* (1747).

> There have of late years been but very few vineyards in England though they were formerly very common, as may be gathered from the several Places in divers Parts of England which yet retain that name, as also from ancient records which testify the Quantities of Ground which were allotted for vineyards to Abbeys and Monasteries for Wine for the use of the Inhabitants; but as to the Quantity of the Wines which were then produced in England we are at present ignorant; and how these vineyards were rooted up and became so generally neglected we have no very good accounts left. Whatever might be the Cause of this total Neglect in cultivating Vines in England, I will not pretend to determine, but such was the Prejudice most people conceived to any Attempts of producing Wine in England that, for some Ages past, every trial of that kind has been ridiculed by the Generality of People, and at this day very few Persons will believe it possible to be effected.

People have not changed much in two hundred years.

> From the success of some modern Essays made near London there would be no great Encouragement to begin work of this kind, so how can we expect Success? I shall humbly offer my Opinion which is founded upon some trials I have made . . . from whence it is hoped that the Prejudice which most People have against a Project of this kind will either be removed or at least suspended until Trials have been judiciously made of this affair.

In the event his name has lived in the annals of English viticulture as being the person after whom the Pinot Meunier variety of grape was called Dusty Miller. Edward Hyams (author of *The Grape-Vine in England*, 1949) reckoned that the Pinot Meunier was the Roman *aminea lanata* and had grown vigorously in Italy and France (where it was classed as *cepages nobles*) for two thousand years—and now in England too.

The first consideration, in Philip Miller's view, must be the choice of soil and situation: sandy loam, a foot above gravel or chalk, and a site on the north side of a river on an elevation inclining to the south. His way of preparing grapes for wine-making was to cut the bunches of grapes off the vine, spread them on wheat straw and let them lie there for three or four weeks to let the moisture 'perspire' from them.

84

In *The Art of Making Wines*, published at about the same time as Miller's book, William Graham 'late of Ware' stated 'it is the opinion of many gentlemen of undoubted experience that the southern part of this island, with the industry of the natives, might produce vines as fertile as those of France either for claret or white wines'. The soil in which they should plant their vines should be of a nitrous sulphurous nature; be black, loose and moist, proceeding from its oily quality or fatness, of which there was great plenty in England. The only manure needed was a little lime mixed with rotten cow dung, 'the one cherishing, the other heating, the roots of the vine.' He volunteered instructions 'To make Wine of the Grapes of The Growth of England.' 'There is a sort of muscadel grapes growing now in many parts of England which may be brought, by the help of a little loaf sugar to feed on, to produce a curious sweet wine little differing from Canary, and altogether as wholesome and pleasant.'

To Rev. Samuel Pegge MA of Whittington the prejudice against even attempting to make English wine was altogether too much, especially when, as in the case of the Hon. Daines Barrington, it was based on a belief that wine-grapes had *never* been grown in England, and that all accounts of their having been cultivated were a myth based on a misunderstanding of Latin. Pegge vented his feelings in two long papers read to the Society of Archaeologists and published in *Archaeologia* in 1763 and 1771. The first was prompted by a report from the Museum Rusticum; but his more vituperative observations came in his answer to the comments made on his first paper by the Hon. Daines Barrington, a fellow member of the Society, who contended that in ancient documents *vineae* referred to apples and pears, cider and perry, and not grape vines and wine. Pegge demolished this theory with detailed historical argument, and I have used much of the fruits of his research in my earlier chapters. But Pegge owes his place in this story to his spirited refutation of the theory that the climate of England prevented open-air vine growing. Did not some of the more austere wines grow in the Rhine or on the Maine in latitudes as high as 49 degrees 'which may equal perhaps in coldness ours of $51\frac{1}{2}$?'

Sir Edward Barry Bt. FRCS, FRS, who also made a detailed study of the subject in *Observations Historical, Critical and Medical on the Wines of the Ancients and the Analogy between them and Modern Wines* in 1775, took the point one further, and made a positive suggestion which someone might well take up to-day. 'No trials with vines have been made in any part of Ireland' he wrote 'where the latitude is the same as England's and the soil and situation seem to be more friendly to vines particularly in the most southern parts of the county of Cork.'

It was hilly country, said Sir Edward, and many of those hills were at a moderate distance from the sea, with a favourable south east aspect to the sun and defended from northerly winds. There were several inland places rather more favourably exposed and warmly defended with large rivers adjacent to them. Both ancients and moderns had observed that wine produced from hills exposed to the sea breezes and those rising from rivers had been chiefly distinguished for their superior qualities, for example, the Falernian wines and wine from the river Champaign.

More support came from 'R.G.' (Richard Gough) in the *Gentleman's Magazine* of 1775 (page 513) with an article 'Wine antiently made in England, contended for'. It was probable that the great monasteries in London, he said, had their vineyards as well as in other parts of the kingdom, and that the places which still retained the name of *vineyard* (that is in 1775) were without the walls of London. He instanced Vine-street in East Smithfield and Hatton Garden; and others in St Giles's in the Fields and in Piccadilly; The Vineyard by Houndsditch, that in Southwark opposite the Tower, a street in Richmond and elsewhere in Surrey.

The title pages of the books by F. X. Vispré, and by William Speechley, the Duke of Portland's gardener who spent seven years collecting vine-varieties from all over the world.

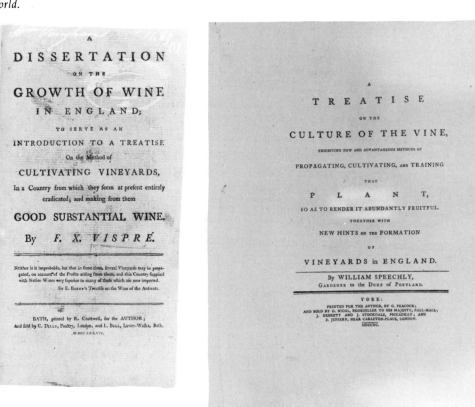

Whoever attends to the stout walls which enclosed the ancient gardens will think no difficulty in keeping a mob out of the most inticing vineyard, whose extent could not be comparable to a modern turnip or pea field. Dr James's vineyard must have been as much terra firma for an orchard, as for a vineyard. But this is only a single instance against many. The site of the monastic buildings at Croyland is too much altered to trace the vineyard there; but a warm S.W. bank at Denney Abbey, situated by Croyland in the fens near Cambridge, still retains the name of the *vineyard*.

Dr James's vineyard at Lambeth was also referred to by F. X. Vispré in the talk he gave to the Society of Arts, in 1784, on 'A Plan for Cultivating Vineyards Adapted to this Climate', a title which showed how far along the road the argument had already gone. It was no longer a question of dismissing the open-air cultivation of wine-grapes because of the unsuitability of the climate; but, given the climate as it was, what were the varieties of vine which *would* grow and ripen in it? This was progress indeed, and two years later (1786) Vispré followed up his talk with a comprehensive book entitled, *A Dissertation on the Growth of Wine in England; to serve as an Introduction to a Treatise on the Method of Cultivating Vineyards In Country from which they seem at present entirely eradicated; and making from them* GOOD SUBSTANTIAL WINE.

Anyone who intended to take Vispré's advice, but knew nothing of what varieties to plant, could have done no better than invest in a copy of *A Treatise on the Culture of the Vine . . . together with New Hints on the Formation of Vineyards in England* by William Speechley, the Duke of Portland's gardener, published in 1789. He had some hundred varieties growing at Welbeck, the Portland estate in Nottinghamshire. It took him seven years to make his collection and write his treatise. His vines came from all over the world, and in his book he grouped them into those suitable for the hothouse, for the vinery and for the wall. Joseph Thompson, who succeeded him as gardener at Welbeck, said that though Speechley was able to list 112 names he entertained great doubts that he would be able to make out fifty distinct kinds.

James Oglethorpe Plants a Vineyard at Godalming, ### 1720 to 1820

So much for the theorists. Who took heed of their theories and put them into practice? Two exercises of the eighteenth century stood out from all

'This Beautiful Spot is nearly inclos'd by a lofty Wall well stock'd with choice fruit Trees, & a noble Stream runs near a Mile long by the side of the Park.' The lofty wall, on the extreme left of this late eighteenth-century picture of Westbrook Place, was built by James Oglethorpe to enclose part of the vineyard which he planted around 1730.

others on account of their size, success and duration: Westbrook and Painshill.

James Oglethorpe (or Oglethorp) was born around 1688. He was the son of a leading Jacobite, Theophilus Oglethorpe, who married twice and had nine children of whom James was the last. For various reasons it was James who in 1718 at the age of thirty came into possession of Westbrook Place, a fine mansion built around 1680 by Sir John Platt (a relation of the Sir Hugh who wrote *The Garden of Eden* published in 1675?) which his father Theophilus had bought in 1688. The house had a classical front with a semi-circular portico and stood in a park of some 80 acres at the foot of a humped, wooded hill. It lay close to the small Surrey town of Godalming, some fifteen miles south of London. The house still stands today.

James Oglethorpe took over the family seat in the House of Commons as Member of Parliament for the Haslemere Division of Surrey. He was an ardent social reformer and made Westbrook the hub of a great philanthropic movement which brought about major reforms in London's prisons.

Shortly after becoming Squire of Westbrook James Oglethorpe built a massive wall up the humped hill and planted in front of it what some authorities are quoted as saying was probably the largest vineyard of its kind that England had ever seen. The wall was of stone, ten feet high and a foot thick with a rounded, bricked top. The part of it which ran up the

hill was some four hundred yards long. He had the ground outside the wall, falling away down the hill, levelled up to form a flat terrace some ten feet wide, and then a step four feet deep down to a second terrace stretching forwards about twelve feet, after which the ground fell precipitously down what remained of the hill to a lake. Along these two straight terraces, stretching the whole four hundred yards in front of the wall, Oglethorpe planted his wine-grape vines. Each terrace was broad enough to take two rows and it is likely that on the upper terrace vines were also splayed against the wall.

From these wine-grapes he made wine; the location of the winery is not known, though it may have been situated in one of the outhouses still standing on the right of the house as you face it. James Oglethorpe established his vineyard and winery between 1720 and 1732 when Westbrook was in its heyday as a social-political centre. The young MP and reformer held soirées and political gatherings almost every weekend, at which the local English wine flowed freely, and his guests enjoyed the delicacy for which Westbrook also became renowned: French snails, which Oglethorpe bred upon the vine leaves. He is also said to have turned loose in the vineyard a barrel of lizards which he had brought back from one of his frequent foreign jaunts.

James Oglethorpe conceived the idea of founding a colony in America as a refuge for people stricken by poverty, including many from London prisons, and for persecuted German protestants. In November 1732 he sailed across the Atlantic with 120 settlers and founded what became Georgia. He stayed for two years, and during that time his sisters occupied Westbrook and made it a hotbed of Jacobite intrigue. But they saw that the vineyard was kept in order, and the annual quota of Westbrook White maintained. James made several visits to England to raise funds and collect further settlers, including John and Charles Wesley who both spent some time in Georgia. James finally left the colony in July 1743. The following year he married an heiress, Elizabeth Wright, and the two of them settled at her estate at Cranham in Essex. He commanded a part of the army which crushed Bonnie Prince Charlie's Forty-Five Rebellion and re-took Preston for King George. He earned the sobriquet 'Brave General Oglethorpe'. He still retained Westbrook, however, and continued to visit it to supervise his affairs. Ironically it is said that, at the invitation of his hot-headed sisters, for a time Prince Charles Edward himself* stayed hidden at Westbrook

---

* Anti-Jacobites spread the rumour that when James II still could not produce a son and heir, he arranged for a live baby to be brought into the bedchamber, where the Queen had delivered yet another still-born child, in a warming pan. This, it was said, had been declared

during the Forty-Five Rebellion. If so, he probably drank to the downfall of the house of Hanover in a beaker of General Oglethorpe's best. For certainly the vineyard and the winepress continued to operate without interruption in spite of political upheavals.

The vineyard remained intact, and the wine-making seems to have continued at least until 1754, when Westbrook was visited by Dr Richard Pococke who noted of Godalming in his *Travels Through England*, published in that year, that it was 'where was General Oglethorpe's, where there is a vineyard out of which they make a wine like Rhenish'.

And it would appear to have survived longer than that, for when the general died in 1785 aged eighty-nine and the estate was put up for sale at Garraways Coffee House on May 2, 1788 (exactly a hundred years after his father had bought it), part of the description of the property on the sale particulars read: 'Also, Gardens and a Vineyard of considerable Extent, divided and subdivided with lofty Stone Walls, and supplied with an abundance of Fruit-Trees of various kinds'. Thirty-five years later it was up for sale again (June 23, 1823 at Garraways) when it was described as having 'A Good Kitchen Garden, part-walled and well planted'. There were also 'Enclosures of Meadow, Pasture, Arable and Wood Land' covering 82 acres, 2 rods and 38 perches. This area was broken down into five sections of which one was:

Vine Yards and Gardens   6a 2r 20p

So it looks as if the vineyard had a life of almost a hundred years. The subsequent owner was one Nathaniel Godbold who made a fortune out of patent medicines and was the inventor of a Celebrated Balsam to which he gave his name. In 1892 Westwood Place was acquired by the Countess of Meath and was opened in August of that year by the Countess of Albany as the Meath Home of Comfort for epileptic women and girls. By then the vineyard was no more, but it seems that until quite late one of the buildings on the estate was still known as 'Vineyard Cottage'. A local resident called Charles Softley, who was born in 1829 and died around 1915, filled several notebooks with personal reminiscences of 'Godalming and Its Neighbourhood' which Stanley Dedman, the borough librarian and curator, reproduced in an edited version in 1968. In the notebook in which he described Westbrook, Softley wrote: 'from the Shell House to the

---

the King's son and Prince of Wales. The substitute baby, who became the Old Pretender and father of Bonnie Prince Charlie, was said to be an elder brother of James Oglethorpe. The story is vouched for in detail in an account written by an old woman called Frances Shaftoe.

"Vineyard Cottage" to the left . . . ran a wall as now, and continuing to the extreme end and parallel to the Eashing Lane as far as and near to Mr Peachey's Farm. It almost surrounded the Estate. In the last named cottage, "The Vineyard Cottage", once lived a farm labourer with wife and four children'! It was Softley who recorded that General Oglethorpe turned lizards loose in the vineyard.

The once-named Westbrook Place was still the Meath Home when I had a walk round the estate—with the kind permission of Miss Jacobs the matron—in February 1977 to see what remained of the plot which, in its day, had been the largest vineyard England had ever seen. I walked round the front of the house, which faced east, to the site where allegedly the Oglethorpe vineyard had flourished for nigh on a century. What would I find? The tall trees grew close together, without leaves at this time of year, but festooned with ivy, shutting out the light and making the grove dark and dank. But there was no mistaking the wall: brown stone, certainly 'lofty' and capped with rounded brick. In front of it the hill sloped steeply down thirty or forty feet to Eashing Lane, which ran parallel to the wall just as Charles Softley had described it. The lane is now the boundary of the Meath Home property and separates it from the railway line which at this point runs into Godalming Station. Beyond and below the line is the lake, fed presumably by the Noble Stream, all of which, long before they laid the railway line, was part of the Westbrook eighty-acre estate. Immediately in front of the wall—that is facing the railway station—were the two broad terraces, the lower divided from the upper by a four-foot vertical step. It was purely earthwork; there was no stone or brick reinforcing the embankment. The path behind the wall up the hill was four feet higher than the first terrace. I walked along the terrace examining the wall on my right as I went. In the wall still were a number of rusty iron nails, held firmly in the masonry, which I like to think had once clutched the tendrils of the General's wine-grapes, though doubtless they had held other wall-climbing fruits as well, such as plums and peaches.

After some sixty yards the wall had collapsed—or had been purposely demolished? For 150 yards it lay in broken chunks which had fallen forwards on to the flat terrace in front. My foot slid into a crevice which had formed between two slabs of fallen wall—mortared bricks it seemed at this point—and, in pulling away the ivy to see what lay beneath, my hand was scratched by thorns. It was a gooseberry bush, alive and well and waiting for yet another spring, planted by who knows who as part of the well stocked garden which replaced the vineyard.

The collapsed wall ran up to the fence which divides the Meath Home property on its east side from the Little Fort, now occupied by Mr and Mrs Richard Flowitt, the old part of which is the only one of the four forts,

built in 1743 to defend Westbrook from anti-Jacobites, to survive. To the west of Little Fort the wall continued straight as ever, picking up the line of the first section in the Meath Home wood. It stretched for another 150 yards to the end of the next property, West Acre, occupied by Mr and Mrs House. There were no trees here; the ground was a well-tended, open garden. The two terraces, which in the Meath Home wood were difficult to discern through the undergrowth, were now clearly defined. The south face of the wall, clean and well-preserved, was pitted with old nails as before. At once it was possible to imagine the whole extent of the vineyard with its two broad terraces, the one four feet below the other looking on to the lake below, starting at the angled 'wing' in the wood and ending four hundred straight yards later at the end of the West Acre garden, possibly the site of Softley's 'Vineyard Cottage'.

Here, in the early eighteenth century, there took place a truly remarkable demonstration of the practicality of growing wine-grapes in the open air in England, and making from them 'wine like Rhenish' which, apparently, was produced in large quantities and satisfied the palates of the men of taste who formed James Oglethorpe's select circle. I was sorry I had to

Much of the wall built by James Oglethorpe in 1730 to enclose his famous vineyard still stands today — here it passes through the garden of a house called Little Fort. The wall was built with two forts, one of which can be seen in this photograph.

92

This illustration is from William Speechley's book A Treatise on the Culture of the Vine *(1790); it was a blue-print for any Ingenious Gentleman planning a vineyard—cautiously relying on the sun's heat being intensified by a wall. The terrace layout is similar to that still to be seen at Westbrook today.*

leave Westbrook without having found any sign of the Press House in which the General made the English wine which I like to think was quaffed and approved by (if Frances Shaftoe's story is true) James's romantic nephew Charles Edward Stuart/Oglethorpe.

The Vineyard of Charles Hamilton at Cobham, 1740 to 80

The second of the 'modern essays near London' to which Philip Miller in *The Gardener's Dictionary* was doubtless referring was the even more famous Surrey vineyard at Painshill near Cobham, some eighteen miles south of the capital.

This lay on the slopes of the high ground about St George's Hill above the Mole Valley. The same itinerant bishop, Dr Richard Pococke who noted Westbrook, came here in 1750. 'We came to Painshill near Cobham, Mr Hamilton's, which is a most beautiful farm improvement . . . There are ten acres of vineyard here in two places; the grape gently press'd makes an excellent champaign, and pressed out and left on the husk produces a very good Burgundy; five or six hogsheads have been made in a year, and it sells at the inns here at 7s 6d a bottle. Cobham is a very small town full of inns.' 'Mr Hamilton' was the Honourable Charles Hamilton, ninth and youngest son of James sixth Earl of Abercorn.

In 1738, when he was 34, Charles Hamilton took a long lease of Pains-hill, a smallish house with a large, wild park of some three hundred acres which, being a romantic at heart, he set about transforming into a magnificent garden complete with the usual 'follies' beloved by all landscapers of the time.

Part of the transformation, consistent with its romantic motivation, included the planting of a section of the southern-facing piece of ground, which sloped down to the lake, with wine-grape vines from which to make English wine. He saw the vineyard as flanking the north shore of the lake for several hundred yards east of the Ruined Chapel, with the vines set in close rows, up the hill with its gravelly, sandy soil and at right angles to the water, from which they were divided by a footpath.

The Hon. Charles Hamilton, son of the Duke of Abercorn, grew wine-grapes and made wine on a large scale at Painshill, Cobham in Surrey between 1740 and 1774—it was then the most famous vineyard in England. This portrait was painted by Antonio David in 1732.

94

The precise year in which Hamilton planted the vineyard is not known, but it must have taken some time to construct the artificial lake—it probably has a tiled bottom—and to complete the mechanical arrangements for keeping it filled with water from the river by means of a giant wheel. So it is unlikely to have been put down in that first year 1738/9, though it will have been seen as an important part of the transformation scene from the start. The vines were certainly bearing grapes by 1748 when Hamilton engaged a French vigneron to come and look after them for him, so they were probably planted between 1740 and 1743.

David Geneste came from a French Protestant ('Huguenot') family who for generations had owned a vineyard at Beziat in Clairac in Guienne. David Geneste was born in Clairac in 1692, some seven years after Louis XIV, King of France, had withdrawn his protection from French Protestants by revoking the Edict of Nantes. David's sister Marie stayed in France, inherited the Beziat vineyard and married André Borderie of Bourgade in 1723. But David decided to flee France along with so many other Huguenots, and at the end of the seventeen-thirties, when he was about forty, he landed in England. In 1739 he sent the first of a series of letters (which have survived) to his sister, now Mme Marie Borderie. He married an English girl called Anne Bateman by whom he had two sons and a daughter. The first Mrs Geneste died in 1748 but how David had supported himself up to then is not known, though it appears from later letters that he had a struggle to survive, and lived in great poverty. In that year however he was taken on as vigneron at Painshill Park by Charles Hamilton.

In a letter to his sister Marie at Beziat written in 1748 he told her he was working five or six leagues from home and earning a *louis d'or* a week: 24 *livres* or about a guinea. The vineyard, he said, was about fifteen *cartonnats* in size: some five acres. The grapes that year were very fine and they were planning to plant about ten acres next year. The park attracted many noble visitors who always gave him a tip. Already he had managed to put aside a nest egg of £50.

It was some time since he worked on the vineyard at Beziat and his recollection of how to manage one was somewhat hazy. Would Marie write and tell him about the most suitable methods and the right seasons for planting and cultivating the types of vine which he had seen growing at home when he was a boy? If he could make a success of things at Painshill, it would mean he could make a good living, as there was no one in England who understood vine-keeping. He found the Hamilton vineyard in a very bad state. Would she also send him some pruning knives which he could get a smith to copy for him?

His job at Painshill, he pointed out, was not merely to look after the vineyard but to supervise the running of the whole estate, apart from the

Charles Hamilton constructed the artificial lake at Painshill Park (shown in this engraving of 1795) in 1740, and on the slope above its north shore he planted his vineyard. The Temple of Bacchus in the background still stands.

kitchen for which there was a housekeeper. The park was full of game birds and it was a pity he did not shoot. A small river (the Mole) which ran through the park was full of fish. The place was as pleasant as any he had ever seen. May God grant that he could keep the job for a few years at least.

Hamilton planted two sorts of 'burgundy' grape vine, the Auvernat, delicate but tender, and 'the Miller Grape commonly called the *black cluster*, which is more hardy' and which, as seen, was the Pinot Meunier. The first year he tried to make red wine by treading the grapes, letting them ferment in a vat till the husks and impurities formed a thick crust at the top and, when the turbulence had ceased, drawing off the clear wine from the bottom.

'This essay' he confessed 'did not answer. The wine was so harsh and austere that I despaired of ever making red wine fit to drink. But through that harshness I perceived a flavour something like that of some small French white wines which made me hope I should succeed better with white wine.'

His experimenting with white exceeded his most sanguine expectations. The wine from the first pressing resembled the flavour of champagne.

'In two or three years more, as the vines grew stronger, to my great amazement my wine had a finer flavour than the best champaign I ever tasted; the first running was as clear as spirits; the second running was *oeil de Perdrix*, and both of them sparkled and creamed in the glass like *Champaign*.' Many good judges of wine were deceived and thought it superior to any champagne they had ever drunk. 'But such is the prejudice of most people against anything of English growth, I generally found it more prudent not

96

to declare where it grew till after they had passed their verdict on it.' He sold it to wine merchants for 50 guineas a hogshead. He sold £500 worth to one merchant who retailed it at 7s 6d to 10s 6d a bottle.

His method of preparing the grapes for vinification was to cut the bunches off with scissors and bring them to his 'Wine Barn' in small quantities to prevent them heating and pressing against each other. He then picked off the stalks and discarded the mouldy and green grapes. Into the press they went within a few hours of picking—none of that laying out on wheat straw, which Philip Miller had recommended in *The Gardener's Dictionary* (1747), for Charles Hamilton. The first running came from the pressure of the weight of the bunches. It was as clear as water and as sweet as syrup. He then applied pressure: the first press; after a second press the liquor would often be reddish. It ran from the press into a large receiver and at once into hogsheads which were closely bunged up. 'In a few hours one could hear the fermentation begin.' The casks would have burst if they had not been cooped with iron. He left the hogsheads in the wine barn all

The Ruined Chapel, marked 'l' on this 1797 map of Painshill Park in the corner of the vineyard (marked 'k'), still exists though the vines have long since gone. Charles Hamilton sold the estate in 1774 but the vineyard was maintained until the early nineteenth century.

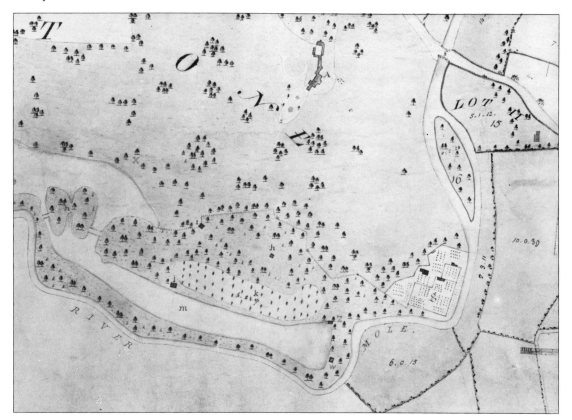

winter. When the noise and the oozing ceased, which told him the ferment-ation was over, the wine was racked off into clean hogsheads and carried to the vaults before a return of warm weather raised a second fermentation. In March he examined them. 'If any were not quite fine they were fined down with common fish glue in the usual manner.' By the end of March it had all been bottled 'and in about six weeks more would be in perfect order for drinking and would be in its prime for above one year'. The sweetness and flavour abated in the second year and gradually declined till it lost all flavour and sweetness. 'The only art I ever used to it was putting three pounds of white sugar candy to some of the hogsheads when the wine was first tunned from the press in order to conform to a rage that prevailed to drink none but very sweet Champaign.'

His success told him that much good wine might be made in many parts of the south of England. 'Main parts are south of Painshill; many soils may yet be fitter to it, and many situations must be so; for mine was much exposed to the south-west wind (the worst of all for vines) and the declivity was rather too steep; yet with these disadvantages it succeeded many years. Indeed the uncertainty of our climate is against it, and many fine crops have been spoiled by May frosts and wet summers; but one good year balances many disappointments.'

In 1750 David Geneste was describing to sister Marie the vines which were growing at Painshill; pied rouge, muscat blanc, muscat rouge, Guillan blanc and Sauvoit, plus a few other quicker-growing vines whose names he did not know. In November 1751 he was expecting to make eight to ten barrels of wine. They had hoped for a larger quantity of grapes at the beginning of the flowering season but the continuous rain that followed caused almost all the grapes to fall off, and the early frosts prevented those that remained from ripening. So they only got two barrels, half of which were mere *verjus*. The same had happened to vine-growers everywhere in England, he said, and he had not heard of any drinkable wine being pro-duced other than David Geneste's. He hoped to be more fortunate next year. His noble master had not been deterred however; on the contrary he had ordered more vines to be planted.

In 1752 David Geneste got an assistant from Bordeaux, to help him prune the vines. This man, recommended at David's request by André Borderie, got five *louis d'or* in his first year and received two more to pay for his journey to England. It seems that David had been asking Charles Hamil-ton to help him get a government post and that the assistant was to be trained to take over from him at Painshill and be in full charge as Master Vigneron. In fact several young vine-growers came over from Bordeaux in 1753 in the hope of getting a job on a vineyard in England—among them Matthieu Potevin and his cousin Paul Ducos, both from Clairac. They

brought David pruning hooks, sharpening stones and a couple of the small spades used for digging around the roots of the vines called *becats*.

In 1754 the Painshill vineyard produced four barrels of wine, two of which it was planned were to be sold as *vin de Champagne* at fifty *piéces* the barrel. On June 16 1754, Hamilton wrote to Lord Ilchester: 'you are such an infidel as to my Vineyard I hardly expect to convert You, even when you taste it, but Lady Ilchester who liked my first so well will be in Love with this; and I'll answer for it 'twill make Miss Cheek laugh and quicken her low spirits' (Surrey Record Office).

On Easter Day 1755 David Geneste told his sister that the white wine of 1753 was sold eight months later by Mr Hamilton for sixty guineas the barrel. He assured her it was esteemed the richest wine of its kind ever seen. Prompted by the fact that his employer was making so much money out of his vineyard, largely due to his French vigneron's talent and energy, David asked Hamilton for a rise. If Mr Hamilton could not see his way to accede to his request, David said he would have to leave. But he had overplayed his hand. His request and the way he made it offended and angered Hamilton who told him he had not the slightest intention of paying him another farthing. David was given notice and started to look for another job. However a month before the day on which he was due to depart Hamilton sent for him and asked him to taste that year's wine. It consisted of ten barrels— five of white and five of red—all of which came from black grapes. The master and his vigneron agreed it to be very good, and the euphoria and the wine combined to make the Honourable Charles relent. It could not surely be possible that David, who had made all this possible, was seriously contemplating leaving? He had always hoped to finish his days at Painshill,

No one knows where on the Painshill estate the wine was made, or what kind of winepress was used, but, judging from the scale of the operations, it probably resembled the wine-press illustrated in this engraving of 1747.

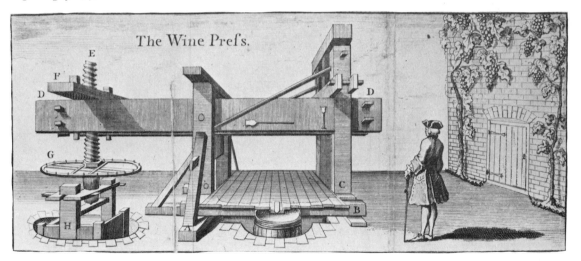

The Wine Press.

said Geneste, and he had only resigned because he could not live on such low wages. They talked it over, and mellowed by the Painshill Red, Hamilton offered to retain Geneste at £15 a year rent free. The Frenchman accepted.

Telling all this to his sister, David concluded 'and thus I shall still be a vinegrower, and if I have the good fortune to make a good harvest this year I hope it will turn to my profit, seeing that there are several gentlemen who are considering planting and I am the only one who can supply the stock'. He had some thirty to thirty-five thousand vine plants at Painshill, more than they had at Beziat. He reckoned that looking after Hamilton's vineyard required between twelve and thirteen hundred man-days a year, not counting the labour of the vine-grower himself who did all the pruning and cutting back. The winter of 1754/55 had been so bad that there still remained three *cartonnats* (about half an acre) to be pruned, which they hoped to finish that week (March 30 1755).

Never had he worked so hard, he told Marie, and thanks be to God he was in good health except for his eyes. Forced to bend for an hour or two every morning he had difficulty in keeping his eyes open. It was the same when he was cutting back the branches.

> You would be surprised if you could see the strength with which the vines grow in this country, the vine being from ten to fifteen feet long and as thick as your thumb. Such a great rate of growth makes for a condition such that the greater part of the grapes drop off, and if the vine is overladen it gives an abundance of grapes which do not ripen. I know M. Borderie understands such problems better than I do. Would you please ask him as a brother and friend to let me have his opinion of what I should do to prevent the wood from growing so strongly? The soil here is as poor as soil can be.

The letter ended with David reporting that the promised tools were seized by the Customs in London five months before, and it was probable that by now they were lost. Would she send him half a dozen wooden clogs? and two sharpening stones with them?

David Geneste was 63 in 1755. His ultimate fate is not known to me, though perhaps it is to his descendants, still living in Clairac, and to Claude Martin, the owner of David's manuscript letters.

By this time however the combined efforts of Charles Hamilton and David Geneste had made such a success of the vine-growing and wine-making that critics were confounded, and writers took it for granted. For Thomas Whately, who described a number of England's largest gardens in his *Observations on Modern Gardening* (1771), the vineyard at Painshill

seemed hardly worthy of remark. It was as if England's country houses had as many vineyards as lakes and mazes—perhaps they had. 'Painshill' he wrote, 'is situated on the utmost verge of a moor which rises above a fertile plain watered by the Mole . . . The house stands at one extremity of the crescent, on a hill which is shut out from the park, but open to the country . . . This hill is divided from another much larger by a small valley; and on top of the second eminence, at a seat just above a large vineyard which overspreads all the side, a scene totally different appears.'

The denigrators of English viticulture were shamed by the success of Painshill; the apologists who peddled empty theories about its impracticability, because of the unsuitability of the soil or mythical changes in the climate, were exposed as ignorant faint-hearts. Philip Miller, author of *The Gardener's Dictionary* of 1747, would have spoken with more certainty had he been acquainted with the success of Charles Hamilton, stated Sir Edward Barry in his *Observations* (1775). The lessons to be drawn from his achievement were self-evident.

'There are not wanting in this country' declared Sir Edward,

> several gentlemen of fortune who make the improvements in agriculture their favourite study and practice. To such no experiments could give a more reasonable and elegant amusement than planting and cultivating a small vineyard in a favourable situation. Nor could the fruits of any plantation afford that cheerful pleasure which they would receive from drinking fine wines of their own production. The prospect of some success even from the first trial, seem almost certain, if conducted by the rules given by Mr Hamilton and Mr Miller, with the necessary assistance of a good *vigneron*, well versed in the mechanic operations of this press. Neither is it improbable but that in some time several vineyards may be propagated on account of the profit arising from them, and this country supplied with native wines very superior to many of those which are now imported.

Charles Hamilton was a rich man: that was evident from the way in which he lavished money on the development of Painshill. From 1743 to 1758 he held the lucrative post of Receiver General of Minorca, Britain's naval base in the Mediterranean, and the even more notoriously lucrative one of Deputy Paymaster General. But even so it seems that at one time he had to borrow £6,000 from an old friend, Henry Holland, and had agreed to pay four per cent interest on the loan. In 1773 Hamilton received a letter from Henry Holland pointing out that payment of the interest had lapsed and that he wanted the loan repaid plus the interest in arrears. It appears that Charles was stumped for the cash—his fortune was in land—and he came to the sad conclusion that he would have to sell Painshill. He did so in 1773 to someone who already owned a great deal of land in Surrey,

Benjamin Bond Hopkins. The new owner paid £25,000 for the estate and was in possession by April 1773. He had decided that the modest residence which Hamilton had occupied all this time was not grand enough for him; he pulled it down (all but a small part still remaining) and replaced it with a more pretentious building. Charles Hamilton wrote to Lord Holland on July 22, 1773 'next week I go to Bath'. Bond Hopkins, he said, would be building immediately.

However Bond Hopkins kept the three hundred-acre garden much as Charles Hamilton had laid it out, including the vineyard. What it looked like at this time, at the height of its maturity, can be judged from the painting, by George Barret (1728–84), of the section of the park around the lake which takes in the rows of vines running down to the water beside the Ruined Chapel, and a gardener with a barrow full of grapes trundling along the footpath at the bottom. This is the only known picture of the Painshill vineyard, and indeed of any eighteenth-century English vineyard.

F. X. Vispré, whose writings on English viticulture have already been quoted, saw the vines nine years after Hamilton had left for Bath. 'In the cold and rainy year 1782' he wrote, 'I visited the vineyard at Painshill; the grapes at the end of October were only changing colour; they did not ripen that year . . . The last year 1785, though very unfavourable to vines in Portugal, was so much better in England that the grapes in the small vineyard in Chelsea were half-ripened in the second week in August.' The vineyard at Painshill, he said, seldom ripened its fruit at the present time as its plants were forty years old and they were chilled by the damp air from the horse chestnut trees bordering it on the north side.

John Adams, who was to become second President of the United States of America in 1797, described Painshill as 'the most striking Piece of Art that I have yet seen' when he visited the park on June 26, 1786, though he had nothing in particular to say about the vineyard, which however was still being cultivated. Thomas Jefferson also visited the garden about the same time. In his book *The English Gardener* published in 1829 William Cobbett (1763–1835) remembers visiting Painshill as a boy: he would only have been ten when Hamilton left so it was probably some time after then. 'The vines there' he wrote, 'were planted in rows and tied to stakes in just the same manner as the vineyards in France; and at the time when I saw the vineyard the vines were well loaded with a black-coloured grape.'

Charles Hamilton died in 1786 at Bath aged eighty-two; thrice married, he was one of the most colourful men of his time and certainly the most enterprising viticulturist. Benjamin Bond Hopkins kept the vineyard going until his death in 1794. He added a folly of his own, a fine circular 'Roman Bath' fed with icy cold water from a spring, prevented from overflowing by a horse-operated pump. There is no evidence of Bond Hopkins

making wine, but what he did with all those wine-grapes, if he did not, is anyone's guess. It is likely that after Bond Hopkins' death the vineyard was neglected, and that the Earl of Carhampton—as Colonel Luttrell he had opposed John Wilkes in the famous Middlesex Election—who owned Painshill from 1804 to 1821, took the view of the majority, that a vineyard was fine for romantic eccentrics like Charlie Hamilton but no less of a folly than a Gothic Chapel without a roof, and out of tune with the utilitarian spirit of the dawning nineteenth century. In their *History of Surrey* (vol II) published in 1814, Manning and Bray stated that the vineyard was no longer kept up. When the estate was auctioned at Garraways Coffee House on September 23 1831, the sale particulars called attention to the 'Beautiful Ornamental Pleasure Grounds, Park, Garden & C', but made no mention of the vineyard. However, three years later J. C. Loudon was able to write in his famous *Encyclopaedia of Gardening*, published in 1834: 'some of the vines which formed this vineyard may still be seen on the original site, now covered with a grove of Scotch pines'.

But I saw no sign of the vines when in February 1977 I went over the ground at the invitation of Norman Kitz, who lives in the beautifully maintained main section (Wedgwood House) of what remains of the mansion which Richard Jupp designed for Benjamin Bond Hopkins in 1773.

We walked down through the Scotch pines and other trees which had seeded themselves during the 150 years of neglect. Some of them had grown through the dilapidated Temple of Bacchus, at last being carefully restored. We passed the round pool which had been the centre of Benjamin's 'Roman Bath', recently dismantled for no particular reason. The horizontal iron rotary horse pump was still *in situ*, and a local industrial archaeological society hope to have it working again very soon. We came to the Ruined Chapel hidden in dark foliage, but easily recognisable as the building marking the extremity of the vineyard in George Barret's picture. We picked our way along the footpath on which, in the painting, the vine-dresser was pushing his barrow-load of grapes, as David Geneste must have done every day during the vendange. On our right the lake sparkled through the hanging branches of the trees in the winter sunshine. On our left the ground rose steeply, and I looked in vain through the shadows for the furrows which once held those lines of delicate but tender Auvernat vines and the 'more hardy' Miller Grape. Horizontal terracing of course, settling into the side of a hill, is likely to resist erosion better than vertical furrows. The outline of what the Romans dug at North Leigh 1400 years ago is still reasonably firm; but of the close lines of earth heaped to take the stakes and vine roots at Painshill there is no sign after two hundred years; although uprooting the trees and clearing the brambles and the ivy might reveal all.

What Sir Richard Pococke meant when he said in 1750 that there were

ten acres of vineyard at Painshill *in two places*, I do not know. The main site is clearly marked on the survey map of 1797, but where the other was is still a mystery—even to Norman Kitz who has lived at Pains Hill (as it is now written) for ten years, and to whom I am very grateful for showing me round. He has done more research into Charles Hamilton's activities than anyone else, and he has found no clue to the whereabouts of this second vineyard or to the site of the 'Wine Barn' where the press was housed and the wine-making took place. And where did Hamilton put all those hogsheads? In his detailed description of his wine-making he omitted to give any hint of where it all happened. Nothing is known of what his press looked like, but it must have been a big contraption if it was to handle the quantity of grapes he gathered each October from his ten acres. If, as he complained, 'the declivity was rather too steep' for successful crops, it must have been a handicap too for easy transport of the loaded baskets to the Wine Barn, assuming it was near the house. So perhaps it was at lake level? In the Ruined Chapel? Or at the top of the vineyard in the aptly dedicated Temple of Bacchus?

It is all conjecture. One day maybe Norman Kitz and the Friends of Pains Hill will clear the site and replant vines in the sandy gravelly soil, steeply sloping south to the edge of the water—and I shall go and help them do so. After five years they will make Painshill Wine once again, and, with the first vintage, we will toast the health of Charles Hamilton and David Geneste; and where more appropriately than in the Hamilton Hall of the Abercorn Rooms of the Great Eastern Hotel at Liverpool Street Station which once belonged to the Hamilton family?

Other Vineyards and Wineries in Eighteenth-Century England

Hamilton was correct in deducing from his own success that it was likely that viticulture could flourish in other parts of southern England. It is not clear to what location Dr John Campbell was referring, but in his *Political Survey of Great Britain* published in 1774 he told of the practice to the west of Surrey and made suggestions on how to dispose of the end-product if it was unacceptable to English taste.

> We have had vines in England in different places and in large quantities . . .
> If our wines in Hampshire may not reach that perfection which is requisite to please our palates or become fashionable here, they might possibly be exported with great profit to our plantations and derive [from] their

passage into warmer climates that excellence which cultivation could not give; and thus perhaps may also make them worth sending home again; nor would the accumulation of freight render them dearer to the consumer than the duties that are now laid on wines of foreign growth.

Here again is a sign of viticulture and wine-making being considered as a commercial operation, notwithstanding Sir Edward Barry seeing the exercise purely in terms of gentlemen of fortune conducting experiments to give them reasonable and elegant amusement.

Westbrook and Painshill, large and successful both, obviously produced more wine than the lord of the manor and his household could consume but the limits of their marketing, it seems, were the inns of Godalming and Cobham: a state of affairs that was to be repeated in the early days of the viticultural revival of two hundred years later.

In his *Ichnographia Rustica* published in 1742 Stephen Switzer said he was confident vineyards could be so cultivated in England 'so as to produce large quantities of grapes and so well ripened as to afford a good substantial vinous juice'. There were grapes in Somerset, he said, and those of the late Sir William Bassett annually produced some hogsheads of good-bodied and palatable wine. These will have come from his vineyard at Claverton which lies a few miles to the east of Bath. Sir William Bassett was MP for Bath for many years until 1693. In the early eighteenth century the vineyard came into the possession of the Skrine family.

The Claverton vineyard was marked in Savage and Meyler's 'Map of Five Miles Round Bath' of 1805, with the vines clearly shown. The site could still be made out in Canon Ellacombe's day (1890): a garden attached to Vineyards Farm. 'It is enclosed on three sides by an old wall, and it contains an old building which Mr Skrine considers to have been the wine-press. The property was purchased in 1701 by Mr Richard Holder and part of the purchase money was £28 for 'four hogsheads of wine of the vineyards of Claverton'. When Dorothy Vinter, an authority on the vineyards of the West Country, paid Claverton a visit in 1966 she found the wall which was the boundary of the vineyard still standing and the site so sheltered that a fig tree was growing in the middle of the wall with fruit ripening on it.

There was also an eighteenth-century vineyard at Bath itself: on the face of a hill half a mile above the Abbey Church. This must have been extremely large if, according to H. M. Tod (1911), it produced in 1718 sixty-six hogsheads of wine which were sold at £10 each. Tunstall's *Rambles About Bath* of 1876 mentioned 'The Vineyards' in the Walcot area and stated that cultivation of the vines ceased about 1730 because of 'alterations in the climate': the same old scapegoat. By then only the name persisted,

as did the name of the Old Domesday vineyard at Stonehouse in Gloucestershire, still marked on a survey map of the manor of 1728. Viney Farm was all that remained of the vineyard at Mangotsfield which Sir David Blount divided into two in 1203. But from a report in the *Gloucester Journal* of 1733 it is evident that there were grapes and not just grass growing in the vineyard called the Sunns at Churchdown near Gloucester. An appeal offered a reward of a guinea to anyone who gave intelligence to contribute to a legal conviction of the thief who stole grapes from the vineyard.

According to Rudge's *Gloucestershire* (1803), a vineyard was being worked at Tortworth in Cromhall Park throughout the eighteenth century: 'a large Plantation of Vines which is said to have produced ten hogsheads of good wine in one year'. Rudge adds that it was 'discontinued or destroyed in consequence of a dispute with the rector on a claim of the tythes'.

This assertion aroused the interest of Canon Henry Ellacombe who hied him to Lord Ducie who owned the land in 1890. His lordship told him all he knew and gave the Canon permission to examine the site for himself. 'Last month' Ellacombe wrote,

> I had the advantage of again closely examining it and taking accurate measurements of it with him and Lord Moreton. The vineyard is in a wood about a quarter of a mile from the present house, and it is in Cromhall Parish. The position is peculiar, and has been admirably chosen for the purpose. It is a steep but not high hill which may be said to form the northern base of an irregular triangle. This northern base is a shallow segment of a circle, the centre being almost due south so that from sunrise to sunset there would be more or less of sun shining on it. The two other sides of the triangle are steep hills sufficiently near to protect the vineyard from winds, but not so near as to prevent the sunshine—so that the result is that the vineyard got the maximum of possible sun with the minimum of wind. The hill is a mountain limestone and the soil seems to be shallow and stony. The terraces begin from the lowest level within a stone's throw of a small brook that runs through the valley, there are seven distinct terraces—divided from each other by walls a yard high, the distance from wall to wall being from 12 to 14 feet—the terraces vary in length according to the slope of the hill, the longest being 320 yards. The walls are built of the mountain limestone of the hill. The spaces between the walls have not been levelled, but follow the natural slope of the hill. The site of the vineyard is now chiefly covered with yew trees and it was the opinion of Sir Joseph Hooker who examined it a few years ago that these yew trees were of comparatively recent growth, none of them probably more than 60 or 70 years old.

Ellacombe made the 'fair presumption' that this dated the destruction of the vineyard as 1820 or 1830.

106

Evidence of eighteenth-century vineyards in the counties to the north of London comes from Suffolk, Hertfordshire and Essex. There is a note on wine-making in a memorandum and account book in the Suffolk Record Office dated 1731. In 1767 land known as The Vineyard at Benges in Herts, near the old church of St Leonard, was described as having been used lately as a vineyard by Thomas Dimsdale, the owner, who planted the vines. Not surprisingly, the great vine-growing county of Essex maintained the tradition in the eighteenth century with a vineyard, which was probably one of many, at Gidea Hall, Romford. That the two parts of it are marked on both sides of an ornamental canal on a map of 1807 indicates that the vines must have been cultivated for some years.

Charles Hamilton was not the only one to look to France for the viticultural experience which was lacking in England. In the seventeen-eighties Sir Philip Cravenleigh planted a vineyard on his Shropshire estate after sending one of his sons to France to learn the art of planting and dressing vines. According to the *Public Advertiser* of September 18 1784, quoted by Vispré, 'they drank wine, good, bad or indifferent as it happened'.

1763: Duke of Norfolk Makes Sixty Pipes of Red at Arundel

Of the precise role of the Museum Rusticum (see page 85) which had spurred Sam Pegge to action I am not sure, but it was to this institution to which he referred his readers who wished to be informed of the quality of the burgundy made by his Grace the Duke of Norfolk at Arundel in Sussex. I cannot refer to the mysterious museum, but the reliable Tod states that in 1763 sixty pipes of burgundy were made from the duke's vineyard at Arundel Castle which he says were 'not equal to the best of Beaune but better than ordinary', though how he knew 148 years later is his own secret. The commune of Beaune, he commented in 1911, 'grows at least three classes of wine, and there is nothing to prevent Sussex growing wine equal to the second of these as well as the ordinary'.

Writing before Tod, Andrew Pettigrew, in 1884, also gave the year 1763 as the one in which the Duke of Norfolk's vineyard at Arundel Castle produced excellent wine. 'I remember some years ago having a conversation with the late Lord Howard of Glossop on vines and vineyards, and his lordship then informed me that his father remembered tasting some of the wine made from the vineyard at Arundel which he said was very good and resembled Burgundy. There were several hogsheads of it in the cellar at that time. The vineyard is not cultivated now [1884] but I believe some of the

original vines were to be seen recently growing on the old site.'

Maps of Arundel Park of 1772 and 1804 give the site of a vineyard which at the time was within the castle precinct. In the only detailed description of the pre-1800 castle, which was partially or wholly rebuilt three times between the end of the eighteenth century and the beginning of the twentieth, there is no mention of the winepress where the 'burgundy' was made. Arundel Castle contains what is probably the second largest

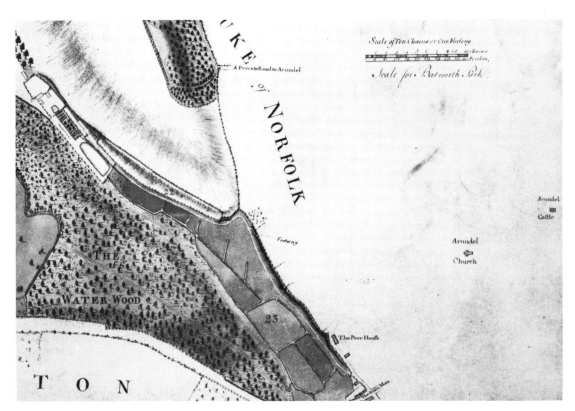

Names of the Fields	By Statute Measure		By 120 Rod 𝓎ᵉ Acre	
	Inmost Content	Outmost Content	Inmost Content	Outmost Content
Nᵒ	A R P	A R P	A R P	A R P
1 The Rewel Field	30 .. 2	31 1 14	40 .. 2	41 3 4 8
21 Carthouse Hanger	2 3 5	3 1 26	3 2 23	4 2 6
22 The Vineyard	2 .. 27	2 .. 27	2 3 17	2 3 17
23 Boggy Meads	16 .. 5	16 .. 5	21 .. 15	21 1 15

archival collection in Britain, and Dr Francis Steer, the Duke of Norfolk's Archivist, has devoted many years to cataloguing the several tons of manuscripts stored in the rooms of the castle tower. He is not half way through the task, but so far, he assures me, he has not come across a single letter, report, account book or journal which makes any reference to the cultivation of the vineyard, the harvesting of the grapes or the making of wine.

To-day the site is outside the wall of Arundel Park and has never been built on. Not only that, but it is a vineyard once again. In 1970 Mr H. B. Evans acquired the land, planted some vines on it, and the ground has proved as fruitful as it ever was. He had no definite evidence at the time that he was re-cultivating the eighteenth-century duke's vineyard, but he at once recognized that he had the ideal site with the classical requirements of a south-facing slope, well-drained and sheltered from the north. And then, when he first ploughed the site, he turned up a large number of old wine bottles which had obviously been in the ground a long time. Old wine bottles still come to the surface from time to time, he tells me. So perhaps the duke's winery of 1763 was beside the vineyard and not in one of the out-houses near to the castle.

Thirty years after the Duke of Norfolk's venture in Sussex, in the adjoining county Edward Hasted was gathering material for his *History and Topical Survey of the County of Kent* published in 1797/9. 'The mention made in the record of Domesday of the three arpends of vineyard in this parish [Certh or Chart Sutton]' he wrote,

> ought not to be passed by unnoticed here, this being one of several instances of there having been vineyards in this country in very early times. I mean plantations of the grape vine; for I can by no means acquiesce in the conjecture that *vineae* universally meant plantations of apples and pears, at least as far as relates to this country where the latter were not introduced at the time nor for some time after the taking of the survey of Domesday.
>
> This parish of Chart among others in the same situation on the side of the quarry hills is peculiarly adapted to the planting of vines, as well as from the warm and nutritive quality of the soil, as its genial aspect, being entirely sheltered from the north and east and facing the south in the declivity of the hill.

In 1763 the Duke of Norfolk made sixty pipes (105 gallons each) of 'Burgundy' from the wine-grapes he grew in his vineyard at Arundel Castle in Sussex. This map of 1772 shows the vineyard site (22), measuring two acres, twenty-seven perches.

He inferred there was still a vineyard at Chart Sutton in the seventeen-nineties; furthermore, 'in my memory there have been two exceeding fine vineyards in this county, one at Tunbridge-castle and the other in Hall-place, Barming near Maidstone, from which quantities of exceeding good and well-flavoured wine have been produced'. Unfortunately he was not prepared to give further information on either of these.

The Vineyards of Eighteenth-Century London

Open-air vines flourished in London in the eighteenth century as well as they had ever done, but since the Middle Ages the City had been widely built over and metropolitan vines were now mostly single, and the grapes for eating. There was little room in the centre for growing rows of wine-grapes, though there was more scope in 'Middlesex': the West End and Greater London of to-day. In *The City Gardener*, which he wrote in 1722, Thomas Fairchild spoke of the vine in Leicester Fields that bore grapes every year, and of the vines in tavern yards: the Rose Tavern without Temple Bar and a coffee house next to Grays Inn Gate. From 1701 he had been selling vines from his nursery in Hoxton, a competitor of his more famous contemporaries James Lee and Lewis Kennedy, whose Vineyard Nursery at Hammersmith (on the site of Olympia) was not devoted to vines as its name might seem to imply, but 'variegated treasures' including the first fuchsias seen in Britain. Though the Vineyard Nursery specialized in exotics (plants not native to Europe), a visitor would have seen vine plants on display, for before Lee and Kennedy turned it into a nursery garden in about 1745 the land had been a vineyard—hence the nursery's name. It is thought that the previous owner was probably one Paul Gervaise. Whether he ran it as a vineyard right up to Lee and Kennedy's occupation is not known. There was mention of a cottage on the land in 1628 called 'Vynehouse', and in 1686 of a wine cooper, Henry Bristowe.

'When Kennedy and Lee took over the land' states Miss E. J. Willson in her study *James Lee and the Vineyard Nursery Hammersmith* (1961), 'there was a thatched house in the grounds, the upper part of which was used as a dwelling house and had been used for selling the wine; there were wine cellars under it. This may be the cottage described as "Vynehouse" in 1628.'

In its heyday the Vineyard Nursery at Hammersmith covered eighteen acres. James Lee may have learnt something of vines from Philip Miller, author of the *Gardener's Dictionary*, under whom he first worked at Chelsea. He certainly seemed to have the reputation of being knowledgeable about their cultivation.

Lewis Kennedy died in 1782 and James Lee in 1795; but the Vineyard Nursery at Hammersmith continued to be operated into the 1890s by their descendants.

David Hughson (pseudonym of David Pugh) told how John Warner made an attempt in 1725 to 'restore' the cultivation of the vine in East Lane, Rotherhithe (William Driver was doing the same thing, but mostly under

glass, in East Lane, Southwark). John Warner had observed that Burgundy grapes ripened early, said Hughson, and 'conceiving they might be grown in England, obtained some cuttings which he planted here as standards'. In spite of the soil not being particularly suited, due to his care and skill Warner was rewarded by success. His crop was so ample that he made at least a hundred gallons of wine annually. Moreover he was able to supply cuttings of his vines for cultivation in many other parts of England.

Another witness to John Warner's prowess as a vine grower was Richard Bradley who became Professor of Botany at Cambridge University in 1724 and wrote a book called *The Vineyard*. Bradley described Warner as 'a man of great curiosity' who boasted he had made a pipe of wine from a hundred and twenty vines in his Rotherhithe vineyard the first year of bearing and continued to make good wine for many years thereafter.

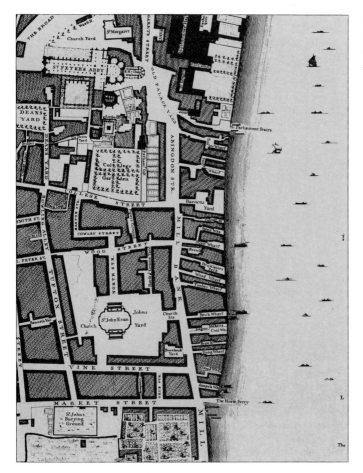

Today's Romney Street was once 'Vine Street', as this section of John Rocque's map of 1746 shows. The street marks the site of the mediaeval vineyard of Westminster Abbey.

Most authorities credit Richard Bradley with having introduced the famous Black Hamburg grape to England, though William Speechley (see page 87) called it 'Warners Grape'. Perhaps Bradley planted the first one at Cambridge but the proving of its suitability for growing and ripening in England was left to John Warner of Rotherhithe.

It was probably from John Warner, the popularizer of the Black Hamburg, that Sir Charles Raymond obtained the plant which he laid under glass at Valentine near Ilford in Essex in 1758. This was the parent of the vine at Hampton Court, which, by 1881, was a hundred and ten feet long and thirty inches in circumference. In that year the Hampton Court vine produced two thousand bunches of Black Hamburg grapes, and of course it still flourishes to-day.

Richard Bradley knew Tom Fairchild's vineyard at Hoxton, and those in Hatton Garden, St Giles's, Coldbath Fields and Houndsditch. He also described how a Mr Rigaud grew grapes without the help of a wall 'in open borders', in the centre of what is now the West End of London, in his garden near Swallow Street which ran from Piccadilly to Oxford Street and which was largely demolished at the end of the eighteenth century to make way for John Nash's Regent Street. Mr Rigaud's vineyard is marked by Vine Street off the small part of Swallow Street that still remains. Vine Street became famous for its police station where Mayfair revellers spent the morning after the night before, and in the nineteen-thirties its cells were full of Bright Young Things arrested in raids on night clubs illegally selling alcohol after hours.

Further west, the walls of Joseph Kirke's nursery at Brompton were covered with Muskadine grape vines, and in the borders in front of the walls grew what Bradley called 'standard vines'. Another vineyard at Brompton belonged to a Mr King. Its reputation led Samuel Pegge to pronounce (in 1763): 'but as to this article of goodness and perfection in the wines here made, something may be seen concerning them in the quotations produced above; the performances of Mr King are known to many'. They seem to have been so well known that he found it unnecessary to expound further.

There was a close of about half an acre known as The Vineyard between the east wall of Camberwell Manor House and the parish church of St Giles which in 1717 was transferred by the landowner 'for her love of the church' to the parish of Camberwell as an addition to the churchyard. I have already referred to the early history of the vineyard at Clerkenwell (see page 49). In the parish Rate Book of 1759 a Mr Samuel Bradford was rated for a summer house, vineyard, fishpond and garden, which would seem to indicate he was actually growing vines.

In his diary for October 18 1765, Peter Collinson wrote: 'I went to see Mr Rogers' vineyard at Parsons Green, all of Burgundy grapes and seemingly all perfectly ripe. I did not see a green half ripe grape in all this great quantity. He does not expect to make less than 14 hogsheads of wine. The branches and fruit are remarkably large and the vines are very strong.'

A Mr Lawrence, the vicar of Hilvertot in Northamptonshire, in the introduction to his *Gardeners Calendar* of 1718, told of a visit to the garden of 'that ingenious encourager of vegetable nature' Mr Ball of Kensington

In 1758 Sir Charles Raymond planted a single vine under glass at Valentine near Ilford, and a shoot from this grew into the famous Hampton Court Vine (right: as it was in 1840). By 1881 it was 110 feet long and produced two thousand bunches of Black Hamburg grapes— 'dessert grapes' for eating, not wine-making.

Dessert grapes were easily ripened by heat generated from stoves in hothouses such as this one from an illustration of 1751. Varieties which grew well in artificial conditions could not contend with the natural, outdoor climate, and this contributed to the myth that the English climate was unsuitable for open-air viticulture.

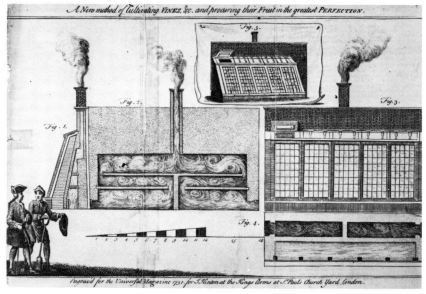

A New method of Cultivating VINES, &c. and procuring their Fruit in the greatest PERFECTION.

Engraved for the Universal Magazine 1751 for J. Hinton at the Kings Arms at S.t Pauls Church Yard London.

who for a trial planted a spot with vines. Lawrence said he saw some very fair bunches of Blue Frontignac tolerably ripe.

Bartholomew Rocque had a vineyard at Walham Green for thirty years in what H. M. Tod described as 'a common field garden'. Although the ground was flat the vines he grew there were 'as good as those of Orleans or Auxerre'.

It is clear that English vineyards had not been entirely eradicated by the eighteenth century as Francis Xavier Vispré had hinted. Compared with the Middle Ages, they did not come so thickly on the ground; but they were as widely distributed over the English counties. No vineyard as big as those at Westbrook and Painshill had ever been seen in England before. The Little Ice Age was over: high summer (July and August) temperatures prevailing in central England in the eighteenth century rose from 15.4°C to nearly 16°C, a level not reached again for two hundred years; but such a change did not provoke a sudden upsurge in viticulture. The activity had not been awaiting warmer summers to bring it to life. This had never been a major factor.

English wine had not disappeared by the eighteenth century, but, because its manufacture no longer held a position at the centre of the English way of life as it once had, the practice of viticulture had come to be regarded as eccentric. It suffered the fate of the dog which stood on one leg in front of Samuel Johnson and provoked the remark that the wonder was, not how well it did it, but that it could do it at all. So false and patronizing a premiss was difficult to discard, and it coloured the attitude to English viticulture for many years to come.

Part IV   To Cheer a November Day

1800 to 1945

FIVE

Full Marks for Keston and Castle Coch then Full Stop

War with Napoleon Reduces the Supply of French Wine

George III's war with the armies of revolutionary France led by General Bonaparte hindered English merchants from trading with the king's enemies, but did not stop them. The concept of total war had not yet arrived. However, when the self-declared 'Emperor of the French' imposed a blockade of Britain, trade was only carried on with the greatest difficulty, and by March 1807 there was virtual suspension of all English shipping to the continent. As a result French wine was scarce in England, but not unobtainable. In any event in a country where the population at the end of the eighteenth century had risen to ten million and a vast middle class had emerged, wine was no longer the drink of all Englishmen except the poorest, as it had been in the days of the Plantagenets. It was a drink only for those who could afford it, and in time of war the circle of wine-drinkers inevitably contracted. The nobility and gentry, the rich tradesmen and professional men, who could not let foreign wars interfere with the business of keeping their place in society, saw to it that the wine supply was maintained whatever the cost. The stocks would have fallen even lower if it had not been for the cases of claret and burgundy captured at sea, and the even greater quantity brought to the coves and beaches of England by smugglers. A wine merchant's list of 1804 shows how expensive it was: Superior Claret at 70s a dozen, Vin de Graves at 66s a dozen.

In the year 1812, when Napoleon's humiliation at Moscow raised the hopes of the Allied Powers that the Disturber of Europe would finally be suppressed, an English medical man demonstrated his irritation at the

continuing high cost of wine from the continent by issuing an *Invitation to the Inhabitants of England to the Manufacture of Wines from the Fruits of their Own Country*. Little doubt could reasonably be entertained, said Dr R. Worthington MD, that 'in a well planted vineyard the grape would flourish with us and yield plentifully'.

'If the vineyard were perfectly defended from the north and disposed on rather a sharp slope open to the south and a little inclining to the east, more especially if fashioned in terraces backing each other, such a quantity of heat would be accumulated and retained as would probably be found quite equal to the office of perfectly ripening the grape; those kinds in particular best adapted to our climate.'

Vineyards had been broken up in the past, he said, not because of their failure but because their tillage for wheat became a more indispensable requisition. Worthington claimed that if they were again established under the improved system of cultivation and of gardening which was the characteristic of the new nineteenth century, the English vintage might on the average of years prove not only considerable but great.

> Would a few men only, of wealth and influence, dispersed through the southern and the midland provinces of the kingdom, take the lead in this attempt, and sanction a well conducted trial, we might reasonably expect, in the advancement of time, a short time perhaps, to see an English vintage becoming general; foreign compositions shoved aside; and the bottle of English grape occupying the place of pride and honor on an English table. None but the man of comprehensive means can now, without ruinous expenditure, support the habit of drinking foreign wine, or hardly even those demands for its introduction which in the intercourse of life are wont to rise; while few, without his example before them, will summon sufficient resolution and dignity to banish it from their tables.

He refused to be side-tracked by arguments about the English climate, and pointed out the mildness of English autumns,

> the finest season of the English year continuing not unfrequently soft and open to the middle of November . . . But I have myself proved that grapes caught by the frost will make sound wine . . . There is more to be apprehended perhaps from foggy or wet weather than frost, but neither of them present any *real objection* against the establishment of vineyards in this kingdom. These existed and prospered centuries ago under the rude untutored hands by which they were cultivated. What therefore might not be hoped for under the present improved condition of natural science and of horticulture!

Terria septē
Sidere uirg
September
Sept.

VI   F

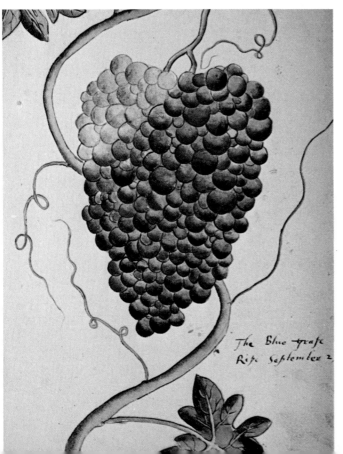

The Blue grape
Ripe September 2

There was the patriotic angle too.

> Let us then—let those more especially I should say whose example would have influence—endeavour to draw from the bowels of their own land and from the warmth of their own sun, that character of wine to which prejudice annexes an importance; and by the acquisition of which vanity will be accommodated. Let them—and their united efforts will not be in vain—let them, on principle of patriotism and humanity, come forward and assert the powers of their soil, and the science of cultivators, by illustrating to our neighbours of the continent that, as we rival them in many things, and far surpass them in others, we are determined to contend with them, as far as it can be done, even in the culture of the vineyard.

In this way claimed Dr Worthington we might possess an English wine which required no 'adventitious help' from sugar or spirit: a dig at the fortified port and sherry which had become so popular. It was therefore a wine which the grower and maker could afford to sell, and *the man of moderate income* store in his cellar at five-sixths less cost than they were paying for wine of similar fruit, so adulterated and disguised as to have lost all flavour of the parent fruit. Foreign wines communicated little sensation of fruit to the palate. A properly prepared English wine, conveying the full and agreeable flavour of the grape, might, on the other hand, 'cheer a November day'.

In the following year (1813) the man of moderate income could even less afford French wine, for the British government increased the duty on it to 19s 8d a gallon: 3s a bottle.

Purists, such as the author of Phillip's *Pomarium Britannicum* (1820), were of one mind on the subject of English wine. 'The idea that we cannot make good wine from our grapes is erroneous' he declared. 'I have tasted it quite equal to Grave wines, and in some instances, where it has been kept for eight to ten years, it has been drunk as hock by the nicest judges.' Mr Middleton, author of *Agriculture in Middlesex*, without a date but of this period, agreed with him. 'It certainly is very possible to make as palatable and much more wholesome wine in England than what is generally imported. It is well known that wine may be made of the English sweet-water grape equal to Mountain.'

With the return of peace after twenty years of non-stop fighting and inhibiting shortages at home, the people of Britain celebrated their escape from Boney with traditional vigour. The upper classes returned to their wine-drinking, and for the lower classes gin once more took the place of ale and beer.

Wartime shortage of foreign wine had not revived an interest in English wine, as it might have done. Indeed viticulture in Britain was in the

*Overleaf (right):
In the Middle Ages, abbeys and monasteries around Bath and Glastonbury ran extensive vineyards, and today the owner of this vineyard at Wootton describes it as 'an English vineyard where wine is made in the traditional manner'.*

*Facing (top):
Nigel Godden mills the grapes at the Pilton Manor Winery. After the milling the 'mulch' goes into the cylindrical winepress on the left.*

*Facing (bottom left):
'Riesling-Sylvaner' or 'Mueller-Thurgau' (far left) white wine-grapes have proved to be the most likely to grow and ripen in the English climate sufficiently well for wine-making.*

*Facing (bottom right):
Wootton Wine from Shepton Mallet in Somerset; the Wootton vines come from the Rhine and Alsace, and the Wootton vineyard has its own winery.*

doldrums. As an agricultural industry which once gave occupation to a large body of labourers in the southern counties it had completely passed away and could never return in its old form. There had been a revival of grape-growing in Sussex—but under glass.

Most famous of the glass grape-houses was the great Conservatory at the Royal Horticultural Society's Chiswick Garden, which in 1857 was emptied of its ornamental plants and filled with vines. Twenty-five varieties were planted in an outside, and partly in an inside, border. By 1859 they were covering three-quarters of the thirty-foot-high roof. They were mostly Black Hamburg, each vine producing ten two-pound bunches. Head of Chiswick Garden was Archibald F. Barron who wrote what became the standard work on viticulture, *Vines and Vine Culture*. This of

John Ward grew ten varieties of wine-grape in the vineyard shown on this map of 1832 of Holwood estate. There was a Roman settlement site known as Caesar's Camp on the estate, so perhaps there had been a vineyard at Keston in Roman times.

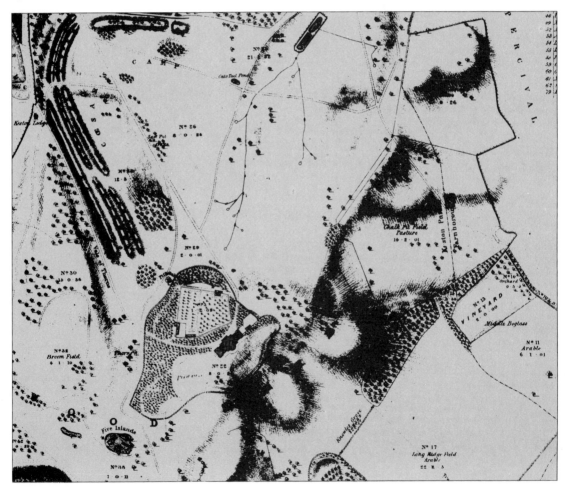

John Ward built Holwood House at Keston when he acquired the estate and planted his vineyard. The house still stands today.

course dealt exclusively with cultivation of dessert grapes under glass, against walls and 'Pot Vines For Table Decoration'. He referred to open-air vineyards in his introduction and gave as an instance one at Bury St Edmunds 'which is still partly in existence (1883)'. This was probably St Peters Vineyard. A builder called Darkin made a pipe to a pipe-and-a-half of excellent wine every year at this time from the grapes which grew on the high walls of St Peters Vineyard, Bury St Edmunds (*Notes & Queries*, November 27, 1869).

Barron attributed the discontinuation of open-air vineyards to the introduction of cheap glass 'giving more satisfactory results'. This will certainly have assisted in the demise of English viticulture as an agricultural industry; but the English tradition of growing wine-grapes vineyard-fashion was never lost sight of, and the knowledge *that it worked* was never forgotten. Charles Hamilton's operation at Painshill, which continued into the nineteenth century, was a success story within the memory of many who, now peace had returned, could indulge their fancies in a way they never could have done in wartime.

Ten Sorts of Vine at a Vineyard in Kent

One such person was John Ward, a London merchant, who acquired an estate at Keston in Kent, some fourteen miles south of London. The house, Holwood, had been the country residence of William Pitt. Ward pulled it down and replaced it with another which was completed in 1827.

Ward spent a great deal of time and trouble in having the grounds landscaped: 'a fine sweep of lawn descends into a wide spreading valley, and the high and distant woodlands of Knole, Seven Oaks, Tunbridge and the hills of Sussex form an extensive amphitheatre of forest scenery and downs as far as the eye can see'. He was obviously just the kind of gentleman of quality in circumstances which would permit him to wait for results, who would be able to add lustre to the English viticultural tradition in the steps of Charles Hamilton and James Oglethorpe.

'In the rear of Holwood' wrote William Hone in his *Every-Day Book and Table Book* (1841),

> Mr Ward is forming a vineyard which, if conducted with the judgement and circumspection that mark the commencement, may prove that the climate of England is suited to the open culture of the grape. Mr Ward has imported ten sorts of vines, five black and five white, from different parts of the Rhine and Burgundy. They are planted on a slope towards the SSE. Difficulties and partial failures are to be expected in the outset of the experiment, and are to be overcome in its progress by enlarged experience and information respecting the treatment of the plants in foreign countries.

I can find no account of the progress or ultimate fate of John Ward's vineyard at Keston: today the house is the headquarters of Seismograph Service Ltd. It seems it was unknown forty years later to the anonymous writer of a piece in *The Floral World and Garden Guide* of 1865, headed HOME-GROWN WINE. He had no doubts. 'English vineyards are things of the past' was his uncompromising opening sentence. The vine did not pay in Britain except as a dessert fruit, he declared. Many who would plant 'open quarters' of hardy grapes were deterred from doing so by the general prejudice which existed in opposition to such enterprises; but wine was being made all over Britain from vines on walls.

> Those who read of the ancient vineyards in this country are sometimes in haste to conclude that the climate of England must have undergone a change for the worse. Such however is not the fact. In times when the open-air vinery was looked to for supplies of wine the crop was as precarious as now. The old vineyard was dependent on occasional good seasons and, as land increased in value, the cultivation of grapes declined—for the simple reason that there was no certainty as to the produce. The vineyard described by Mr Cyrus Redding in his recent work [which I have not been able to trace] produced wines such as modern palates would refuse to touch.

If the practices of rural life had improved, had the vine had its share of attention? he asked. 'Further, has the manufacture of wine had any

attention at all in this country during the last two hundred years? The answer must be No.' He was obviously not as well informed as he might be. However, his assertion, though without foundation, led him to put forward an interesting suggestion. Though nothing had been done in England, great progress had been made in America, he said. So why not introduce some American varieties to grow in the open air in Britain? Might we not follow in the wake of our transatlantic cousins and become to some extent independent of the foreign supplies of the most invigorating and wholesome of all the beverages used by man? He commended the idea as commercially worthy of the attention of those who had suitable sites. European vines were no good in the northern states of America owing to the severity of the climate. However,

> if the native vines yield abundantly and if their produce is eminently adapted for wine making, it follows that in the more genial climate of the southern counties of England and Ireland, those same American vines would be more likely to afford satisfactory results than the varieties we have hitherto regarded as the hardiest. Nay, we do not see why even to the Orkneys the American grape should not be found adaptable; for on their prairies and mountain slopes they have to endure severe winters, and they appear to be partial to a dry, poor, rocky soil.

It seemed a good idea, but there are no signs of anyone taking it up. It was in fact a better idea than the author of 'Home-Grown Wine' knew, and for a reason unconnected with their hardiness. Obviously his knowledge of viticultural activities in other parts of Britain was not great, and it is probable therefore that he had not heard of the appearance in 1863 at Hammersmith—on the old Lee and Kennedy site?—of a rare insect imported, unknowingly, from America which had a catastrophic effect on vine roots, the phylloxera vastatrix: from the Greek *phyllon* (leaf) and *xeros* (dry).

The following year the killing disease, known as phylloxera, broke out within the dense vineyards of the Department of the Gard in the South of France. Within twenty years it had spread to the whole country and very nearly wiped out its entire ancient wine industry. One and a half million out of two and a half million hectares of vines were destroyed. Whereas in 1875 France produced eighty-three million hectolitres of wine, in 1889 it could only muster twenty-three million. In 1880 the phylloxera vine pest struck in Italy.

The insect had no effect on the roots of American vines because they had evolved a resistance and adapted to survive in spite of phylloxera. Vine roots in other countries which had evolved in phylloxera-free soil had no resistance to attacks by the insect, they just weakened and died. Thus

the recommendation in *The Floral World* of 1865 that anyone proposing to start an open-air vineyard in England should plant American vines was very apposite.

1875: Lord Bute Plans a Vineyard at Cardiff

The recommendation was not followed by the Marquess of Bute when he decided to embark on an ambitious scheme in South Wales.

John Patrick Crichton-Stuart, third Marquess of Bute, was Scots. He was the great grandson of George III's unpopular favourite, the third Earl of Bute. He was born in 1847 and succeeded to the title when his father died suddenly the following year. In 1872 he married Gwendoline daughter of Lord Howard of Glossop, a kinsman of the Duke of Norfolk whose vine-growing and wine-making activities at Arundel Castle have already been noted. He was immensely wealthy, the owner of some 117,000 acres, a London house in Regents Park, Mountstuart in Rothesay, Dumfries House in Ayrshire, Falkland House in Fifeshire, Old Palace of Mochrum in Wigtownshire and Cardiff Castle. He was closely associated with the cultural life and commercial property of Cardiff, carrying on the work of his father, 'creator of modern Cardiff.'

The third Marquess was nothing if not independent. He engaged in a variety of activities ranging from translating the novels of Turgenev to investigating psychical phenomena. He worshipped the past and was fascinated by the ritual and ceremony of guilds and orders, the heraldry and the dressing-up. He dreamt of reconstructing Cardiff Castle as it had been around the thirteenth century when it was built; and in 1865 he commissioned an imaginative architect, William Burges, to draw up plans for a no-expense-barred exercise in what the Italians call *scenografia*. Work began shortly afterwards but it was twenty years before the curtain went up on the finished transformation scene.

Also part of the Cardiff estates inherited from his father was the ruined Castell Coch—the 'Red Castle', so named because it had been constructed of unfaced red sandstone. It lay some five miles to the north of Cardiff near the tiny hamlet of Tongwynlais and commanded the plain of Cardiff to the south and the narrow gorge of the river Taff immediately below to the west. It had also been built at the end of the thirteenth century but had been un-inhabited and neglected for three hundred years. It was completely over-grown and a favourite spot for Arcadian picnics; but here was obvious raw material for a second flight of fancy, and in 1871, with the Cardiff Castle scheme well under way, Lord Bute arranged for the ruins of Castell Coch

Opposite: Castle Coch lies some five miles north of Cardiff overlooking the River Taff. In 1875 the architect William Burges began to reconstruct the ruins of the castle, neglected for three hundred years, giving it the full mediaeval treatment and turning it into a 'costly folly'.

124

to be cleared of undergrowth and rubbish, and had Burges make a thorough survey with a view to reconstructing it in all its mediaeval glory. The faithful architect had plans ready by the following year and in 1875 work began on the construction of a building which conformed, in Burges' imagination at least, to the likely appearance of the castle in the days of Richard the Lion Hearted, of troubadours and minstrels, of jousting and feasting.

To be consistent, the surroundings, as well as the castle itself, had to be mediaeval. Did not the marquesses and bishops and abbots of the Middle Ages grow their own wine-grapes vineyard-fashion in the parks of their castles and abbeys? Did they not make native wine as good as any from the banks of the Rhine or Moselle? Would it not complete the picture for the Marquess to do the same beside the Taff at Castell Coch? Was there not a tradition that in this very parish of Sully there had been a vineyard in those far off times?

So, one day in Scotland in 1873, the year after he married, the twenty-six-year-old nobleman called in his head gardener, Andrew Pettigrew, and told him of his Great Plan to plant a vineyard at Castle Coch. He would leave the precise location until Pettigrew had had the opportunity of judging the best position and giving his opinion about the suitability of the soil.

Some weeks later Pettigrew journeyed to South Wales to view the proposed site which he at once reported to his lordship was to his liking, though he had to admit he had no experience of the climate of South Wales. The ground selected was to the west of the castle at a somewhat lower level, with a gentle slope to the south. It was 150 feet above sea level. From the nature of the ground it required no natural drainage. It was protected from the north by a large plantation which covered the breast and summit of the hill behind. It was also protected from the east and west by smaller hills close by, and lay open to the south, overlooking the Bristol Channel some four or five miles away. The soil, which was two feet deep, was of a light fibrous loam overlying limestone.

Lord Bute was determined not to leave anything to chance. He wrote to a number of his friends in France asking them to recommend an intelligent young man versed in the ways of choosing, planting and pruning vines who would be ready to come to South Wales to help plant the vineyard, run it and make wine from its produce. No doubt he had read of Charles Hamilton's successful employment of David Geneste at Painshill and thought to emulate him; but in spite of generous offers and promises of excellent conditions, 'we learned that it would be extremely difficult to induce a person of the class wanted to leave his home and friends to come here on any consideration'.

So his lordship despatched Andrew Pettigrew on a tour of the princi-

pal vineyards of the Medoc and elsewhere to pick up what information he could. 'It was rather a perplexing duty to one totally unacquainted with the French language' Andrew Pettigrew told members of the Cardiff Naturalists Society in 1884, 'but furnished with letters of introduction to wine merchants and the principal vineyard proprietors in France and others, I set out in the latter end of September [1874] in time to see the vintage of the year.'

He first saw the vineyards around Paris, and more from his guide's gesticulations than his words he learnt the details of French propagating, pruning, planting and the rest, which he was able to relate to his existing knowledge of growing vines in England against walls. He then went to Chalons-sur-Marne in the champagne country with a letter of introduction to a man named Jacusson who was the proprietor of one of the largest champagne 'manufactories' in France. They had, Pettigrew was told, five million bottles of champagne stored in cellars cut into the chalk hills. From there Pettigrew went to Bordeaux where the head of the large firm to whom he had an introduction put him in the hands of one of his clerks who hailed from Scotland but could speak French like a native. They toured several vineyards in the Medoc and witnessed the vintage at the Chateaux Latour (103 acres), Lafitte (165 acres), and the Margaux (197 acres).

When Pettigrew returned to Castle Coch he reported that he had been strongly recommended by the vine-growers around Paris to try the varieties known as Gamay Noir and Mille Blanch; these were the two, they said, most likely to suit the climate of South Wales. They were grown all around Paris, in Burgundy and in the colder wine districts of France. The plants had a strong constitution, a reputation for producing fruit freely and for making very good wine. Lord Bute took his gardener's advice and ordered the recommended French vines. That winter Lord Bute and Pettigrew trenched and levelled a three-acre site in the chosen position, and the following March (1875) they planted the vine shoots from across the Channel 'on the French system': each three feet apart in north to south rows separated by three-foot gaps.

Bute and Pettigrew decided to adopt the 'low stem' system practised in the colder districts. It meant pruning every winter to within a few inches of the ground, and training the annual growths to low stakes as they developed. In this way foliage and fruit were kept close to the ground, both benefiting from its warmth.

The Castle Coch vineyard, and Lord Bute's intention to make wine from it, was greeted with jeers in *Punch*. It predicted in 1875 that if ever wine was produced from Glamorgan it would take four men to drink it: the victim, two others to hold him down and a fourth to force the wine down his throat. *Funny Folks* remarked that 'Lord Bute has, it appears, a

The vines planted by Lord Bute and his gardener Andrew Pettigrew in the Castle Coch vineyard in the 1870s came from the colder wine districts of France.

Bute-iful vineyard at Castell Coch near Cardiff where it is hoped such wine will be produced that in future Hock will be superseded by Coch, and the unpronounceable vintages of the Taff. Coch-heimer is, as yet, a wine *in potentis*, but the vines are planted and the gardener, Mr Pettigrew, expects no petty growth.'

However in *The Garden* of September 1875 there appeared a more sober assessment of the experiment's chance of success—from the pen of the master vigneron himself, Andrew Pettigrew.

> The two thousand vines planted at Castle Coch, in the Vale of Glamorgan, on the 20th of March last, have broken well, considering the long journey which they had from France, and the time during which they were out of the ground. Most of them have grown to the top of the stakes, and they look strong and healthy; many of them showed two bunches of grapes, which were taken off during the operation of tying. All feel quite satisfied with the progress they have made this season, so far as growth is concerned. I propagated two thousand vines this spring from eyes saved from the prunings. They are in robust health, about three feet high, and I purpose planting them this autumn, or probably next spring. I may here mention that, through some typographical error, the varieties of Grapes planted at Castle Coch were wrongly named. The black Grape used there is Gamais Noir, and the white one Le Miel Blanc. Mr Fenn, of Woodstock, writing to me the other day, says: 'With myself there can be no question but

that good home-made grape wine can be manufactured in England now as well as in former times', a statement with which I entirely agree. Indeed, I purpose making a quantity of wine this season from grapes grown on the castle wall here. The vines which were planted some six or seven years ago are now bearing heavy crops of tolerably good-sized grapes, which have ripened very well during the last two years. The portion of the wall on which they are growing is about a hundred yards in length . . . The variety principally grown is Royal Muscadine; but a great many others were planted, perhaps by way of experiment, or simply to cover the wall till the others (Royal Muscadine) grew larger. Among those were Black Hamburgh, Lady Downe's Seedling, Black Alicante, Mrs Pince, and Trentham Black. Black Hamburgh fruits freely, but does not ripen well; and I may say the others have been failures, with the exception of Trentham Black, which fruits freely and ripens well.

For the first four years, with four good summers in turn, the vineyard consolidated itself, and the vines were able to make themselves at home in their foreign soil. 'They grew well and made strong canes which ripened thoroughly' Pettigrew told the Cardiff Naturalists' Society in 1884. 'Gardeners and others who came from a distance to see the vineyard were surprised at the luxuriance of the vines growing in the open air, and simply

In March 1875 Andrew Pettigrew trenched and levelled a three-acre site and planted two thousand French vines. He planted them according to the 'French system', three feet apart in north to south rows separated by three-foot gaps.

Lord Bute's Vinyard Castle Coch.

129

130

trained to stakes in the way raspberry plants are trained in this country.'

'The sight about the end of July is a novel and interesting one,' continued Pettigrew.

> Long rows of vines, as straight as a line, in a curved slope down the hill, and the tops of the canes all neatly stopped at the height of four feet from the ground, with their large dark-green glossy foliage almost meeting in the rows, was a sight not to be seen anywhere else in this country. I was very well pleased with the progress the vines made for the first three or four years . . . The vines were growing vigorously and there were no signs of the dreaded phylloxera so common in many places in this country now. The only pest that attacked them was a kind of fungus called 'Oidum Tuckerii' which was soon got rid of by picking the affected leaves off and burning them.

Castell Coch 'Still Champagne' is Made at Cardiff Castle

Two years after planting they attempted to make some wine. There was nowhere for doing this at Castle Coch and all the wine-making took place at Cardiff Castle; but no one knows where. The crop of 1877 was not a heavy one but, said Pettigrew, they brought the grapes down from the vineyard to 'the gardens in Cardiff', separated the berries from the stalks, crushed them in a machine which they had made for the purpose, added a little water to the must, which then lay for twenty-four hours in a wooden vat before being put in the winepress. They added three pounds of cane sugar to every gallon of liquor, and then it was all put into a barrel to ferment. Strong fermentation lasted for about twenty days, after which they put the bung in, gently at first, and then, when fermentation had ceased altogether, driven hard in. The wine was racked off several times during the following spring and summer, and it was finally bottled after having lain for a little more than a year in a barrel. They had made some forty gallons of white wine which filled 240 bottles.

Though the location of the winepress at Cardiff Castle has never been determined, it is known that Castell Coch wine, once bottled, was stored in the Cart Shed Cellar, the Park Hall Cellar and the Mushroom House Cellar. The only hint of the owner's role as a vine-grower and wine-maker in the decoration of the castle interior was the carved stone banister with a dome above it, representing the fable of the Fox and the Grapes, outside the door to the roof garden.

The 1878 crop was better still, though far from being full; they made three hundred bottles of wine. 'The vines broke well in 1879 and showed an

'Gardeners and others who came from a distance to see the vineyard were surprised at the luxuriance of the vines growing in the open air' wrote Andrew Pettigrew of the Castle Coch vineyard. 'The tops of the canes all neatly stopped at the height of four feet from the ground, with their large dark-green glossy foliage almost meeting in the rows, was a sight not to be seen anywhere else in this country.'

131

abundance of fruit in the latter end of May but with the cold and sunless wet summer that followed the fruit all dropped off, and we did not gather a bunch of grapes from the vineyard.'

There was total failure the next year too on account of the wood not having ripened the previous season. There was a good crop in 1881, however, and a first-class white wine was made, which sold at £3 a dozen bottles. Castell Coch Wine was at first offered for sale at the Angel Hotel which belonged to Lord Bute and was situated opposite the castle. In those days there was another row of houses between the castle and the hotel, two streets where to-day there is the single, wide Castle Street. The Angel still stands and is a fine example of the grand hotel architecture of its day (1880).

H. M. Tod drank a glass or two of the 1881 vintage at the Angel and described it as 'still champagne'—which is what Charles Hamilton liked to call his Cobham wine. 'It was the palest in colour and the best', added Tod. Every bottle of the 1881 wine was sold, except for a few dozen which were salted away in the Cardiff Castle cellars. Archibald Barron, head of the Royal Horticultural Society's Chiswick Garden, included a chapter on the Vineyard at Castle Coch in his book *Vines and Vine Culture* (1883) and mentioned that there had been a good crop in 1881. 'The wine was of the best quality, and pronounced by the Fruit Committee of the Royal Horticultural Society to resemble a first-class still champagne.' It was the last Castell Coch wine for two years, for 1882 and 1883 were again blank owing to the successive bad seasons.

Summing up the progress to date in 1884, Andrew Pettigrew said the period of the experiment was the worst they could have hit on for twenty or thirty years. There was nothing in the condition of the soil or climate to hinder the healthy growth of the vines, but the absence of sunheat had prevented the development or ripening of the fruit. 'It has yet to be proved whether in a succession of ordinary good seasons a better result will be arrived at. I am myself hopeful that it may be; and that it may yet be found that the out-door cultivation of the vine may be prosecuted in favourable situations in this country (at least on walls and gables of houses) with not much greater risk of failure than in the case of ordinary garden fruits.'

His optimism was justified; there was a general improvement. Both in 1884 and 1885 1,500 bottles of Castell Coch Wine were produced, and they began selling the wine directly from the castle gardens as well as at the Angel. Lord Bute not only refused to be discouraged by another failure in 1886 but told Andrew Pettigrew to plant two other vineyards on other parts of the estate. So Pettigrew prepared another five acres at nearby Swanbridge on sloping land facing south west within half a mile of the Bristol Channel, and a smaller one at St Quentins near Cowbridge. Swanbridge proved a good choice, but the vines were taken up at St Quentins after a few

Previous page: a group of grape-pickers gather beside a cart laden with black grapes from the Castle Coch vineyard. The grapes were taken for milling and pressing at Cardiff Castle.

A contemporary photograph of Lord Bute's home, Cardiff Castle, where the grapes from the Castle Coch vineyard were made into wine.

years' trial since the position, being open to the channel, was too windswept.

The summer of 1887 was one of high temperatures and light rain, and a record 3,600 bottles were made. In the third edition of *Vines and Vine Culture*, which came out in 1892, Archibald Barron also saw fit to remark that in the Jubilee Year of 1887 the vintage at Castle Coch produced 'nine hogsheads of excellent wine'. The crop was the largest and best ripened since the vines were planted, he said. The sturdiest variety was Gamay Noir. But then the cycle repeated itself: two bad years followed by a third bumper year. With slumps in 1888 and 1889 they made 2,000 bottles in 1890; then only 900 and 600 respectively in 1891 and 1892.

Quantity may have been low but evidently the quality was of the highest. In his diary of July 1892 Lord Bute noted: 'The Mayor of Cardiff has bought three dozen of my 1885 wine, like, but in his opinion, better (and I really think it is) than, my Falernian here.' That year Andrew Pettigrew told members of the Royal Horticultural Society about Castle Coch and its wine. He brought some samples with him and a well-known chemist who tasted them stated they were 'most excellent as a British production; not only of full alcoholic strength, but containing an agreeable amount of acid tartrate, as well as aroma far in advance of grape wines generally manufactured in this country'. This remark probably referred to the home-made fruit drink listed as Grape Wine in Frederick Bishop's book of recipes, *The Wife's Own Book of Cookery* (1860), and which most probably used eating grapes, or to the commercially manufactured drinks like 'Onomosto',

It is not known where
in Cardiff Castle the
winepresses were
located. There was a
vertical press (right)
for pressing Castell
Coch wine, as well as
the horizontal one
(above). In 1877 forty
gallons of white wine
were made (240
bottles). In 1885 they
made 1,500 bottles and
in 1887 3,600.

made by Thos. Grant & Sons of Maidstone from imported grape juice and retailing at 2s a bottle.

Castell Coch White was in a different league. Wine-drinkers as well as wine-analysers testified to its quality by being prepared to pay an increased price for matured South Wales vintages. In 1893 the Birmingham wine merchants Ludlow, Roberts & Willes sold four and a half dozen of the 1881 vintage, which cost £3 a dozen in that year, at £5 15s a dozen.

Lord Bute Makes Red Wine and Appoints an Agent to Sell It

In 1893 Lord Bute decided to make red wine. By then it is probable that he was growing the one variety of vine only, Gamay Noir, which produced purple berried bunches in great abundance.

In the early years of wine-making at Cardiff Castle a simple cog-rollered mill was used through which the bunches were passed and crushed —berries, stones and stalks together. The pulp produced in this was immediately taken to the press and the wine made from it always turned out white. In 1893 however, new apparatus was introduced. By using what Andrew's son A. A. Pettigrew called an *égrappoir*, into which the bunches were fed in bucketfuls, the berries were stripped of their stalks before being passed through rubber-coated rollers; in this way the seed-stones remained unbroken, and the resulting pulp was of pure fruit. New after-treatment was introduced at the same time. Before being pressed, the pulp was heaped into an immense vat and here, during several days, the first fermentation took place. The juice therefore took on the colour of the skins and the result was red wine.

Tod thought 1893 was Castle Coch's finest year, which is not unreasonable considering that the fine weather and enormous crop combined to produce forty hogsheads of must which made 12,000 bottles of wine. A doctor who tried some at the Angel liked it so much he bought a dozen cases on the spot. He paid the usual 60s a dozen. When he died some years later the cases which he had not consumed were sold along with the rest of his cellar for 115s a dozen.

This was an exceptionally high price. When John Searcy & Sons joined forces with G. Tansley & Co in 1898 to form Searcy, Tansley & Co, they issued a General Price List offering an 1886 Pommard at 42s a dozen and a Chambertin 1885 at 66s. A bottle of vin ordinaire claret could be bought for a shilling, but a dozen bottles of Lafite 1874 cost 148s.

Lord Bute was fanatical about allowing his grapes to prove that they could ripen in their South Wales vineyard, and produce juice of a sweetness suitable for wine-making, *without other stimulation*. Looking back on the vineyard of Castle Coch's forty-five years of life, Andrew Pettigrew's son, A. A. Pettigrew, said that only in seven of the years was thorough ripening of the fruit attained.

In 1897 Lord Bute appointed Messrs. Hatch, Mansfield & Co., a London wine merchant as the agency for his 'Castell Coch Wine'. The approach was cautious: though the wine did not have the delicate aroma and flavour of the best foreign wine, it was 'eminently honest and wholesome'.

The remaining seasons were merely indifferent when only partial ripening was attained, or thoroughly bad where there was no crop at all. And even in those seven years the production of sugar in the apparently mature fruit was insufficient for the requirements of fermentation! In that memorable year 1887 considerable quantities of cane-sugar had to be added to the freshly pressed juice. In 1893, another gloriously fine year when the record quantity of forty hogsheads of must was produced, a deficiency of three degrees of saccharinity was recorded. In spite of this deficiency, Lord Bute refused to allow the addition of sugar, with the result that only a vinegary liquor was produced from that year's vintage.

Fortunately phylloxera never made its appearance at Castle Coch throughout the whole of the forty-five-year period. But in 1895 Vine

*Lord Bute's wine was
professionally marketed,
and these labels were
designed for the bottles.*

Mildew (*Uncinula necator*), which had been noticed on a few vines here and
there for some years before, broke out with such virulence that the whole
field was affected and the crop of fruit entirely ruined. Spraying with
Bordeaux mixture—in later years dusting with flowers of sulphur—became
part of the routine both at the main vineyard and at Swanbridge, although
the disease did not appear as an epidemic at the latter until some years later
and the effects were never so destructive.

H. M. Tod thought Swanbridge was in the much more favourable
position of the two vineyards. He paid regular visits up to 1897 and was
flattered when Andrew Pettigrew invited him to suggest names for some
of the Castell Coch wines. This presented a difficulty, confessed Tod, because of the want of definiteness in style and character; some were stronger
than others and some reminded him of a mixture of incompatible sorts.
When it came to the point, he was unable to think of anything peculiarly
Welsh (or English), and could suggest nothing less derivative than 'Calca-
vella', the name of Portuguese white wine.

It was also in 1897 that Lord Bute decided to make a serious attempt
to promote the sale of Castell Coch wine by appointing a well-known
London wine merchant as the agency for its sale, Messrs Hatch, Mansfield
& Co., established in 1802 and still operating at Cowcross Street, EC1, 'wine
merchants to the City of London'. In their catalogue under the heading
'Welsh Wines; Canary Brand'—which showed that Tod's Portuguese

suggestion had not gone unminded—they stated that 'although the wines cannot yet be said to possess the delicate aroma and flavour of the best foreign wines, they are eminently honest and wholesome'. Eight sorts were listed with such descriptions as: 'big soft wine, medium dry' and 'full rich wine'. Prices ranged from 48s a dozen for an 1885 wine to 36s a dozen for a wine of 1892. A. A. Pettigrew commented: 'fair business resulted at first; soon, however, to fall off'. To-day's managing director, Hon. Ralph Mansfield, tells me that a fire at their offices in 5 Pall Mall East shortly after the war destroyed their records, so no documents remain relating to the firm's activities as the agents of Castell Coch. 'But' he said 'I do well remember my father telling me of an experiment in selling Welsh wines which was not exactly a success!'

Tod was inspired by the success of the Bute/Pettigrew venture to start growing vines vineyard-fashion at his own nursery at Wisley in 1891, 'and I found that I could ripen their grapes as well that way as on open walls'.

John Patrick Crichton-Stuart, third Marquess of Bute, was an immensely rich landowner closely associated with the cultural and commercial life of Cardiff, carrying on the work of his father, the 'creator of modern Cardiff'. The third Marquess was twenty-six when, in 1873, he planned to plant a vineyard beside Castle Coch, near Cardiff. He died in 1900, but the vineyard continued to be cultivated until 1920.

The End of Castle Coch

The third Marquess of Bute died in 1900 and was succeeded by his nineteen-year-old son who took as much interest in the vineyard as his father. Tod paid a visit to Castle Coch in 1905 after an interval of some years and was amazed to find 63,000 vines in fruit. He arranged to have some Muscat Hatif de Saumur vines from the vineyard sent to Wisley. There was another outstanding summer in 1911, but even in that year the South Wales vignerons had to add three and a half pounds of cane sugar to every gallon of expressed juice. Owing to the impossibility of obtaining sugar during the Great War, no attempt was made at wine-making after 1914. But the vines still grew both at Castle Coch and Swanbridge all through the war and were only finally uprooted in 1920 when his lordship decided to put the land to other use. In the forty-five years during which the vineyard flourished, as A. A. Pettigrew vouched in 1926, 'the late Marquess's interest in it never flagged, and no expense was spared by him or by the present Marquess that could in any way promote its success'.

The Wine and Vintage Book of Cardiff Castle (Castell Coch and Swanbridge wine), 1887–1902, deposited by the descendants of the Marquess's agent at the time (and now in Glamorgan Record Office, Cardiff), contains a record of the quantities, bottling, storage, price and sale of the wine produced at the two vineyards over this period.

A. A. Pettigrew's final verdict on the forty-five-year saga of the Castle Coch vineyard seems unduly pessimistic. 'Cardiff lies in latitude 51.5° N and has a mean annual temperature of 49.1°F. It may be asked why has it proved impossible to mature a good wine-producing grape here, when excellent wine is produced along the northern European line already indicated.'

He considered the northern limit of the cultivation of the grape vine as a line starting from the mouth of the Loire (lat. 47° N) in the west, reaching its most northerly point (52° N) in the vicinity of Frankfurt in Germany, and southward to Odessa on the Black Sea (47° N). 'For several degrees northward of this line the vine is perfectly hardy and grows vigorously but —other than in exceptional situations and seasons—is unable to produce or ripen fruit capable of being made into wine.'

He answered his own question by saying that the vine required not a high temperature averaged for the whole year but a higher temperature and more sunlight during the summer season than the British climate afforded. It hardly mattered how low the winter temperature fell. In

Europe the lower mean annual temperature was due to a balance between very low winter but high summer temperatures.

> The conclusion to be drawn from the Glamorgan experiment would seem to be clear, that here viticulture holds out no promise of success. There is obviously something wrong with the climate when even in the most favourable of seasons it has been found necessary to resort to the artificial addition of sugar* or (as in some cases) of alcohol.
>
> Quite tolerably good wines have been made here by the expedients described, but they were not the genuine products of our soil. Moreover it is clear that they can never compete in the market with wines imported from countries enjoying more suitable climates.

The fourth Marquess of Bute disposed of the greater part of his South Wales estate in 1938. He died in 1947, and the following year Cardiff Castle was conveyed, with certain reservations, by way of gift to Cardiff Corporation for the benefit of the town's citizens. Castle Coch is now in the hands of the Department of the Environment and open to the public to admire or deplore. The two vineyards are council house estates. The twentieth century has taken over for good.

Twentieth-Century 'British Wines'

H. M. Tod's comprehensive work *Vine-Growing in England*, from which I have quoted copiously, was published in 1911, and he is perhaps the first to deal with the subject historically on so large a scale. He named 2,265 types of vine in cultivation in various parts of the world in 1911, and gave the following list of wines grown in England for the purpose of making English wine:

---

* The relatively cold climate of Germany, whose vineyards straddle the 50th parallel approximately on the latitude of Newfoundland and Labrador, does not give their grapes a high sugar content either. Most German white wine is low in alcohol, seldom exceeding 11 per cent. At best, state Alexander Dorozynski and Bibiane Bell in *The Wine Book* (1969), 'this gives them freshness and contributes to the bouquet, and at worst it makes them too tart, too acid and lacking in body and alcohol. On the whole, German wines are scrupulously well made. But many nevertheless receive the "sunshine of Frankenthal"— Frankenthal being a large beet-sugar producing centre.' A German wine district with an international reputation is Maximin-Grunhause on the river Ruwer, but if the light Moselle produced there turns out too acid there is no hesitation in sugaring it before putting it on the market.

The Miller
Miller's Burgundy
Common or Royal Muscadine
Black Cluster
Experione
Cambridge Botanic Garden
Moore's Early
Ironclad
Duchess
Dutch Sweetwater
Brandt (*which was of American origin and Tod claimed to have introduced to Britain in 1886*)
Chasselas Vibert: white and red

In 1911 wine-making still had three years to go at Castle Coch, but most people in Britain would have denied that grapes grown on British soil were capable of making wine. It was with some confusion therefore that they learnt of the existence in their midst of something called the British Wine Industry and its product 'British Wine'.

Bottles were advertised and could be seen on the shelves of grocers throughout Britain with labels bearing such legends as 'British Sherry', 'British Ruby', 'British Tawny' alongside bottles of 'tonic wine' with trade names like Sanatogen. These were the twentieth-century versions of Ono-mosto. They did not claim to be champagne but the kind of fortified wine which for so long had been made at Jerez in Spain and Oporto in Portugal, and shipped to Britain for consumption by the upper classes before and after lunch and dinner: sherry and port. These sherry-type and port-type beverages were 'Made in Britain' indeed, but not from English or Welsh grapes. Their base was imported grape juice concentrate or imported raisins. They cost a good deal less than the Real Thing, because on the latter the Government charged import duty which was handed on to the consumer in the selling price. These imitations became so popular that at the end of the nineteen-twenties sales of the Real Thing fell in a way that greatly reduced the revenue which the Government derived from customs duty. To restore the balance the Board of Trade in 1927 imposed an excise duty of a shilling a gallon on 'British Wines', which however was still very much less than the customs duty on the wines from Spain and Portugal over which they therefore retained a considerable advantage. Twelve months later (in 1928) the excise duty was increased to 1s 6d, while the customs duty on real sherry and port stood at 8s a gallon. It was still less than the preferential customs duty imposed on wine made in the British Empire—the dominions and colonial territories—'Big Tree Burgundy' and the rest, which was 4s a gallon.

There was no such thing as a light English table wine in 1928; but if there had been it is likely that the legislators would have made a distinction between 'British Wines', made from imported concentrate in the tradition of Onomosto, and 'English Wine' and 'Welsh Wine' made from English and Welsh grapes harvested in vineyards as an agricultural crop in the tradition of Meare, Ely, Rayleigh, Hatfield, Westbrook, Painshill, Holwood and Castle Coch. The two would not have been in competition, and since both agricultural labour and wine chemists would have been involved in English wine production, it is likely that a British government would have wanted to encourage it in every way it could.

Sloth won the day after 1920. The cynical mood of the Cocktail Era of a Britain recovering from the unprecedented chaos of the 1914–18 War was hardly conducive to sponsoring an uncertain activity such as viticulture and wine-making, in which the risks seemed great and the rewards, however promising, were far from immediate. The upheaval which the war occasioned meant that the world of 1920 was totally different from that of 1910. Four years had been enough to bring down the curtain on so much that had gone before. English wine? Not really mentionable in what they called Society. If Soames Forsyte had told his friends he was using his property for vine-growing and wine-making, he would have forfeited his reputation as a Man of Taste; it was hardly what a gentleman would do. It was good copy for the satirists; perfect material for a comic passage in a short story in next week's *Strand* magazine by P. G. Wodehouse or Dornford Yates.

1920 to 1945

During the nineteen-twenties and -thirties, the circumstances, which had made possible the production of English wine for 1,900 years, did not change; English vineyards could still yield English wine-grapes capable of making English wine distinctive from any other, just as the constant American ambience produced a distinctive American wine, the German ambience produced a distinctive German wine, the Italian ambience a distinctive Italian wine. The vine plants, if anyone had planted them, would have behaved in the same way as they had for the Roman officer who occupied the station villa of Vindomis, for Hamo, Bishop of Rochester at Halling, King Richard at Windsor, Lord Salisbury at Hatfield, Charles Hamilton at Cobham. The soil was the same; the pattern of hills and valleys and rivers, the sea breezes, the summers, the autumns. The knowledge was there for anyone who had the urge to tap it.

There will have been several curious enough to try it out against the tide of fashion and risk the label of eccentric; but unless they capitalized their eccentricity and wrote a book about it, their vineyard and its wine went unchronicled. To what extent he was alone in his endeavour I do not know, but in 1939 George Ordish planted a vineyard in the garden of his house at Yalding in Kent, and kept it going through the holocaust which in that year struck the world once more; but except for him and any others whose sites are unknown, it would seem without doubt that between the closing of Castle Coch in 1920 and the end of the Second World War in 1945 there was a twenty-five-year gap in English viticulture of a kind which had never occurred before.

1945 to 1967

SIX

Transformation Scene: the Researcher, the Writer and the Grower

The Tradition Had Become Quaint

With so long a period of suspended animation it was natural that viticulture should appear 'quaint' to those who had only heard of it as an old wives' tale. Stigmatized as old-fashioned, it was still too recent to belong to the romantic past which went under the name of 'English History'.

It was English viticulture's misfortune to have gone underground in a period when social change was so comprehensive. To those who lived through to 1945 anything which belonged to an unreal era called 'Before The War' found little acceptance in a world in which the password was 'Contemporary'. The concept of English wine was decidedly *not* contemporary, any more than silent movies or Oxford bags.

Apart from a certain amount of commercial growing by professional market gardeners, the cultivation of grapes in England and Wales was thought to be an upper class, if not aristocratic, activity carried on by old retainers in stately homes. Commercial and private growing of English dessert grapes was not in the mainstream of English life. With the allegedly 'wrong' climate the 'correct' heat had to be sustained by intensifying the sun through glass or introducing hot steam through pipes. These operations put the activity beyond the means of the majority.

Wine-drinking was even more rarefied than grape-eating. An exalted few had an account with a wine-merchant and what they referred to as 'my cellar'. No one who spoke of his wine-merchant needed to put the word 'grape' before the noun, since everyone knew he was talking about the alcoholic drink made from fermented grapes. If however he had talked of

146

his aunt's wine-making they would have assumed he was referring to her boiling of fruit and flowers and the bottling of mixtures which she labelled Elderberry Wine, Dandelion Wine and Turnip Wine.

For those to whom wine meant grape-wine only, the application of the word to an alcoholic drink made from the fermentation of *any* fruit, flower or vegetable was unfortunate because it brought to 'real' wine-making all the pejorative overtones of the term 'home-made', and lent it a cottage industry image which it has never been able entirely to shrug off. It generated a disbelief that the term 'wine-making' could, in England, ever have been applied to any activity other than the making of fruit wines, or could ever have referred to anything as un-English as making a drink associated with chianti, chablis, hock and the rest.

In England the association was not with peasants' feet treading the grapes but with the lady-like hands of straw-hatted spinsters presiding over trestle tables at village fêtes. Ignorant that there was ever a time when English wine had a distinctive character which no one regarded as a second-hand imitation of a Real Thing made only in Europe, the wine snobs subscribed to what they believed to be a tradition that it was Bad Form to admit to a liking for 'English wine', let alone to drinking it regularly or serving it to one's guests.

1946: Scientist Ray Barrington Brock Adopts a New Approach

In 1946, however, no such consideration influenced Ray Barrington Brock. He was a scientist who liked gardening. Until 1938 he had been a Senior Research Chemist in the Ilford photographic group, and in 1946 he was managing director of one of the large instrument manufacturers. At his house at Oxted in Surrey he was delighted to see how well his peaches ripened out of doors, without the aid of glass. If peaches, he asked himself, why not other fruit not normally associated with England: grapes for instance? This was just the kind of problem his scientific mind was aching to wrestle with. In his new job he was no longer able to apply his mind to the disciplined and exciting procedures of research in which he had been trained. So in 1946, with no previous knowledge of viticulture or wine-making, without prejudices or inhibitions, he set himself a project: to discover which varieties of grape would grow and ripen in England in the open air. He plunged into the subject with the fanatical energy of a convert, but also with the methodical approach of a scientist who takes nothing at face value. He

147

was as much concerned with eating-grapes as wine-grapes; indeed the accent in the early days was on the former.

First of all he repaired his ignorance of the subject by reading, but none of the books he found could explain why the vineyards which once had flourished were no longer to be seen. He then came across a book written at the end of the nineteenth century by a twenty-four-year-old Australian, Francois de Castella (still alive and well in 1945), *Viticulture in the State of Victoria*. This described very clearly how methods of cultivation changed according to the climate, whether hot in the south or less hot in the north. From de Castella's reasoning Ray Barrington Brock was able to deduce the probable requirements for a climate such as England's. He gleaned all the information he could from continental literature and visited viticultural research stations in France and Switzerland (Lausanne), and later in Germany. He got in touch with one of Britain's most distinguished writers on garden matters, Edward Hyams, the author of *The English Garden, Irish Gardens, Pleasure from Plants* and many novels, who was doing literary research for a book on English viticulture.

A few vineyards dotted round the countryside here and there had saved English viticulture from total expiry during the war, notably the one which George Ordish had planted at Vine House at Yalding in Kent in 1939. Soon after the war Edward Hyams put down a vineyard not far distant from Yalding, at Shottenden near Canterbury. These vineyards were helping to restore the English viticultural tradition and to create the kind of practical background against which Ray Barrington Brock's research could be shown to be far from academic. In the garden of a cottage in the Kent village of Wrotham, Hyams found a vine which closely resembled the old Pinot Meunier or Dusty Miller type which had been a feature of English viticulture for a hundred years or more. It had adapted itself to the English climate very much better than the standard Pinot grapes of France which Barrington Brock found unsatisfactory when he tried to grow them at Oxted. It was the Pinot Meunier which Hyams identified with the Roman *aminea lanata* (see page 84). He took a cutting of his find and it became the father of the now-famous Wrotham Pinot of which Ray Barrington Brock soon had a row for experimentation. 'The Wrotham Pinot is a consistent cropper' he was later able to report,

> and ripens here in good years in the open vineyard. It is probable that it would be suitable for a really high-flavoured Burgundy type of red wine in favoured sites in the south of England, but is not suitable where conditions are not very good. It is a borderline case as regards ripening, although it does give consistent cropping. The quantities of course, as with all very high quality grapes, are not very great.

Edward Hyams published his book in 1949. It had the title *The Grape Vine in England, The History and Practice of the cultivation of Vines in England; an account of their origin and introduction; a guide to the plantation and care of Vineyards to-day; a refutation of the notion that English weather is hostile to the Vine; a description of the way to make wine.* It was the most comprehensive book on the subject since H. M. Tod's *Vine-Growing in England* of 1911 and played an important part as the propaganda arm of Ray Barrington Brock's scientific work at Oxted. To the new post-war generation it put English viticulture in its proper perspective, gave them reason for taking it seriously and pointed to its commercial potential. A main message of the book was that in his view the English climate had not changed for a thousand years. It was still what it had always been, an island climate which distinguished it from parts of the continent of Europe on a similar latitude. The climate was temperate, humid and gentle, and because of this English wine could claim the distinction of being an island wine with qualities of a different sort to that made from grapes grown on the continent.

Ray Barrington Brock's researches on the continent showed him that in the vineyards of northern Europe the custom was to restrict the size of the vines more and more, and plant them closer and closer as the climate became colder. In the South of France they were spaced as wide as ten feet, but in some of the Champagne vineyards they were planted only one foot three inches apart. A bigger crop usually followed a hot summer. In northern climates south facing hillsides were considered best; vines never seemed to suffer from drought in the north once they were established. Good wine was made from semi-ripe Riesling grapes which, on the banks of the Rhine, ripened a fortnight or so later than most.

His reading and questioning over, he determined on a plan of action. His first step was to write to the Royal Horticultural Society to ask for their help in securing samples and cuttings of every sort of eating- and wine-grape vine then growing in Britain, whether under glass in hothouses or out of doors against walls. They poured in by the hundred, some labelled, some not, and most of the former wrongly named. It was obvious that no one had ever embarked on a similar operation before and that a major task was going to be replacing myth with fact, traditional assumptions with a degree of scientific knowledge hitherto foreign to English viticulture.

Not one of the vines he received from growers in Britain proved to be entirely suitable for growing out of doors vineyard-fashion, though most succeeded under cloches and many were borderline cases which were fine under glass but doubtful in the open. From the labels there were some hundred different names but on examination they represented in fact only about fifteen to twenty varieties. Many examples of a bad American hybrid vine arrived which were labelled 'Royal Muskadine'. Apparently they had

149

been disseminated throughout the British Isles under this name for many a year, in spite of bearing no resemblance whatsoever to the famous 'Royal Muskadine'.

Barrington Brock's second step was to invite continental research stations to send him cuttings of vines which they thought were likely to grow and ripen in England. In the spring of 1946 he planted a selection of these in a section of his Oxted garden on the top of a ridge some 450 feet up on the North Downs which, after the name of his house, he called the Summerfield Vineyard. With the aid of an assistant, Mr E. G. Walker, whom he engaged for the purpose, he laid out the vineyard into six plots, the last of which, Plot F, was specifically set aside for wine-grapes, with two and a half feet between vines and two feet between rows. They were: Pinot Meunier, known in England as Miller's Burgundy and famous as an outdoor grape for centuries, Seibel 13053, Pinot Noir, Seyve-Villard 5/276, Blue Portuguese, Riesling Clone, Riesling-Sylvaner (which later became known as Mueller-Thurgau). On all six plots he had some forty-five varieties from which of course he could draw no conclusions for three years. It was not until the fourth year that he was able to say whether the grapes held promise or not. He then grew each variety for at least a further three years while he assessed the usefulness of the grape, in the hope of establishing, in a scientific way, which grapes grew and ripened best in the open air vineyard-fashion. He hoped Surrey could be taken as typical an English county as any, though he was aware that his vineyard was 450 feet above sea level.

Later it became clear that further west the warmer and longer summer gave far superior ripening, and that in Dorset and Somerset there was consistent ripening of varieties which were borderline cases in Surrey. One of the greatest of the red varieties which Barrington Brock thought would never ripen in Surrey produced a first-class wine in the Bristol area. The Thames Valley, later, also proved to be much better than Oxted.

He found that soil had very little effect on ripening. 'With the exception of one or two people who appeared to have slight trouble with absolutely water-logged clay, nobody seemed to find any real difference with any particular type of soil.' Twenty years later Anton Massel was to confirm this in his book *Applied Wine Chemistry and Technology* (1969).

The structure of the soil will depend on its geological origin; in regard to the quality of the wine its importance is often overrated. Basically it will be agreed that the soil must provide a suitable habitat for the vine's roots. The main characteristics of a good soil are good drainage, with a sound structure to retain moisture for the roots . . . That the soil has less influence on the quality than the grape variety and the climate, is demonstrated by the vines

grown in the Douro valley and the Moselle valley. The soil is similar but the wines are totally different.

After a summary of soil conditions of Europe's vineyards Massel concluded however: 'It can be seen that the best wines are grown in soil rich in minerals, but poor in nitrogen. The saying that the best wines come from the poorest soil is consequently not strictly true. It can however be said that the poorest wines come from the poorest soil.'

1949: the First Data from Oxted Viticultural Research Station

With the experiment well under way Ray Barrington Brock named the Summerfield Vineyard the Oxted Viticultural Research Station and instituted regular Open Days to which people began to come from all over the country to see progress and to tell him of their own experiences.

It was a laborious but fruitful operation of trial and error. The first year in which data became available, 1949, was very hot. One of the first conclusions to be established was that the continental order of ripening, calculated on the mean of the Royal Chasselas vine, was not the English order. It was going to be no use applying French data to English viticulture. England had enough sun and ample warmth, but not every variety reacted to the same stimuli in the same way. By chemical analysis he discovered that some would not ripen at all if they did not get enough sun; while others would ripen well. It was a question of selecting from those which did not need so much sun. When there was a lot of sun the French data might apply; otherwise not. A number of varieties sent over by French research stations were classified as early ripeners *in France*, but in England were late ripeners because of the lack of sun. One Italian vine on the other hand went on ripening even if the sun never shone from one day to another. The determining factor was the length of time during which the plant actually lay in the path of the sun's rays: the ultra-violet light as opposed to the warmth. Vines needed both, but there was a threshold *for each variety* below which they would not grow and did not ripen. There was no *general* threshold for vines in England; and each variety behaved differently.

Most of the plants sent over from the continent grew, but not all accomplished the changeover from acidity to sweetness: the ripening for which a certain proportion of ultra-violet light was needed. To find out how much ultra-violet light each variety of grape vine required was the basis of the whole of Ray Barrington Brock's research and his major contri-

151

bution to the subject as a whole. This research had never been done before. From his scientific analyses Barrington Brock was able to pinpoint why the figures from the continent were of no use in England. He experimented with means of preventing and curing vine diseases, the effect of soils and manures and different pruning and training methods; but he was mainly concerned to find out what would ripen and what would not. His 'major scientific discovery', which he saw as having far-reaching results, was 'to show quite conclusively that vines respond differently to the amount of sunshine that they receive, quite irrespective of the warmth of the climate in which they are growing.' It appeared that on the continent it was normal for the vines to get an adequate supply of sunshine even in a bad year when the average temperature was low, with the result that the factor had not been noticed. In Britain however, where there were far longer periods of heavy cloud with the sun obscured for weeks on end, he found that there were a number of varieties which were capable of continuing to ripen without sunshine, if the weather remained sufficiently warm. 'Others, like the Blue Portuguese or Meslier Precoce, are quite hopeless unless the sun shines a reasonable amount. This has meant that we have had to recast completely all ideas received from the continent as to earliness or otherwise of varieties which might have been thought suitable for this climate.'

In 1949 he published the Viticultural Research Station's first report: *Outdoor Grapes in Cold Climates*. As the Summerfield Vineyard developed, he said, they had received more and more enquiries from interested visitors for the information he had procured from the continent and elsewhere. 'There appears to be a very real demand for information on the possibilities of cultivating the vine in this country on the lines of the northerly European vineyards, and this book has been written purely as a preliminary description of the work in hand.'

By the time the next report was out he hoped to be able to enlarge on any points which were not sufficiently clear. It was obvious that he had a very long piece of research on his hands and that recommendations made in 1949 might easily have to be completely amended after a few years. 'Suffice to say however that we are already certain that some of the lesser known vine varieties will give us excellent results out of doors in southern England. Only research however will show us how to overcome the troubles we shall certainly experience in obtaining results.'

The most striking feature of his research into wine-making so far was the information from the Swiss Research Station that grapes for wine-making needed to be riper than grapes for eating. In Switzerland they sold the Golden Chasselas for eating three weeks before it was considered sufficiently ripe for wine, when it was almost sickly sweet.

Barrington Brock gave particulars, in the first report, of the varieties being tried out at Oxted. He cautiously prefaced his chapter headed 'Recommendations', making it clear that they were intended solely to assist people to make a start and should not be taken as very definite.

Ray Barrington Brock's right-hand man at Oxted was E. G. Walker. In this photograph he is working the American-style winepress which the research station used for experiments—one gallon a squeeze. No wine was made at Oxted commercially.

So little is really known of the troubles which are sure to arise in an established vineyard, and of the difficulties of cultivation of many of the most promising varieties that it may well be that in a few years time we shall have to amend many of these recommendations. We have for instance already found in 1948 that Ascot Citronelle, which was the most promising variety in the vineyard and grew better than anything else, bloomed well and yet set hardly any fruit at all. This bad setting was in fact so serious that we cannot recommend this variety until we have had further experience and a number of other very promising varieties have been excluded for the same sort of reason.

Ray Barrington Brock published the results of his research in a series of Reports, the first of which appeared in 1949. The four pioneering reports from the Oxted Viticultural Research Station, together with Edward Hyams' book The Grape Vine in England, *gave the English wine revival its scientific basis.*

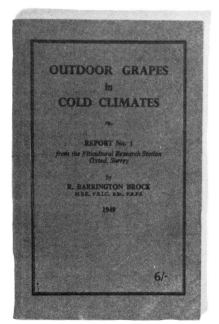

OUTDOOR GRAPES
in
COLD CLIMATES

REPORT No. 1
*from the Viticultural Research Station
Oxted, Surrey*

by

R. BARRINGTON BROCK
M.S.E., F.R.I.C., B.Sc., F.R.P.S.

1949

6/-

He also experimented with cloches and was able to recommend the varieties which were best suited to them. He studied the various pruning methods and came to prefer that devised by M. Guyot, the author of the sage dictum that the finest wine was only made from correctly ripened grapes on correct soil, correctly vinified. Barrington Brock advised against the use of powerful fertilizers and advocated planting only one-year-old vines which the nurseryman could guarantee were free from phylloxera.

It is interesting to note that in this first progress report of 1949 Ray Barrington Brock was able to say:

> Apart from these types [a list of six recommended wine-grapes] which are likely to be successful under adverse conditions, there is the possibility that Riesling and Riesling-Sylvaner [Mueller-Thurgau], which are the varieties used for Hock and Moselle, may be possible over here. They are however rather late ripening and we would at this stage rather recommend Madeleine Royale or Gamay Hatif as being more likely to ripen under our conditions. We shall however know rather more about this matter in 1951.

In 1946 Ray Barrington Brock set out to discover which vine varieties would grow and ripen in England in the open air. He carried out his research at his own expense at his house, Summerfield, at Oxted, Surrey, over a period of thirty years. This photograph was taken in the 1950s.

154

Among the varieties of wine-grape vine tried out at Oxted in the 1950s was the Riesling-Sylvaner, today usually known as Mueller-Thurgau, from which most English wine is now made. In 1949 Barrington Brock tipped Riesling-Sylvaner as likely to be a winner in England.

This early tip that Mueller-Thurgau was a likely winner was a measure of Ray Barrington Brock's perspicacity, for twenty-five years later more Mueller-Thurgau had been planted in England and Wales than any other variety, and its grapes were the base of most of the English wine made in the nineteen-seventies.

One of the more promising ungrafted varieties Ray handled came from the USSR. He heard that the Russians had successfully crossed a very early ripening Siberian grape, the *Vitis amurensis*, with other internationally well-known vines. He contacted the government-controlled Caucasus Viticultural Research Station through an intermediary. He was told they were not allowed to sell any of their plants, but if he liked to send them fifty ball point pens, of which there was short supply in the Soviet Union, and a couple of good secateurs, they would see what could be arranged. The barter was organized and the Siberian cross-bred vines duly arrived at Oxted. Two of them turned out to be superlative—he named them Russian Early July and Russian Early Violet.

From 1950 he was able to shift the emphasis of research away from eating-grapes. By then he had a number of table grapes of all seasons to offer, though he had found that in general eating-grapes were not very satisfactory in the open vineyard in England's climate, not because they would not ripen but because there always seemed to be storms about the time when they were ripening which banged the berries about and made them look disreputable. This did not matter to the private consumer but for the commercial grower it meant they were unsaleable. From 1950 on-

wards he concentrated on wine-grapes, but these did not, of course, crop sufficiently to make reasonable quantities of wine until 1955.

Ray Barrington Brock Turns to Wine-Making

With wine-grapes 'ripe' means sweet enough to make wine from. So to obtain data on ripening Ray Barrington Brock had to make wine. No one would have believed his figures if he had only taken sugar content, with the result that he found himself involved in wine-making, though this had not been part of his original plan. He soon discovered it required very much more skill than vine-growing.

Setting up a winery would be expensive, so he asked the Government for a grant. The ministry told him that if his tests proved successful they would consider a grant! So he scraped up enough of his own money and built an inadequate underground winery at Oxted, to which eventually he installed proper temperature control, and in which he was able to carry out comparative tests. He began selling cuttings on Open Days and the income from this paid about half of Mr Walker's salary. Of the six hundred or so varieties he had grown by the nineteen-fifties only some fifteen or so proved any good. The Siegerrebe and the Riesling-Sylvaner were the best.

On most varieties he reckoned they ought to get two pounds of grapes to a vine in a normal year, about one bottle of wine as a fair average; but some grapes contained much less juice than others. To obtain independent judgements on the quality of his wine he invited members of the Institute of Masters of Wine, a post-war body, to come to Surrey and pronounce on bottles of Oxted and continental wines labelled only by numbers. From the marking of the Masters, to Ray's delight, it became evident that he was beginning to make a liquor which matched, and was often better than, the average French product.

Other pioneers of this time were Dr A. Pollard, who planted a vine-yard at Bakewell near Bristol, and Mrs S. M. Tritton whose husband wrote a book *Grape Growing and Wine Making From Grapes and Other Fruits* which was published by Grey Owl Research Laboratories in 1951. In his intro-duction he justified bringing out such a book on the grounds that 'in recent years much interest has been shown in the art of outdoor grape growing and in wine making'.

In 1952 George Ordish wrote a book about the open-air vine-growing he had been doing in Kent since 1939. It was called *Wine Growing in England* and published in 1953. His vines continued to flourish at Yalding until he moved to St Albans in the nineteen-sixties.

This of course was vine-growing by enthusiasts as a hobby, and of

the many other similar operations at this time I have no knowledge; but in 1952 a grower of a different sort entered the scene, and succeeded in transforming it.

1952: *Sir Guy Salisbury-Jones Plants a Vineyard at Hambledon*

The success of the eighteenth- and nineteenth-century projects of Charles Hamilton, James Oglethorpe, the Duke of Norfolk, John Ward and the Marquess of Bute failed to fire the imagination of contemporaries, let alone inspire a 'movement', but the decision of Major-General Sir Guy Salisbury-Jones GCVO, CMG, CBE, MC, to plant a vineyard at Hambledon in Hampshire set in train a sequence of events which stimulated interest in English viticulture on an unprecedented scale; new votaries joined the ranks in increasing numbers every year. The atmospheric climate had not changed: what had changed was the social climate—and communications. These were responsible for the chain reaction which followed Hambledon, whereas the previous exercises had been isolated and unproductive of anything other than wine.

'I am often asked what induced me to plant it' Sir Guy told members of the Royal Society of Arts whom, like F. X. Vispré, he had been invited to address in March 1973.

I think that it all goes back to 1917. One day, in the cold wet autumn of that year, the division to which I belonged attacked alongside the French, and at the end of the day we found ourselves sharing a muddy slit trench with some French soldiers. These splendid 'poilus', as they were called, seeing that we had no wine ration took pity on us and shared with us their own, thereby greatly boosting our morale. Never has wine been more welcome, and on that day was consolidated my love, not only for France, but for her wine.

More than thirty years later, as we looked down on the sun-drenched slopes below our house, it occurred to my stepson, who knew of my love for France, and wine, that the site would be ideal for the cultivation of the vine. A wild suggestion, so I thought at the time. Shortly afterwards however I was introduced to the writings of Edward Hyams and Barrington Brock on the possibility of viticulture in England. These are the two men who are the real pioneers of the revival of British viticulture, and it was they who inspired me to have a try. Shortly afterwards I set out with our gardener, Mr Blackman, for the vineyards of Burgundy where I already had contacts, to have a look round. Without the co-operation of Mr Blackman I could have achieved nothing.

157

It so happened that our visit coincided with a banquet given by the Confrerie des Chevaliers du Tastevin at the former Cistercian Monastery of Clos-Vougeot. To this banquet we were both bidden, and I have often thought since that it was under the influence of Burgundian hospitality that I ordered four thousand vines, the number I calculated would be required for the one and a half acres which we had available.

He wanted an early ripening variety, but was uncertain whether to buy one with its own root or one grafted on to American root stock.

Most vines on the continent are now grafted on American root stock to enable them to resist phylloxera ... Having decided I would plant grafted vines, I had to seek advice as to the best root stock that would be resistant to our chalky Hampshire soil, and since the soil in Champagne is similar, I ordered vines grafted on the same root stock that is used in that region. The actual vines which the French recommended were a hybrid called Seyve-Villard 5/276 grafted on 16149. But in order, as they put it, to ajouter un peu de noblesse' they also suggested that I plant a few of the noble Chardonnay and Pinot Noir.

The latter was a black grape, but his French hosts advised him against making a red wine in England's northern climate.

'You may well imagine the excitement when the vines arrived. To suit our small tractor, we planted them in rows four feet apart, with three feet between the vines in each row. This worked out about 3,500 vines to the acre.'

He built himself a press house and winery at Hambledon and on the door of it he had inscribed this passage from *Old Men Forget*, the memoirs of A. Duff Cooper (Viscount Norwich):

WINE TO ME

has been a firm friend and a wise counsellor. Often wine has shown me matters in their true perspective and has, as though by the touch of a magic wand, reduced great disasters to minor inconveniences. Wine for me has lit up the pages of literature and revealed in life romance lurking in the common place. Wine has made me bold but not foolish, has induced me to say silly things but not to do them. Under its influence words have often come too easily which had better not been spoken and letters have been written which had better not have been sent. But if such small indiscretions standing in the debit column of wine's account were added up, they would amount to nothing in comparison with the vast accumulation on the credit side.

The winery cost him £6,000, but altogether Sir Guy reckoned his total outlay, together with a cellar, was in the region of £15,200. The inaugural Hambledon wine went on sale in 1955. It was the first commercially made wine of the British Isles to be produced since the final Castell Coch vintage from Lord Bute's winery in 1915. The forty-year gap had at last been bridged.

'Although here we cannot expect to produce any wine commercially if we are to continue with our research' wrote Ray Barrington Brock referring to his activities at Oxted,

> it is naturally of tremendous interest that somebody should be doing this [producing fine quality wine in Hampshire and elsewhere] and we are taking every step that we can to assist these commercial vineyards to get going . . . There is no longer any reason to doubt that the quality of the wine we can produce in southern England is excellent and can be compared safely with imported wines . . . [and this] has naturally been a factor in deciding people to start commercial vineyards as a serious experiment. (Report no 3, 1961.)

English Wine Acquires a Touch of German Wein-Chemie

The year after the first Hambledon wine became available, there came to England the young German I have already mentioned, Anton Massel, who had just completed the two-year advanced course in *wein-chemie* at the old-established, state-run Hoehere Weinbau Institut at Geisenheim, the leading viticultural college in Germany. Anton Massel arrived in England in 1956 to head the laboratory established in London by the German wine-making equipment firm of Seitz, and to help sell their filters and other machines to British importers of bulk wine. Though his business lay with buyers, sellers and bottlers of foreign wine, when he heard of the pioneering English wine-making efforts of people like Sir Guy Salisbury-Jones he put at their disposal the knowledge he had so recently acquired in Germany. He was able to instruct them in the latest techniques of making wine from German-grown grapes which had ripened in conditions similar to those of England. At this early stage in the development of the new English viticulture, his advice, geared to what Ray Barrington Brock had discovered and made known during his ten years of research at Oxted, was very welcome, and played an important part in ensuring that the incipient wine-chemistry of England evolved on lines which were both professional and scientific.

Fresh from college in 1956 Massel saw wine-making through the eyes

159

of a newly qualified chemist; though, in 1976, he confessed to me that over the years his views on how to make the best wine had veered towards the minimum chemistry and the maximum of letting Nature have her way. The art of making wine, as Massel sees it now, is the art of guiding natural processes.

Below left: Sir Guy Salisbury-Jones planted a vineyard at Hambledon in Hampshire in 1952. Here Sir Guy adjusts the winepress for the grapes harvested from his French vines.

Below right: Anton Massel (left) gave valuable professional advice to pioneering English vignerons. Here he helps Alan Rook to gauge the sugar content of the wine-grapes grown at the Stragglethorpe Hall vineyard.

I now tell the people who come to me for a course on wine-making how little they should interfere. Certain interference is necessary of course if the wine is not to spoil. The proper use of sulphur dioxide as an additive is the main skill to acquire. It is still the best protector against premature oxidization—premature ageing, that is. It will keep the wine from going too dark and losing its flavour. Of course if oxidization is accompanied by bacterial infection then the wine is a write-off. Immediately the grapes are crushed, sulphur must be introduced to stop instantaneous fermentation. The prime mechanical necessity is good filtration. Impurities must be given twelve hours to sink to the bottom, and then the 'must' should be racked off. Sulphur and Filtration are the main artificial aids to wine-making; otherwise, interfere as little as possible.

Massel visited Sir Guy Salisbury-Jones at Hambledon and was able to give him good advice, based on the outcome of the first vintage, on how to improve his vinification processes, and also on the running of his vineyard.

Helpers gather at the Hambledon vineyard. Sir Guy Salisbury-Jones marshals them into an efficient corps of pickers for the vital harvesting operation when the crop must be picked in the shortest period of time and with minimum wastage.

Next page: the grape harvest at the Hambledon vineyard in the sixties.

He suggested for instance, that to be properly commercial the plot should be at least three acres, and, acting on this advice, Sir Guy enlarged the vineyard to four and a half acres.

From supplying the English wine-makers with imported equipment, Massel soon added to his service the importation of vine plants, which his experience told him should be of the type grafted on to American roots.

This is not the place to digress at length on the grafted or non-grafted controversy—George Ordish has written fully about phylloxera in *The Great Wine Blight*—but its history is interesting as I have already hinted. The disease *came* to Europe, whereas it is indigenous to America where the vines adapted themselves over the centuries to live and grow without the insect having any effect on them. At first grafting plants on to American roots affected the grape which came from the vine, but in time the French managed to discover which vine varieties were compatible with which root stocks, and now grafting has no effect on the vine or the taste of the grape that grows on it. There is no question of a grafted vine producing a 'second class' wine; but the vine may not live so long. A vine on its own roots will last a hundred years or more, but a grafted vine may die after twenty years

161

while still in its prime. Apart from that, the ungrafted lobby contend that a vine on its own root will grow and ripen on *any* soil, and that this is the main recommendation for planting it in England and Wales. A grafted vine, they say, is very choosy: it may not like chalk for instance. This does not worry the French and Italians as by now they know exactly which graft suits which type of soil. Grafting is easy for those who know how, but Ray Barrington Brock considers it a time-consuming bore that the reviving English viticulture, which should be insistent on not aping continental practices, could well do without.

1958: Margaret Gore-Browne Replants a Five Hundred-Year-Old Site at Beaulieu

Sir Guy's activity at Hambledon was a one-off operation which attracted the attention of the Media because it came under the heading of Eccentric and therefore News, but of no one else, let alone farmers or commercial fruit growers, let alone the Wine Trade or the Government. Sir Guy had not embarked on his project in order to give a lead to others; he did it purely for his own enjoyment. There was no mastermind to stimulate interest. Ray Barrington Brock was 'available', but took no positive steps to promote a general revival or enlist revivalists. When the revival came it was entirely haphazard—a Happening not a Movement. Moreover it arose behind the backs of the Authorities who only became aware of it many years after it had acquired a dimension which even busy civil servants could not fail to notice, and then of course only with suspicion.

What low-powered momentum the revival gathered in the years following the opening of Hambledon came from people who found themselves with a piece of land and said 'Let's plant a vineyard!' The second phase of viticulturists were to say 'Let's plant a vineyard!' and then set out to find a suitable piece of land. But nothing as logical as that had prompted Sir Guy Salisbury-Jones, or Mrs Margaret Gore-Browne who was second in the field.

Colonel and Mrs Robert Gore-Browne had spent most of their lives in Central Africa. They had seen the ill-fated Ground Nuts Scheme come and go, so they knew something about making the best use of 'unusable' acres. Back in England in 1956 they were looking for a home: they looked over a mansion on the Beaulieu estate. Robert disliked the house; besides what would they *do* there? And then as they came out of the drive they noticed the name of the house written on the gate: 'The Vineyards'. 'There', said Mrs Gore-Browne, who was determined to buy the house,

Mrs Gore-Browne with her godson, Lord Montagu's son Ralph, in the Beaulieu vineyard in 1975; in 1958 Margaret Gore-Browne replanted the vineyard which the Abbots of Beaulieu Abbey had established in 1269.

'someone must have grown vines here at some time for it to have that name. So that's what we'll do. *We'll* run a vineyard.'

The someone who had grown vines there was the Abbot of Beaulieu Abbey, in 1269 as seen in Chapter Two. Robert's dislike of the house was unaffected and he could raise no enthusiasm for the vineyard scheme; so Margaret bought The Vineyards with her own money and proceeded to have two acres at the bottom of the estate cleared, drained and deep-cultivated. She went to see Ray Barrington Brock at Oxted and took his advice on which varieties to plant; she consulted Anton Massel on wine-making. In 1958 she planted four rows of Mueller-Thurgau and Seyve-Villard. She persuaded Archangelo Lanza—a cousin of filmstar-singer Mario Lanza—to leave his home in Southern Italy to come and be her vine-keeper and wine-maker. Angelo's wife Santina did the cooking and helped run the house.

Their landlord, Lord Montagu, offered to restore the ancient building which formed part of the abbey ruins and where the Cistercians may have made wine 750 years before. One day in 1959 the Gore-Brownes went with Lord Montagu to view the abbey.

From the ruined walls a flock of jackdaws fluttered wildly. There was no roof, but one realized it had sloped sharply down almost to the ground, in consonance with the pattern of the parent abbey of Citeaux, where marshy ground had prohibited digging for a cellar, and a thick thatch had to serve instead of the coolness of earth. A long mound, where visitors to the National Motor Museum now lie on the grass, is all that is left of a cart track along which grapes were carried from our vineyard to the press.

The colonel was finally won over and became a partner in his wife's project. In 1960 they built a well-equipped winery at the end of the drive round the corner from the front door. The first pressing was in 1961: a rosé.

These were the days of improvisation which have since passed into English viticulture folk-lore: the Gore-Browne Bird Scarer for instance. Margaret tried artificial hawks swinging on hydrogen balloons, fireworks, rattles and gramophone records in quick succession. All were effective to a certain degree, but none proved the dependable horror of which all black-birds and thrushes would be permanently scared. The 'different' device which answered her specification was the laundry basket which she set in

Below left: Lord Montagu and Franciscan Brother Simon admire the 1964 crop of grapes in the Beaulieu vineyard.

Below right: the grapes being loaded into a barrel at the Beaulieu vineyard will have become the Beaulieu Rosé chosen for the first British Festival of Food and Wine at the Hunting Lodge restaurant in London in 1972.

the branches of a tree filled with six young sparrow hawks ready to leave their parents but not yet old enough to fend for themselves. She fed them with dead day-old chicks, of which she kept a supply in plastic bags in a deep-freeze. As the little predators grew older they adopted the vineyard as their territory. Blackbird is their favourite food, so the grapes were well protected until the time came for harvesting. By then the birds had become fully grown and flew to fresh fields far away. A new brood was installed the following year.

Though set in motion by amateurs, the operations at Hambledon and Beaulieu were strictly commercial from the start. But the establishment of a third vineyard was a very much more calculated move.

1962: Jack Ward of Merrydown Begins to Make Wine from Grapes

In 1958 a half-acre vineyard was planted at Horam in Sussex, small in size but instigated by a man whose influence on the revival of English viticulture was to be enormous. This was J. L. Ward who had no agricultural or horticultural background but had planned a career in music. After the war, when Jack Ward was 36, he set up in business with a neighbour Ian Howie. The two of them started making cider on a fifty-year-old cider press in the garage of his home near Rotherfield which was called Merrydown. They then launched the Merrydown Wine Company which soon produced fruit wines from fermented fruit juice other than apples, and became a major operator in this field. Soon after the manor at Horam was destroyed by fire—all except its ample cellars—Jack Ward and Ian Howie acquired what remained of it and built themselves a new headquarters and factory. Progress from fruit wines made of gooseberries, blackberries and the rest, which achieved wide sales not only in Britain but overseas, to wine proper, and the planting of their own experimental vineyard, was a natural step. In time they added to the original half-acre and in 1962 began growing Riesling-Sylvaner (Mueller-Thurgau) and trying out some dozen other varieties, from which they made small quantities of wine.

The little group of English viticulturists looked to the Oxted Viticultural Research Station for most of its information, but others, like Anton Massel, as noted, Charles Wheatley of Wantage and N. F. J. Schembri, who had had experience of vineyards in Malta and now operated from Reading, were also contributing to the new data on which the activity could build. Ray Barrington Brock did not sell any of his wine, but as he stated in his third report *Progress with Vines and Wines* (1961) the sale of vines had helped

to pay about one-third of the cost of the research. Until 1960 he made a calculated loss of a kind he felt justified in spending on his hobby. The loss would have been higher if he had not been granted tax relief; but in 1960 this was withdrawn and he had to adjust his operating costs accordingly. For the first time he had to ask people writing for information to send a stamped envelope for the reply.

He was in no doubt that such rewards as he might be able to earn would only come in the long term. 'During the years under review [1951 to 1960]' he wrote in his third report, 'we have been able to register some real successes, and it is quite clear that if we continued for another twenty years or so we shall be able to give information which is of very real value.' The Royal Horticultural Society had awarded Oxted the Jones Bateman Cup for its work on vine research. 'This cup is awarded every three years for original research in fruit culture and it was encouraging to receive this evidence that the work so far has been useful.'

What constitutes 'typical' weather in England is anyone's guess. But for Ray Barrington Brock that of the fifties was 'very extraordinary'. From 1951 to 1954 inclusive it was 'average' but 1954 to 1958 were a succession of very bad years. South of London the weather was well below the average

The English wine revival received an injection of professionalism from J. L. Ward, chairman of the Merrydown Wine Company, makers of fruit wines and cider. In 1958 Merrydown planted a half-acre vineyard at their headquarters in Horam, Sussex. They added to it year by year and in 1962 began growing Riesling-Sylvaner and a dozen other varieties as an experiment.

of the previous fifty years and it culminated in 1958 with an exceptionally cold and wet year.

> In 1958 in the middle of July, we decided that there was no hope of getting a useable crop for wine at all, and the eating grapes were just about as bad, except under cloches. Nevertheless 1958 did redeem itself with quite a nice warm spell in the autumn, and a number of varieties, although the berries were small, did come up to reasonable ripeness. We managed to make several types of wine, some of which proved to be of quite reasonable quality.

Then 1959 was scorchingly hot, and 1960 exceedingly wet.

Summerfield Vineyard had now been going for over a decade, long enough for the experience of David Geneste and Andrew Pettigrew to start repeating itself.

Others who read of the activity at Oxted, Hambledon, Beaulieu and Horam were spurred to jump on a wagon which had been standing forgotten all these years but was now on the move once again, refurbished and re-equipped in a style befitting the second half of the twentieth century; no longer a museum piece attracting the patronizing attention only of folklorists and social historians, but restored to the English way of life of which it had once been so familiar a part.

In spite of Ray Barrington Brock's warnings against the danger of taking continental data at its face value, many of these revivalists inevitably based their vine-growing on continental practices—planting 3,000 vines to the acre and in rows so close they could not use modern machinery. They learnt their lesson to their cost but to the benefit of those who followed on. Lord Bute had laid out his South Wales vineyard 'on the French system' at a time when communications were bad and means of exchanging information was undeveloped, but in the nineteen-sixties circumstances favoured the building up of a corpus of purely *English* viticultural experience which had no need to pay court to European practices or to the past. Gradually it became less amateur, less romantic; less the hoe and knapsack sprayer; more cost-conscious, profit-orientated, professional, commercial.

No State Aid in the 1960s

It was in 1960 that Harold Macmillan's Conservative Government introduced a Horticultural Improvements Scheme under which grants could be made to full-time, experienced fruit and vegetable growers, and in particular to those with glasshouses, who had at least two years in horticulture,

168

earned at least the minimum agricultural wage and ran a holding of at least four eligible acres. The legislation was designed to aid producers supplying the wholesale fruit market. A commercial grower of dessert grapes who sold his crop to a wholesaler was eligible for a grant provided he met the other qualifications. But in drafting this legislation no account was taken of those who grew wine-grapes in the open air vineyard-fashion, since their numbers were negligible and uncoordinated. They did not yet constitute a measurable or predictable sector of horticulture which the administrators of the scheme could regard as an entity (as the hop growers had become under the aegis of the Hop Marketing Board). The thinking behind the 1960 scheme—and it never changed with the many subsequent amendments—was that the area deserving state aid was strictly horticultural, and that any follow-on activity outside that, such as the processing of tomatoes into ketchup or grapes into wine, either did not require state aid or did not deserve it.

A business which was part horticultural and part non-horticultural was classified as a mixed business. The horticultural part of a mixed business could attract a grant if it constituted a minimum of four eligible acres of commercial horticulture over the past twenty-four months and could satisfy the livelihood test. The men from the ministry, had they been asked, would have been ready to consider the case of the English vigneron who was prepared to split his business into two: 'a horticultural production business', within the meaning of the Act, which owned and operated a vineyard whose end-produce was grapes—and so would qualify for a grant; and a separate company which bought the grapes, took them to a winery, which it or someone else owned, and had them processed into wine. This separate company would not be eligible for a grant.

However few English vignerons were ready to negotiate that sort of deal in 1960, quite apart from meeting the general qualifications of size and length of horticultural experience, and in fact none did. Putting their vineyards into shape was an all-consuming task without dissipating energy wrestling with a government department over the interpretation of what they were doing, with a remote hope that they might be blessed with state aid. The laudable aim of the legislators had been to concentrate the small funds available in the chosen area and not have them diluted by allowing them to spread into others. There had to be rules and a ministry had to administer them, even though, when definitions have to be made so as little as possible can be left to 'discretion', inevitable absurdities arose. An orchard owner could not get a grant for a motor mower to cut the grass between his pear trees as it might also be used to mow the football field. Genuinely early potatoes were classified as a horticultural crop and available for a grant; main crop potatoes not. Hop growers could obtain a grant for putting up

hop poles (under the Farm Improvement Scheme), but not raspberry growers for their trellises. Hops are an agricultural crop so far as grants are concerned.

Inside the offices of the Ministry of Agriculture it probably made sense, but it was unfortunate that a scheme with this basic concept should have been introduced when there was no association of vine-growers and wine-makers to influence the framing of legislation from which they could have derived welcome benefit. The English viticulture revivalists needed all the encouragement, aid and clear thinking they could get; but as with research at Oxted, the Government did not see its role as backing unlikely winners before they had proved their form. So English viticulture was not a candidate for public money even at a time when the nation, as the prime minister had been at pains to point out, had never had it so good.

Large numbers of grapes were being grown of course by those who did it for the pleasure it gave. Ann Roest bought a vine for twelve and six in 1962, planted it in front of her house in Chalfont St Peter, Buckinghamshire, and found it grew at a rate of thirteen inches a week and fruited richly every September. Within six years what she described as 'this science fiction monster' was completely uncontrollable, and had covered a third of her house. She made ten gallons of must each year from which she made enough 'cottage wine', without watering, for herself and her neighbours, to whom she sold it for 4p a bottle.

This was part of another tradition—a once-aristocratic one which had spread from the big country house to the small country cottage—worthy and fun, and happily extending all over Britain; but those who are the concern of this story are the people who pursued the more difficult course of cultivating the wine-grape vineyard-fashion; and this required an effort obviously unnecessary for the undemanding Monster of Chalfont St Peter.

Gathering Momentum with Gillian Pearkes, Alan Rook, Graham Barrett, Ken Barlow, Nigel Godden et al

An early successor to the pioneers of Hambledon and Beaulieu was Philip Tyson-Woodcock who planted a vineyard at Broad Oak near Brede which he later sold to Derek Thorley. Another was Mrs P. Smith who in 1963 started a vineyard at Fletching Common. Both of these were in Sussex. Also in 1963, Gillian Pearkes decided to conduct her own trials in East Devon 'to see if I could ripen grapes satisfactorily that were too late in other well-tried vineyards'.

Miss Pearkes planted her vineyard in an old walled garden which by

tradition occupied the site of a nunnery dissolved by Henry VIII. It was in the grounds of her part-Tudor, part-William and Mary house on the site of an earlier Saxon manor in Hawkchurch, Axminster. It was halfway up the valley of the river Axe and had a south-westerly aspect. The soil which had been tilled for hundreds of years was light fertile loam with a sand sub-soil. She planted most of the varieties which Ray Barrington Brock had shown to be suited to English conditions—Riesling-Sylvaner, Madeleine Sylvaner, Seyve-Villard 5/276, Madeleine Angevine—which first cropped in 1966. She cut all well-ripened cane, after the January pruning, into short lengths and planted it in trenches to provide an inexhaustible supply of vines which she sold to help cover her costs. People came to visit the Hawkchurch vineyard from all over Britain, as they were visiting Hambledon and Beaulieu.

> I find viticulture a most absorbing and deeply interesting occupation. I do not allow my vineyard to rule my life however, as it so easily could if one had a greater area under the vine than one could happily manage; it is this factor which rules the size of my plantation. I have often thought about enlarging my present site (1967) but find that I can now comfortably keep it under control during the summer with regard to hoeing and weed control, and constantly tying in and pinching out laterals and sublaterals. Perhaps more than with all other plants and crops one feels with a vine that one is at all times working and preparing for the following season. This is espe-cially evident when one trains the replacement canes carefully, corrects soil deficiencies with various substances from which it sometimes takes many months for the vine to reap any benefit, feeds the weak growing vine, brutally prunes the weak grower to assist it to find its feet, and likewise starves the over-vigorous vines that make too much growth at the expense of fruit; I think I have a great affinity with the vine, which accounts for the feeling I have for my vineyard as a living organism which if properly and regularly attended will repay one with rich and bountiful reward.

The English viticultural revival was creating not only devotees but poets.

The final aim of Gillian Pearkes, who took to the pen to spread the word about the delights of running a vineyard in *Growing Grapes in Britain* (1969), was 'to produce fruit fitted to create a really good quality wine'. This was the aim too of wine merchant turned vigneron Alan Rook, similarly urged to demonstrate the joys of an activity by which more and more were being smitten, in *The Diary of an English Vineyard* (1969).

The family firm of Nottingham wine merchants, Skinner, Rook & Chambers was founded in 1847, the year Lord Bute was born. In 1964 Alan Rook planted 2,500 vines in the walled, one and a quarter-acre kitchen garden at Stragglethorpe Hall near Lincoln, land which had once belonged

to the Priory of Sempringham. It was at Lincoln that the Romans once had a vineyard, as I have shown in Chapter One. On the 53rd parallel Major Rook and the commander of the Ninth Legion shared the distinction of having the most northerly vineyard in the world.

Rook attended a one-day Fermentation and Wine-Making Course at Anton Massel's Oenological Research Laboratories at Ockley, and Massel, whose firm had supplied the equipment for the winery, came to help with the first vintage at the end of October 1967. They finished with eighty gallons of grape juice; fermentation began on November 12; and by June of the following year they had forty-three and a half dozen bottles of white wine: 'Lincoln Imperial'. The yearly cycle had begun.

'The 1967 vintage was made at the end of a splendid summer' Alan Rook wrote in *The Diary of an English Vineyard*,

> and . . . produced a wine better in every respect than I had allowed myself to hope for. In Lincolnshire we shall not produce a great wine. What we produced in 1967 was a wine which was dry, clean, golden, fruity and full of taste and character—in every way a serious, even a considerable wine. Naturally I wondered what the 1968 wine would be like which was grown in an almost continuously wet, cold, miserable summer, with rain all through the flowering, and continuously through the ripening period . . . By its showing on Sunday it was superb. A fine clean, well-made wine with a lovely vinosity—one I should be delighted to drink anywhere in the world. I like it better than its predecessor, the 1967, because it has more elegance and style. The pity of it is that there were only about twenty gallons as against some one hundred gallons in 1967.
>
> Our first vintage in 1967 has convinced many of my friends that it is possible seriously to make wine in England—even as far north as Lincolnshire. On the showing of our first bottle, the 1968 will certainly convince them that it is also possible to make an elegant wine in Lincolnshire. If I had tasted it blind I feel sure I should have placed it as from the Loire.

In Wales, where Andrew Pettigrew had been laughed at for his efforts at Castle Coch and Swanbridge, a number of vineyards were planted around 1964: some twenty-five in the next four years. George Jones—'Jones the Grape'—was the father of the revived Welsh Viticulture, and his vineyards at Wangara, near Llanelli, and most particularly at Pembrey in Carmarthenshire, roused others to Wales' potential as a vine growing area. Jones the Grape presented a bottle of Pembrey '67 to the Prince of Wales for laying down in the Buckingham Palace cellar against the day when he would come of age in 1969. It was said at the time to be like a Loire red wine, reminding one, in the opinion of Michael Broadbent, Christie's Master of Wine, of a Bourgeuil to be drunk by itself rather than with a meal, a thin, summer wine not a classic dinner wine, to be drunk chilled like young

Beaujolais.

Dr Idris Thomas planted five varieties of vine at Werndeg, Llanarth in Cardiganshire; Lewis Mathias planted a two and a half-acre vineyard at Lamphey Court, Pembroke. Margaret Gore-Browne, who originally came from Neath, and Anton Massel, tried to induce the Welsh Development Board to take an interest.

In England Graham Barrett and his wife Irene started growing a few vines in their garden at Hornchurch, Essex as a hobby. When Graham was left a legacy, he spent the money, in 1965, on buying a plot of land at Cricks Green near Felsted in order to make it into a proper vineyard. The following spring the Barretts planted a quarter of an acre with some thirty sorts of vine for the propagation of stock, and the hobby was well on the way to becoming the prevailing passion of Graham Barrett's life.

A scientific approach to the selection of a site came from Kenneth Barlow, a research consultant on coffee, cotton and tobacco growing, whose first step was to make a thorough study to discover what part of the south of England received the most sunshine. His conclusions led him to the Isle of Wight, and in 1965 he planted what must have been the most southerly vineyard in Britain at Adgestone near Brading.

This was also the year in which the Long Ashton Research Station of Bristol University started to take an interest by planting a half-acre vineyard to try out varieties; and in 1966 Fisons put down an experimental half-acre

In 1965 Graham Barrett bought a plot of land near Felsted, Essex, and began turning it into one of the most successful of modern English vineyards. The quality of his 'Felstar' wine has been widely acclaimed, not only in Britain but on the continent.

The Abbots of Glastonbury grew wine-grapes at Pilton in Somerset as early as 1235. At Pilton Manor today Nigel Godden grows vines from which he makes English wine of a quality that wins him many awards.

at Saffron Walden in Essex. In 1966 English viticulture received its first recognition from the continent when the Belgian Academie du Vin gave a banquet in honour of Hambledon wine. Commercial vineyards appeared in a variety of counties, so that the spread of English viticulture began to resemble the halcyon days of the Middle Ages. Joy and Trevor Bates planted four thousand vines on a three-acre plot at Nettlestead in Kent; Robin Don, a Master of Wines, laid out an eighth of an acre at Dereham in Norfolk; Jack Furness planted a vineyard at Bridgnorth in Shropshire, ex-barrister Jack Edgerley planted one at Kelsale near Ipswich, and Walter Cardy another at Pangbourne in Berkshire.

Nigel Godden took over a mediaeval site when he laid out The Pilton Manor Vineyard at his home near Shepton Mallet in Somerset, where the abbots of Glastonbury had grown grapes in the open at least as early as 1235. He opted for the German system of five feet between rows and four feet between vines. The vineyard is on the west side of the village of Pilton in an open valley running east to west among the foothills leading to the Mendips, eight miles from Glastonbury.

Though there seems to have been a Pilton Manor in the eighth century belonging to the Bishop of Sherborne, Nigel Godden's manor house dates from the thirteenth century, built by Michael of Amesbury, Abbot of Glastonbury, in about 1240. So the house must be contemporary with the original vineyard. To make wine from the grapes of the twentieth-century Pilton vineyard, Godden installed an up-to-date winery and engaged Angelo Pizzi, an Italian wine chemist, to run it.

Commercial operators such as these had to make bulk orders for vines from Anton Massel or direct from the continent; but small operators, such as K. Hudd who put down thirty cuttings for a private vineyard at Bristol in 1965 or Sir William Hart who planted thirty-six at Brackley in North-amptonshire, could have bought from Mr Walker at Oxted who by now had a wide choice of plants, all proved to possess a high degree of compati-bility with English conditions. Two varieties of Russian Amurensis Hybrids, topically named Gagarin Blue and Tereshka, could be bought for 40s each; a number of German hybrids, Madeleine Angevine and Madeleine × Syl-vaner at 17s 6d each. The Riesling-Sylvaner also sold at 17s 6d: 'a regular cropper with us over ten years and has always ripened and given very fine wines—in a good year the crop has reached 500 gallons per acre'. Edward Hyam's 1950 discovery, the Wrotham Pinot, cost 15s.

1967: the English Vineyards Association is Formed

The movement—for such it could now be called—was gathering pace at a rate that required control and steering; and in 1967 a body was registered called 'The English Vineyards Association' to present a combined front to government departments and to any body which could aid or thwart development of an activity which now represented a sizable investment.

The idea of an association had been discussed throughout 1965 by Anton Massel and Norman Cowderoy, a London shipbroker who grew outdoor vines on a two and a half-acre plot near Haywards Heath in Sussex. Cowderoy consulted his solicitor William Van Straubenzee, who also happened to be the local Member of Parliament, gained the support of Jack

Ward of Merrydown, and on October 23, 1965, at the invitation of Margaret Gore-Browne, called a first meeting at The Vineyards, Beaulieu to consider launching an association with the aim of 'promoting the intelligent cultivation of wines for commercial purposes in England'. It would have to be formed, they decided, with the approval of the Ministry of Agriculture and Fisheries under the terms and conditions of the Agricultural Central Co-operative Association Limited. A Steering Committee was appointed on November 15, 1965.

It took the Board of Trade a year to approve the title and at the first annual general meeting on January 18, 1967, at Ockley in Surrey, where Anton Massel had his viticultural equipment firm, Sir Guy Salisbury-Jones was elected President, Lady Montagu of Beaulieu Vice-President, Jack Ward Chairman, and Mrs Irene Barrett Secretary. On March 8 the association was formally registered. Other officers were P. Tyson-Woodcock, Vice-Chairman, and R. S. Don, Director. Anton Massel was Technical Adviser. Apart from the officers there were eight full members in 1967 from Sussex, Kent, Berkshire, Somerset, Worcestershire, Middlesex, Nottinghamshire and Surrey, and twelve associate members.

The objectives of the Association were

> to propagate, graft, grow, cultivate, purchase and sell grape vines and to develop new varieties of grape vines; to buy and sell and to process, whether for the making of wine or grape juice or otherwise, grapes grown from vines planted in the United Kingdom only; to buy and sell grapes grown in the United Kingdom; to set standards for all the foregoing objects and to carry on any other trades, industries, and businesses which may seem calculated to further the above objects, including the purchase of machinery and the marketing of such products.

It was hoped to arrange for members and associate members to obtain special discounts on equipment and fertilizers as a result of co-operative and bulk buying, and to exchange experiences, results and technical information. But Jack Ward saw the first responsibility of the Association to be to persuade the Commissioners of HM Customs and Excise to take a new look at the excise duty on 'British Wines' with which the unheard-of English and Welsh Wine had been lumped willy-nilly.

In March 1966 Lewis Mathias and others formed a Welsh Vineyards Association independent of the English counterpart. It was sponsored and encouraged by the Development Corporation for Wales and by Mrs Margaret Gore-Browne of Beaulieu who was of Welsh ancestry. None of the half dozen members were producing commercially; their numbers failed to increase and in fact gradually dropped. 'Efforts to encourage farmers and possibly other growers proved unsuccessful, as it was a new

and strange venture, and the capital outlay for vines and winery equipment is very high' Lewis Mathias told me.

The pioneering work of the Oxted Viticultural Research Station was coming to an end. The circumstances which now favoured the formation of an Association of enthusiasts were largely of Ray Barrington Brock's creation, and he saw it as the moment to make a planned withdrawal from a scene in which the peculiar excitement of the lone outrider establishing precedents on which others could build, which had attracted him in 1946, was no longer present. That his message had been received and understood by the leader of the new Association was evident from the penultimate paragraph of Jack Ward's piece in the first Association *News Letter*: 'It should not be forgotten that the industry is new in this country, so that any advice coming from the continent may have to be modified to suit our own peculiar conditions.'

Ray issued a fourth report, *Starting A Vineyard*, in 1964 and continued to issue price lists and sell vines which had proved their staying and ripening power in the Summerfield Vineyard into the nineteen-seventies. But as he said in his third Report 'I am afraid it is not generally realized that the Research Station is an entirely private venture, and all the technical work has had to be done in the evenings after a normal day's work. It has meant that it has taken up so much of my spare time that it was not possible to carry on the work and also write reports'. It also became increasingly clear that in spite of being on a beautiful south slope the Oxted vineyard was in an unfavourable position.

> The difficulty seems to lie in the height. At Oxted we are 450 feet above sea level and it used to be said that every hundred feet of height represented three days' lateness of ripening of ordinary fruit. This seems to be quite borne out because we now know that vines grown in the Thames Valley, i.e. very nearly at sea level, and yet within fifteen miles of here, ripen at least two weeks ahead of us. This makes all the difference between ripening in Devon or the Bristol area. In that area red wines have been made from Siebel 13053 and also from other grapes in virtually every year since 1952. This has been done in many cases with varieties which we have not been able to use successfully here. It appears therefore that any recommendations we give from Oxted as to ripening times are, if anything, pessimistic for areas which are not quite so high near London, and for similar areas which are further west.

The most interesting conclusion of his twenty years research was perhaps the 'certainty' that good red wine of the Beaujolais character could be made in all good sites in the south of England.

This can be done with reasonable certainty in three years out of five, but when we started we always said that we did not expect to get any red wine.

At the same time we have been getting more and more information as to the commercial possibilities of wine-making in this country. Again, when we started, we felt it was unlikely that a commercial wine could be produced here, because we thought the crops would be rather small and we were under the impression that our labour charges would be very high relative to the French. We now know that labour charges need not be any higher than is customary in France.

From an acre of Riesling-Sylvaner (Mueller-Thurgau) and Seyve-Villard 5/276 he expected a yield in a normal year of more than 400 gallons of wine to the acre, and in a better year 500 gallons.

Few gained more from the research which Ray Barrington Brock did at Oxted than Margaret Gore-Browne* who in 1967 gave her account of her pioneering essay at Beaulieu in *Let's Plant A Vineyard*. She said that the late Alfred Langenbach had told her 'climatically you should make good wine; your chances depend purely on viticulture'.

'Nothing has since transpired to alter my faith in his judgement. A congenital pessimist can point to failures. In one case a herd of Welsh mountain goats ate every vine in a Glamorganshire vineyard. In Carmarthen, and later in Pembroke, healthy imported vines died mysteriously. Later it was learned that vibration and drying out at the grafting point had caused the casualties'. She told the story of a Carmarthen farmer's wife who, protesting her soil was too stony, nonetheless planted three hundred vines which shot up like beanstalks with lavish, richly green leaves. The stones were slate. 'I thought of the Moselle valley, where every thimbleful of slatey top-soil washed into the ravine is gathered into baskets and carried by hand up precipitous slopes. People will pay £4 a bottle for a fine Moselle. Will slate be as bountiful to Wales as coal formerly was?'

The point was taken up by N. F. J. Schembri in his contribution to the English Vineyards Association's first *New Letter, The New Era of English Wines***. The thinking behind the revival of English Viticulture was Oxted's, he said. Therefore the ignorance which always accompanied any movement where fools rushed in for reasons based largely on emotion and enthusiasm received a leavening from which the revival of English viticulture, and the establishment of a British viticultural method, greatly benefited.

---

* Mrs Gore-Browne died in August 1976, aged 86, only some two months after I had spent a morning with her at Beaulieu talking about the vineyard, which she left to her godson, Lord Montagu's fifteen-year-old son, Hon Ralph Douglas-Scott-Montagu. Lord Montagu's company, Montagu Ventures, had been managing the vineyard in recent years; and Mrs Gore-Browne left the winery to Lord Montagu.

'Contrary to the common belief,' wrote Schembri,

the success or failure of wine-growing** in Britain does not depend entirely on the local environment—climate, soil, etc—but also on the choice of the vine varieties and particularly on the cultivation know-how. The British viticultural method is not necessarily similar to that of a hot region, since the circumstances are often different. The cultivation problems vary considerably from vineyard to vineyard in any region whether the climate is hot, warm or cold. For instance the local conditions such as micro-climate†, aspect, elevation, soil type, air and soil drainage and rainfall may vary even over short distances . . . Probably what injures the vine more than the British climate is wrong cultivation, lack of know-how, or even too much kindness to plants. Several amateur viticulturists have failed in Britain most probably because they do not understand the basic principles of viticulture —when in Rome grow vines as the Romans do, but when in Britain grow vines as the British do.

Much effort has been made over the past few decades to lay the foundation upon which British viticulture is to be established. In other words British viticulture has to be made, and thus created by British vine-growers. As a matter of fact, the good work already done by some notable British growers has paved the way to present-day viticultural activities. British viticulture has already started to shape out.

In the next ten years, from 1967 to 1977, the shape became firm in outline, and English and Welsh wine re-emerged with the distinctive character impressed by a non-continental, island ambience, which in its two thousand-year history no other vine-growing area of the world has ever been able to capture.

** I would like to see the plural kept for every kind of fruit 'wine' other than that made from grapes; i.e. 'wines' when elderberry and gooseberry concoctions are meant; 'wine' when claret and port are meant. I also object to the word 'wine-growing'. I have never seen wine growing in a field, any more than I have seen spaghetti or bread. You grow grain and you make bread from it; you grow vines and grapes and you make wine from them. So 'vine-growing' and 'wine-making' and 'English Wine' (which includes wine made in Wales!) and 'British Wines'.

† A word coined to describe climatic conditions inside a small area such as those existing between two rows of vines.

Part V   The Grape Rush

1967 to 1973

SEVEN

Energy Replaces Amateurism: Respect Replaces Mockery

The Pioneers are No Longer Alone

Membership of the English Vineyards Association grew to fifty within a year of its inauguration in 1967, and by 1969 there were eighty-three members. In 1970 a 'South West Vinegrowers Association' was formed after an inaugural meeting at Pilton Manor. The revival was acquiring a degree of cohesion and common purpose.

But 'English' had no identity as yet, in the way that Burgundy, Moselle or Alsatian had. England With Wales looked like eventually becoming the region with which to compare the Rheingau or the Nahe, but in these early days the divisions were much smaller. Each vigneron hugged his patch and proudly proclaimed it on his label. Sir Guy Salisbury-Jones's wine was 'Hambledon': his wicket and cricket bat emblem was copied from the stone monument on Broad Halfpenny Down which the vineyard overlooked, commemorating the part played by the eighteenth-century Hambledon Club in developing cricket. Alan Rook called his wine 'Lincoln Imperial' after the imp which was the city's ancient emblem (with no pretensions to empire status either Roman or British). However, there were traditions, inherited from Europe, about the naming of wines, and these were adhered to in England. When, in 1969, Graham Barrett made his first wine from his Essex grapes, he wanted to call it 'Felsted', but tradition required that to qualify for that name the wine would have to made in Felsted—'estate bottled'. As it had been 'bottled', that is 'made', in Horam he had to settle for 'Felstar'. Ken Barlow's wine, however, of which he made a first six thousand bottles in 1969 and a further 30,000 in 1970, could

be called 'Adgestone' because he had made it in the Isle of Wight. Everyone avoided any naming which would indicate that English viticulture was merely a 'branch' of the continental wine industry. The label also had to make it quite clear that inside the bottle was 'English Wine' not a flavour of one of the many 'British Wines' nor an empire wine 'type'. The eighteenth-century wine makers could think of no way of guiding consumers except to tell them that the contents were similar to Gascon or Rhenish. The twentieth-century revivalists wished their product to be judged as *English* wine, not better or worse than foreign wine, but to be enjoyed for its own, unique characteristics.

In the summer of 1968 the largest wine-producing area in England was the five and a half-acre vineyard owned by Margaret Gore-Browne at Beaulieu Abbey, which had an annual yield of between five and eight thousand bottles. It was larger than Hambledon; Sir Guy found four and a half acres more than enough to maintain, and in 1966 had engaged a full-time manager, Bill Carcary. Hambledon's 1969 vintage was 'outstanding' according to one expert: 'with character between a delicate dry Vouvray and a first-class crisp Moselle'. It was impossible to stop the comparisons, however flattering, but in a more enlightened vein another expert declared that in its gentle bouquet there was a sweet waft of English flowers. 'Hambledon 69' sold at 22s 6d a bottle (112p).

Sir Guy and the Gore-Brownes were now far from alone. They found themselves, though without ambitions in that direction, the pace-makers for a band of professional enthusiasts who swelled not only in numbers but in the size of each of their operations. The Barretts, encouraged by the quality of their first wine of 1969, were planning to increase their four acres at Cricks Green to eleven by 1971. One of the largest of the new vineyards of 1969—six acres—was the one owned by Peter Baillie-Grohman at Hascombe near Godalming, the place which James Oglethorpe had made 'traditional' in the eighteenth century by his successes at Westbrook. Kenneth Macalpine devoted eight and a half acres of his large farm, at Lamberhurst in Kent, to vines.

By 1969 forty English and Welsh acres had been planted with open air vines, yielding an average of two thousand bottles of wine each. Each vine plant cost six shillings (30p). If 2,200 vines were planted four feet apart with five feet between rows, the cost of an acre was about £665. So it was expensive; but many now regarded it as a good investment, particularly as a hedge against loss from other less dependable agricultural activities. Bernard Theobald had a hundred milking Friesian cows on his farm at Pangbourne, where Walter Cardy, one of the first members of EVA, had run a vineyard for many years. In 1970 Theobald added a vineyard in order to keep his farm going. He planned to have eight acres under cultivation by

1973 and five more in 1974, and he reckoned that these would produce more gross profit in a year than his cows; he estimated his vines would bring in an annual £3,000 an acre, whereas each of his cows produced £250 worth of milk: £36,000 from wine as against £25,000 from milk (both on twelve acres).

The cottage industry image was fading and the joke about Red Biddy from grapes on grandad's allotment was a less reliable generator of instant laughter. Jokes which associated English wine with cheap red wine from supermarkets and replaced the more upper class jokes about Cooking Sherry, were a step in the right direction. At least it was 'wine' and not 'wines'. The very scarcity of English wine precluded it from ever being regarded as plonk or its producer as a plonkiculturist.

In August 1970 English wine was the centre of attraction at a gather-

Nigel Godden produces five tons of wine-grapes an acre from his efficiently run four-and-a-half-acre vineyard at Pilton in Somerset. He has turned viticulture in English climatic conditions into a fine art.

ing of the International Wine and Food Society. Nine varieties of white wine and a rosé, all made by members of the EVA, were selected to win recognition for the new race of English vignerons at the Society's first-ever English Wine Tasting. The press were invited, and mockery was significantly absent from most of the next day's headlines and accounts. The tasters were 'clearly surprised with the quality, individuality and presentation of the wine' wrote the *Guardian* correspondent. There was general agreement, he said, that the wine was well above *vin ordinaire* standards. They liked the 'Brede Riesling-Sylvaner 1969', made from grapes grown by Derek Thorley of Broad Oak near Rye; also Nigel Godden's 'Pilton Manor 1969' from Shepton Mallet. It had been a late summer and the fine autumn of 1969 had greatly helped this first combined demonstration by EVA members. The sceptics who tasted English wine for the first time were at least savouring the product of ideal conditions. Bad first impressions might have delayed acceptance, but these 'experts', who came to the gathering expecting to confirm their prejudgement of English wine, found themselves unable to do other than admit to a 'surprise'. They were impressed, and the British media were impressed that they should be impressed. From

Graham Barrett uses a tractor to spray the vines at his Felsted vineyard. The distance between rows of vines is determined not only by considerations of the effect of the micro-climate created by closeness but also by the ease with which a tractor can pass between the rows.

1970 onwards the concept of 'English wine' was treated with considerably more respect than hitherto. Via the media the news began to infiltrate—very slowly—into the hotel and catering world, and to lap the conservative stronghold of the wine trade. The modern communications system, absent in earlier centuries, began to clear the fog of suspicion and prejudice which had previously prevented English viticulture from being either appreciated or accepted.

In 1969 a leading light of the wine trade had completed the third vintage of Lincoln Imperial. In concluding his *Diary* that year Alan Rook confessed that in the six years since he had planted his vineyard he had got nothing but pleasure from it.

> To watch the young vines slowly maturing, to care for the plants and keep them free from pests, to see the first fruit set and after that to live with the whole cycle of bud burst, growth, flowering, fruit set and the gradual ripening of the grapes, up to the final moment of harvest and the making of the wine is, for me, at least, to be constantly and vividly aware of the changing seasons and in touch with the miracle of life and growth. Many of my friends told me at the beginning that the whole enterprise was impossible, especially as far north as Lincolnshire. There have been moments over the years when I have wondered if they might not be right. They were wrong. I took a risk, succeeded and have enjoyed every moment of it.

Unashamedly attracted by the romantic aspect of it all, Alan Rook, the wine merchant, had his doubts about the chances of it being a commercial proposition.

> I believe some people think that it can. I am not so sure. In our present stage of knowledge the following points would have to be weighed carefully.
>
> (i) We haven't yet got sufficient records to show how often we could expect an average to good crop, and how often we should get a bad year and a small yield. Too many bad years would interrupt the continuity of supply, and make the harvest an expensive one.
>
> (ii) In England the cost of labour is high and (at least until we have mastered the problem of chemical weed control) a vineyard needs a lot of labour.
>
> (iii) I would imagine that a commercial vineyard would need to be not less than 10 to 15 acres. I reckon mine cost about £2,000 an acre to bring to production. At this rate the capital investment for a large undertaking would be considerable.
>
> (iv) The protection of the ripening berries from depredation by birds is a problem we have not yet solved, and is serious. My small vineyard can be netted. This would be impossible in a larger one.

187

Above left: the principal grape variety harvested at the Merrydown two-acre vineyard is the Riesling-Sylvaner or Mueller-Thurgau.

Above right: harvesting the grapes at Hambledon in Hampshire.

1969: Merrydown Offer a Co-operative Wine-Making Service at Horam

Many growers at the beginning of the 1967–1977 decade felt they should first get the viticulture right and graduate to the art of vinification later; but they had to have an end product with which to judge the success of their viticulture. It was here that Jack Ward saw he could bring the resources of Merrydown to the service of the re-born English wine industry by offering, in 1969, co-operative wine-making facilities. Merrydown had turned Derek Thorley's Broad Oak grapes into the Brede Riesling-Sylvaner, which had so pleased the judges at the International Wine and Food Society tasting; and they had made the first 'Felstar' from grapes grown at Cricks Green.

As a corporate member of the English Vineyards Association the Merrydown Wine Company is anxious to assist and encourage viticulturists and members of the association to promote the planting of vineyards in England and the general cultivation of vines out of doors. It is appreciated that an enterprise of this nature is beset enough with technical difficulties and capital expenditure without the prospect of an uncertain market for the disposal of the produce; it is further understood that growers might be

somewhat dismayed by wasting the fruits of their labours, through lack of adequate wine-making equipment and insufficient experience of oenological techniques. The Merrydown Wine Company has therefore evolved a scheme which it is hoped will be attractive enough to encourage the fruit grower or farmer, the enthusiastic amateur, however meagre his resources, or possibly the business man who may be looking for a pleasant occupation on retirement. Clearly many growers would welcome the opportunity of being able to drink and offer their friends a finished product from their own vineyard, and provision has been made in the scheme to ensure this, provided quantities of fruit produced are sufficient to warrant individual handling.

Under the Merrydown Co-operative Scheme the owners of vineyards harvested their grapes, piled the baskets on to a lorry and drove with them as fast as they could to Horam where Merrydown pressed and processed them into wine. The vineyard owner collected the majority of the bottles of 'his' wine, but left a proportion as payment to Merrydown. If he insisted on taking the lot, he could pay for the processing in cash. Merrydown made a blend of all the surplus wine and bottled it as 'Anderida'—the name of the ancient forest which once covered the Weald of Sussex. It was sold under this label to distinguish it from the 'estate bottled' wine

At the Hambledon vineyard grape-pickers bring in the raw material which will make the season's vintage of Hambledon Wine.

made exclusively from the grapes grown on their own Horam vineyards. This was called 'Merrydown *Riesling Sylvaner*'—or after whatever variety of grape from which the wine had been made.

The first vineyard at Horam had been short-lived because the site had had to be sold for development; but it had been quickly succeeded by a second and a third, though the whole area under cultivation never exceeded two acres. In September 1971 Merrydown installed a new, modern wine-press and produced 18,000 bottles of wine.

Had it not been for the introduction, in 1969, of the efficient, well-devised co-operative processing scheme at Horam, many would doubtless have sheered away from viticulture, itself an unknown quantity, for fear of having to grapple with the still less known wine-making operation. As it was, the acreage of open-air vines in Britain increased from fifty in 1970 to two hundred in 1971.

English viticulture grew not only in extent but in reputation. In his *World Atlas of Wine* (1971) Hugh Johnson devoted a page to 'England and Wales', albeit the last one. His intention in writing the book, he said, had been to take the reader to the top of a mountain and show him all the vineyards of the earth. 'The idea of English wine is usually greeted with mockery or disbelief' he wrote. 'It is commonly thought that England lies too far north for grapes to ripen—and besides that there is too much rain.' He described the quality as 'satisfactory'—praise indeed. 'It only needs a more

Those who grow wine-grapes in England but cannot make their own wine send their crop to Horam in Sussex where, under the Merrydown Co-operative Scheme, the grapes are made into wine. The milling (right) crushes the grapes in preparation for pressing.

After the grapes have been milled they go through the process of 'pressing' to extract the juice. At Horam this takes place in the large cylindrical presses shown above.

helpful attitude by the government who at present charge duty on English wine as though it was imported to make possible a small but serious wine industry in England.'

In 1971 the Wine Society, with seven thousand buying members, put Hambledon 69 in its list. Members took six hundred bottles which, as Jack Ward remarked, could not have been all out of curiosity. In that year too Cunard offered Sir Guy's produce to the mainly American passengers on the ocean liner Queen Elizabeth II. In the summer of 1971 the EVA decided to support the first English Vineyards Fair, at Botesdale Lodge, Diss, which was conceived and organized by EVA member Grenville Powney.

1971: Anton Massel Gives a Word of Warning

No one expected the path of the English Vineyards Association, England's first association of vinekeepers, to be a smooth one. Anton Massel's con-

viction, born of his experience, that English vine-growers would be well-advised to plant only phylloxera-resistant grafted stock was not shared by the rest of the Board. Contemplating the set-back which he believed members would suffer from planting non-grafted varieties in the absence of any official EVA warning, if not ban, he considered the best course was to resign as Technical Adviser. And when he felt that some members might think that his allegiance to grafting was not unconnected with his business activities as an importer of vines from the continent, he dropped this side of his business entirely and concentrated on vinification, both as a dealer in equipment and a consultant on processing.

Anton Massel was a forceful propagandist, though taking a less popular, cautionary line: a counter-balance to the over-optimism in some quarters. Recent press reports had highlighted not only the public interest in viticulture over the previous fifteen years, he told members of the Nuffield Scholars' Association in December 1971, but also its apparent profitability.

> Unfortunately the picture has been painted far too rosy, and although it is not my intention to dampen enthusiasm one must look at these factors objectively.
>
> If one considers an investment capital of labour and materials to the end of the third year of approximately £2,500 per acre and on the assumption that existing farm machinery is employed (without giving consideration to expenditure on the basic land) it can be seen that profitability on an average one-acre vineyard with a yield of say 3,000 bottles of wine, which may be sold to the wholesale trade at 80p a bottle, is acceptable. Deducting the production cost of say 50p a bottle (including duty and bottling charges), the income an acre amounts to about £900, less marketing expenses. There is of course a risk of crop failure and viewed in this light, viticulture becomes feasible but offers no exorbitant profit margins. However, viticulture also makes returns in the form of the enormous fun one can have growing the grapes and making the wine, not to speak of the ultimate enjoyment of drinking it.

In his introductory remarks Anton Massel made the point that in the past it was more difficult for the British vigneron to compete with his continental rival because the vine varieties then did not facilitate the production of such a wide range of wines as was known to-day. 'In recent decades many new varieties have emerged and these thrive under varying climatic conditions. The British wine-grower is thus given a chance to select from a wider range to match local micro-climatic conditions. As a result, the quality of the wines that are produced is of a high standard and some wines can even be described as outstanding.' It would be wise in his

Non-alcoholic grape-juice is turned into wine in fermentation tanks. An efficient wine-making plant requires considerable capital investment which few can afford. These tanks are installed at the Merrydown Co-operative winery where English vineyard-owners can have their grapes made into wine at reasonable cost.

opinion however to concentrate on white varieties since red grapes required just that extra amount of sunshine to develop the colour pigment and antho-cyanine essential for the quality of red wine. Red wine was produced in Germany—in the valley of the Ahr for instance—but most experts agreed that German red wines could not compete in quality with that of their French neighbours.

193

1971: the Pros and Cons of Joining the EEC

In 1971, with Britain's acceptance as a member of the European Economic Community becoming more and more likely, English vine-growers and wine-makers were faced with having their parochial operation linked willy-nilly with the viticultural traditions and laws of the continent; and with being obliged to conform in a number of ways, all of which might not be to their advantage.

In 1971, in the six countries forming the Community there was a law which stated that wine production from hybrid vine varieties did not qualify for the wine trade's seal of quality VQPRD: *vins des qualités produits dans les regions délimités*. Connoisseurs on the continent thought that wine from hybrid vines had a distinctive taste not to everyone's liking; the Germans definitely regarded it as inferior and feared that any relaxation of the law would lower the quality of the total market. With Britain's admission to the EEC now a matter of negotiation, viticulturists were worried about what effect this rule would have on the fast-growing English industry where the most prolific grape-producing vine had proved to be the hybrid Seyve-Villard 5/276, which EEC countries liked to call Seyval Blanc. In anticipation of Britain becoming a Community partner, the EVA took steps in 1971 to seek a 'seal of approval' of its own. Many were also concerned about the EEC's regulation restricting the planting of new vineyards, but they were reassured to hear that it was not being applied with any strictness to member countries with small acreages like Belgium and Holland.

For the infant English viticulture the timing of Britain's negotiations for admission to the European Community was highly fortuitous. Britain had a chance of joining a club where vine-growing, wine-making and wine-drinking had always been a central part of living, and a *serious* part. Making wine from grapes might be a joke to a citizen of the United Kingdom, but it could not possibly be to a citizen of Europe. It was a heaven-sent, Heath-negotiated opportunity for synthesizing the embryo English viticulture, concentrating its thinking and accelerating its growth.

England and Wales were now producing a hundred thousand bottles of wine a year from some seventy vineyards. Sixty-year-old Arthur Callow of Axbridge turned his strawberry beds in the Mendip Hills to vines; Bill Greenwood made a start at Purleigh in Essex, hoping to have fifteen acres under cultivation by 1975 producing twenty tons of grapes; Gruff Reece planted ten acres at Gamlingay near St Neots. In April 1972, Ian Paget and

his brother Andrew planted 10,000 Mueller-Thurgau vines on a five-acre slope at Singleton in Sussex, overlooking the site where the Romans supposedly had their vineyard at East Dean.

The Paget brothers' enterprise at Chills Down, Singleton, lay on chalky ground above a disused railway line. They followed the German system and planted the rows six feet apart with plants three and a half feet apart. The following year they switched to the French system and planted 4,000 Reichensteiner and 5,000 Chardonnay, the classic white grape of Champagne and Burgundy, but this time in rows only four feet apart. With the aid of their own version of a broad-based French picking basket, they gathered in one and a half tons of fruit in 1974, which Sir Guy Salisbury-Jones and Bill Carcary made into the first 'Chilsdown' wine. The following year they harvested twenty and a half tons from their seven acres which Merrydown turned into 17,500 bottles of 'Chilsdown 75'.

The Problems of Marketing

In the early nineteen-seventies producing English wine was probably easier than selling it. Although there was co-operative processing there was still no thought of co-operative marketing. Each vigneron sought local outlets for his own small quantities. For him it was a short-term operation, and the main object of the exercise was to get back his outlay as quickly as possible. It was no one's business to generate acceptance of 'English Wine' as a product nationally, but in 1971 the picture was improving. Many hotels and restaurants in the south of England stocked English wine for the first time. Wine merchants jumped on the wagon; Saccone and Speed became sole agents for 'Kentish Sovereign' the wine made from the grapes which Joy and Trevor Bates grew at Nettlestead Green near Wateringbury in Kent; Deinhard & Co, shippers of fine wine from Germany, became agents for Kenneth Barlow's 'Adgestone' wine from the Isle of Wight. 'Adgestone' had found its way on to the wine list of the Dorchester Hotel in London and other five-star hostelries.

The main check to the marketing of English wine was that the United Kingdom was just not a wine-drinking country—*any* wine. The UK consumption of wine in the first six months of 1971 was twenty-two million gallons of which sixteen million were imported. The major part of the six million gallons not being imported were of course the 'Dessert Wines', the port and sherry types like 'Barchester' British sherry made by J. E. Mather of Leeds, in which Bass and Watneys had a stake; mixtures like 'Scotsmac', wine and whisky, made by Charles Kinloch (Courage); tonic wines like

'Wincarnis' from Reckitt & Colman, and 'Sanatogen' from Allied Brewers.

These British beverages still received a degree of protection in relation to imported wines. The excise duty on a bottle of British 'sherry' was 25p if the gravity was kept below 27° proof spirit or 29p if it was stronger, whereas there was a duty of 45p on a bottle of real sherry from Spain and a duty of 37p on 'empire' port and sherry types. With this aid the 'British Wines' industry had become big business and highly profitable. Its products accounted for a quarter of all 'wine' consumed in Britain in any year.

Research Programmes are Initiated by Wye College and the Royal Horticultural Society

Ray Barrington Brock's spare-time research had put the English wine industry into orbit; efforts from other quarters now took it through the next stage. In November 1971 the Hop Research Department of Wye College, London University's agricultural college near Ashford in Kent (site of the Domesday vineyard of Chart Sutton), suggested that they might undertake a research programme for the benefit of the many would-be

A feature of the Merrydown service is the guarantee that the wine sent to a vigneron has been made from his own grapes. At the winery there are barrels which can cope with fairly small tonnages (right) as well as large vats (left).

vineyard-keepers and wine-makers of Britain. Obstacles would have to be overcome, but if whatever scheme they produced met with the approval of the vine-growing community, the staff of Wye College would guarantee full co-operation. The research programme would have to be subsidised by a grant from outside London University. When the Government declined to subscribe, the EVA appealed to its members: the programme at Wye, it told them, would include the testing of new varieties selected from those propagated by European institutes for cultivation in northern latitudes, the examination of methods of pruning, plant management, manuring, and protection against disease most suited to the climatic conditions of England and Wales. The merits of grafted vines and rooted cuttings would be compared.

The response was immediate and enough money was raised during 1972 to enable Wye College to make their plans, and, in the spring of 1973, to start putting the ambitious programme into action.

In the spring of 1972, H. A. Baker, Fruit Officer of the Royal Horticultural Society, had a number of vines planted in the fruit field at the Society's garden at Wisley near Woking in Surrey. There were also a number grown under glass. Altogether he had some seventy different cultivars at Wisley. The vines in the vineyard which were cropping five years later, included four types of early white grapes: Madeleine Sylvaner 28/51, Précoce de Malingre, Siegerrebe, and Madeleine Angevine 7972; two mid-season white grapes: Riesling-Sylvaner and Seyve Villard 5/276; three early black grapes: Noir Hatif de Marseilles, Tereshkova of Russian origin and Pirovano XIV; and two mid-season black grapes: Seibel 13.053 and Brant, a hybrid of Canadian origin.

The number of people who were to benefit from the research being carried out at Wye, Wisley and elsewhere increased every month. By the summer of 1972 there were a hundred commercial vineyards in the United Kingdom, all of them planted but only a minority fully fruiting.

Costs had now come down appreciably. Investment was generally put at £450 to £850 an acre, plus a further £200 to £400 on wire and posts and an amount for rent, labour, chemicals, equipment. An outlay of some £14,600 would be needed over the first three years on a five-acre vineyard, was the view of Ken Gofton writing in the *Financial Times* of July 8, 1972. The first income would come in the fourth year when the first wine was marketed. This might be anything from 10,000 bottles at 70p, making a loss on the year of £1,290, to 15,000 bottles at £1 which would bring a profit of £5,200. On an average the four and half acres at Hambledon produced about 10,000 bottles; in 1970 Sir Guy had made 12,000 bottles and in 1971, 7,000. Ken Barlow produced 25,000 bottles of 'Adgestone' in 1971.

Members of Parliament, who attended a tasting of English wine at the House of Commons, expected it to be cheap; they were reminded that the cost of sending wine in bottles to London from the west country might well exceed the cost of transporting wine in bulk transporters from France. Representatives of the English wine industry told MPs that English wine was never intended to be plonk. If a comparison had to be made then it could be said perhaps to match Blue Nun or Mouton Cadet.

1971: the EVA v. the Government: the Problem of Exercise

Persuading Parliament to take English wine seriously was one thing; putting the case for reducing the excise duty on it, if and when Britain joined the Common Market, was a more urgent and difficult task. The stance taken by the Government was not intolerant; it seemed merely that they wanted to avoid the inconvenience of changing the legislation which treated British Wines and English Wine alike, to suit what they rightly considered to be a tiny minority. The Treasury had always excused its attitude on the grounds that, owing to the General Agreement on Tariffs and Trade (GATT), entered into by the British Government in the nineteen-forties at a time when there was no English wine industry, there was a binding and irrevocable commitment which made any alteration in tax structure impossible.

English vineyard owners were disturbed at the possible effects of Article 5 of the EEC draft directive (Article no. 99) which gave each Member State the right to determine its own rate of duty, for this gave the British Government the right to keep things as they were. Jack Ward described this as 'sacrificing a genuine if tiny emergent industry for the benefit of maintaining an easy source of revenue'.

What Jack Ward and the English Vineyards Association wanted the Government to do was to face the consequences of admitting that the production of English wine from English grapes was agricultural, and treat the operation differently from the production of beer and spirits. To this end, in 1972, Jack Ward drew up a twenty-two-page memorandum which was sent, on behalf of the EVA, to selected Cabinet ministers, MPs, the National Farmers Union, Customs and Excise Office staff, and EVA members, enumerating British tax anomalies compared with other EEC producers, and suggesting that someone find a more equable system of levying taxes. The proposed internal revenue duty—excise—was unacceptable for it was a form of tax that was not normally applied to an agricultural

product and was contrary to the Treaty of Rome. If the Government felt obliged to continue the 25p excise for the sake of the country's revenue as a whole, at least they could encourage English and Welsh vine-growers by handing back even a small proportion of it in the form of grants with which to buy equipment, or as contribution to research of the kind about to be instituted at Wye College.

The message got through to the extent of James Prior, Minister of Agriculture in Edward Heath's Tory administration, agreeing that when the total under cultivation topped 250 acres he would hold a vineyard census; and one was in fact held in June 1974.

No Longer a Joke: English Wine is Accepted Outside England

The main cause for the support of English viticulture was being put daily by the product itself. In 1971 Hermann Guntrum of Nierstein am Rhein, who owned a hundred-acre vineyard, asked that Felstar, of which ten thousand gallons was made in that year (£70,000 worth), should be exhibited at the Stuttgart Trade Fair. It was very well received. Felstar was also one of the three English wines at the press conference/wine tasting given in Stuttgart in 1972, following the reception given by the Prasidium Des Deutschen Weinbauverbandes and attended by personalities from wine-producing countries of five continents. The other two wines were Hamble-don Seyve-Villard 1969 and a 1970 Somerset Riesling-Sylvaner from the Shepton Mallet vineyard of Nigel Godden. All three, which were intro-duced by Anton Massel, were judged of excellent quality. One of those present commented that they could be classified halfway up the German 'Kabinett Wein' quality, which was one above the Tafelwein quality to which most English wine aspired.

In 1972 the Feucht Fröhliche Neustaadter, the wine club of the German town of Neustadt, presented the city of Lincoln, its twin town, with three hundred vines to mark the nine-hundredth anniversary of Lincoln Cathedral. The city fathers planted them in the garden of the Old Bishop's Palace. Was it the only civic vineyard in the world? Maybe; with Alan Rook's at nearby Stragglethorpe Hall, where the wine from it was eventu-ally made, it was perhaps the most northerly.

An English rosé from Beaulieu and Anderida 71 were the choice at the first British Festival of Food and Wine at the Hunting Lodge in London (which many will remember better as the famed Hungaria) organized by that restaurant in conjunction with Merrydown.

All seemed in the ascendant in 1972 except the weather. There were cold winds at the time of flowering which stopped the vines from ripening and devastated the crops. The appalling summer made the 1972 vintage the worst for twenty years. The best yield was in Essex, but even there the crop was fifty per cent down on 1971; in the west country it dropped twenty per cent. Both quantity and quality were down. There was very little English wine to sell that year and existing stocks were exhausted.

'Where can it be obtained?' pleaded Jack Ward. 'With such a miniscule production it is not surprising English wine is difficult to find in the retail shops. That such rarities tend to make their way into the more discriminating establishments is not to be wondered at; that sales of these wines are being monopolized by an enterprising minority is hardly surprising when it is clear that the total national production could be gobbled up by one large catering firm.'

However the bad weather of 1972 had no effect on the numbers who hastened to order vine plants by the thousand and join the EVA to keep themselves informed. There were now three hundred members with 250 acres planted, though not all 'bearing' yet. John Astor planted a vineyard on his two thousand-acre estate at Inkpen, Berkshire. Kevin Fitzgerald and James White pooled their resources to form Suffolk Vineyards Limited, journeyed to France to study how to do it, bought 15,000 grafted vines there, another 7,500 cuttings from an English vineyard and planted them in the seven-acre vineyard they established at Cratfield. At their Orchard Farm they planted another 4,500 root stocks for future development. They planned to build a wine-making plant to handle 250,000 bottles a year with automatic presses, machinery, laboratory and store. They offered to process other growers' grapes as Merrydown was doing, and sold propagated vines at 10p each. They also acted as consultants who would plant a new vineyard to a customer's specification, and supervise its operation each year up to the picking and processing.

Reresby Sitwell, grandson of Sir George Sitwell and a London wine merchant by profession, planted 180 vines at Renishaw Hall, the family seat in Derbyshire. David Carr-Taylor planted the whole of his twenty-one-acre farm at Westfield near Hastings with vines in 1972. 'I found that vines would give the best return for agricultural investment' he said, 'partly because wine is one of the few agricultural products where you can control the selling price.'

The established vineyards were attracting the curious by their thousands. There were twelve thousand visitors to Hambledon during Sir Guy Salisbury-Jones' August and September Open Days. Most of them bought a bottle of Hambledon wine from the shop on their way out: which saved packaging and freight. Some Hambledon wine found its way to the United

States, Japan, Germany, and even to France, but in 1973 Sir Guy was not seriously considering the export market. 'Apart from other considerations' he told his Royal Society of Arts audience in March 1973,

> the formalities of the moment are too complicated. For example, the cases we recently sent to France were needed in a hurry, so that we had to send them by air. Our local customs and excise officer produced the necessary forms to complete, but when the cases reached Heathrow the authorities there said the forms were wrong. After some delay our own local officer was proved to have been right and off went the wine. But the frustrations of bureaucracy had only just started. On arrival at Orly Airport the wine seems to have aroused the suspicions of the French Douane who could not believe that England produced wine. There was further delay therefore before the wine could be cleared.

Others of the old guard were turning to new ventures. After a buyer from Atlanta took the whole of Graham and Irene Barretts' 1972 Riesling-Sylvaner Felstar 72, and they had a bumper crop on their ten and a half acres in Essex in 1973 (with the expectation of 7,500 bottles an acre), the Barretts turned their minds to sparkling wine and planned to plant grapes of the kind that produced French champagne. In the middle of the night of November 30, 1973 Graham Barrett picked a crop of eiswein (icewine) grapes in five degrees of frost, pressed them at once and made seven gallons of ice wine. Ice wine has only been produced eleven times in Germany in the last hundred years; in 1973 German eiswein was selling at £150 a bottle.

Their less heady Felstar 71 won a silver seal at the Club Oenologique's international wine and spirit competition in London in May 1973. The gold seal went to Nigel Godden of Pilton Manor, and the bronze to Cranmore Vineyards in the Isle of Wight. Jack Ward received the club's gold insignia for his contribution to the development of English viticulture.

Graham and Irene Barrett were not alone in aspiring to make 'champagne'. Ray Barrington Brock, who brought his twenty-seven years of research at Oxted to a close in 1973 (when the invaluable Mr Walker died), considered it was easier to make sparkling than still wine as, in England, there were more years when grape juice was more suitable for 'champagne' than for ordinary wine. Good 'champagne' could stand a very much higher acidity and required a grape with a neutral flavour. Remember that, in the eighteenth century, people liked to call the Painshill wine 'still champagne'.

Ray sold his stock of vines to Jackman's nurseries in Woking, one of many for whom the selling of vine shoots offered an increasingly large market every year. It was a profitable new line of business. The cost of the ten thousand plants needed to stock a three-acre vineyard, considered the minimum commercial size, was in the region of £3,500; and the number

of potential customers mounted annually. Membership of the English Vineyards Association had reached 317 in 1973, and they accounted for 750,000 bottles of English wine a year. The wine shop at Merrydown were offering twenty-three brands. Some forty acres were being harvested, but another 140 were under cultivation, working out the three- to four-year waiting period before a full crop could be harvested. In the spring of 1973 another hundred acres of vineyard were added; and these included many extensions to early plots. More vignerons were reluctant to shoulder the risks personally and formed limited companies.

With land costing between £3,000 and £4,000 an acre it was the sensible thing for Alan McKechnie to do when, with John Thornburn, he decided to plant a half-acre vineyard at Dymock in the Severn Valley. Their operation was run by the McKechnie Wine Company of Newent, formed for the purpose in 1973. They chose Reichensteiner and Mueller-Thurgau vines, and the following year extended the vineyard by another two and a quarter acres. When their first vintage was made for them by Merrydown in 1975 they called it 'Three Choirs'.

Sir Guy Salisbury-Jones planned to add to his vineyard at Hambledon in 1974/75 and to raise his annual output to 20,000 bottles. This required mechanization and he bought a 'tracteur-enjambeur Jacquet' of the kind used in French vineyards. He demonstrated the tractor to his friend Mon-

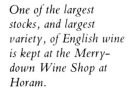

One of the largest stocks, and largest variety, of English wine is kept at the Merry-down Wine Shop at Horam.

sieur Christian Pol Roger who visited Hambledon for the vendange of 1973, the year Britain finally entered the EEC.

1973: Britain's Entry into the European Community Benefits English Viticulture

It was a time for Member States to have a look at each other's progress, and in September Jack Ward made a tour of European vineyards. He returned more convinced than ever that Britain must have its own seal of quality independent of the continent; but in 1977 negotiations were still going on. The Department of Trade said a chemical test formula would carry more weight than merely tasting, but Jack Ward insisted that there should be both. A chemical test could be reduced to figures, whereas an organoleptic test (tasting) depended on the ability of a panel to give a proper—human— assessment.

In his 1973 Budget the Chancellor of the Exchequer made a number of alterations in the alcohol duties to coincide with the introduction to Britain on April 1 of Value Added Tax. For English wine this meant a reduction

Nigel Godden (left) offers visitors to his vineyard 'a unique opportunity to wander at leisure . . . and to taste the wine from the estate in the relaxed atmosphere of a bygone age'. He encourages tourists to visit Pilton Manor Vineyard (above).

in the rate of excise duty from £1.4875 a gallon to 75p; but the consumer had to pay VAT which was levied on the net cost of the wine, plus the reduced duty and the trade mark-up. Cheaper wine benefited, but anything above £1.30, which applied to most English wine, cost more. VAT worked out at about 15p to 17p on a bottle of wine, whether it was English wine made from English grapes, British wines made-up from imported grape concentrate, or a foreign wine.

'How soon will EEC duties be "harmonized" downwards?' asked Edmund Penning-Rowsell in the *Financial Times* of March 13, 1973. The Wine and Spirit Association of Great Britain held a meeting to explain how the wine trade would be affected by Britain's accession. It was known that there was to be a harmonizing period before definite decisions were reached, but speculation was rife. Sir Guy Salisbury-Jones had reasons for optimism, for in February the French head of the Wine Division in the EEC visited

205

Hambledon. The visit was followed up by a letter in which the work at Hambledon was referred to as 'more worthy of consideration in that it has aroused in Great Britain an awareness of the importance of viticulture as much on economic as on human grounds'.

'It seems curious' commented Sir Guy, 'that it should have taken a Frenchman in Brussels to take us seriously. But "a prophet is not without honour save in his own country".'

Confident mastery of the techniques, and the quality of the end product no doubt contributed to English viticulture being taken seriously, but it was the *size* of the industry which would gain it official recognition.

The southern counties of England and Wales are on the same latitude as the vine-growing areas of northern Germany and the vineyards of Luxembourg.

Britain, the northern part of West Germany, Luxembourg, Belgium and the Netherlands—for the purpose of 'permitted oenological processes'—form 'Zone A' of the European Economic Community.

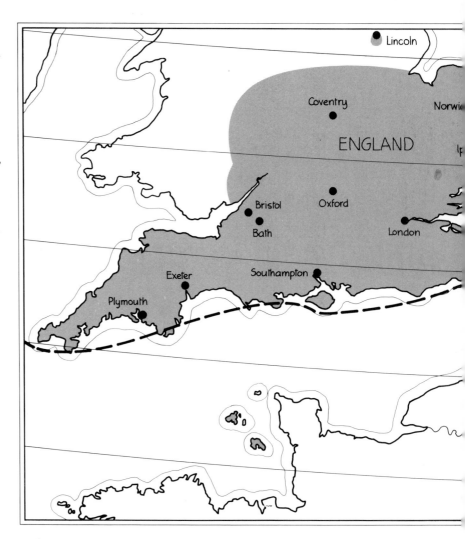

While the terms of Britain's entry into the Community were being nego-
tiated, it was apparent that Britain's small wine industry had no need to fear
that it would at once be forced to conform with EEC common agricultural
policy. It was not large enough. The Six agreed to exempt from the admin-
istrative controls of their wine regime any country with less than 100
hectares (247 acres) of vineyard.

However by August 1973 the picture had changed; in that month a
Statutory Instrument (no. 1341) was laid before the British Parliament by
the Minister of Agriculture, empowering him to bring into operation on
September 1 the Common Agricultural Policy (Wine) Regulations, 1973

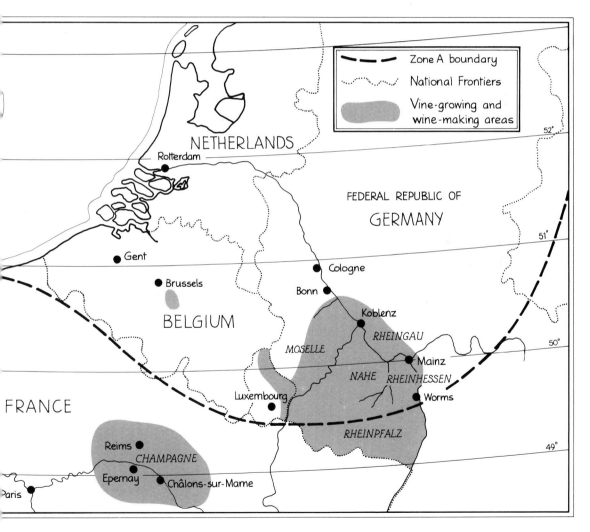

concerning the production and marketing of wine. The schedule of S.I. 1341/1973 listed sixteen 'Community Provisions' which were to become part of the law of the United Kingdom. Failure to comply invoked a fine not exceeding £400. The regulations covered such matters as enriching, acidifying, de-acidifying, sweetening, adding sugar ('chaptalization') and other alcohol. Two regulations concerned the preparation of a register of vineyards; another two set out the general rules for the classification of vine varieties; and one regulation concerned the measures to be taken for examining the suitability of certain vine varieties for cultivation. The Community partners were grouped into 'wine-growing zones', and UK became part of Zone A which also included the northern part of the Federal Republic of Germany, Luxembourg, Belgium, and Holland.

According to Monsieur J. Gourdon, of the Wine, Spirits and Derived Products Division of the Directorate General for Agriculture of the Commission of the European Communities in Brussels, adjustments were made to existing Community wine legislation to fit English viticulture into the Community framework, though subsequent to accession it became subject to far more comprehensive Community wine legislation.

For instance there was rigid control of the varieties of vine which a Member State could plant. It was restricted to those varieties classified as 'authorized' or 'recommended' except for cultivation experiments or scientific research. However the Community recognized that to all intents and purposes *all* British viticulture at this stage was a cultivation experiment, and ruled that the planting of varieties not included in the classification for its zone was for 'experimental purposes' and therefore permissible.

The sixteen regulations given in the schedule of S.I.1341 were in fact only the first of sixty-one EEC Council Regulations which were collected into one volume under the title 'European Communities, Secondary Legislation, Part 41, WINE'. The transitional stage was to end in 1978 when the UK became a full member of the EEC.

1972: English Wine Does Not Merit State Aid

The lowering of the excise duty brought about a number of alterations in the Merrydown Co-operative Scheme for making wine from the grapes of members of the EVA who had no processing equipment of their own. How much wine Merrydown kept as payment—and put into the blended wine they sold as Anderida—depended on a fair evaluation of the quality of the wine-grapes as a commercial crop, the current costs of processing and

bottling, and the excise duty levied on English wine and British Wines. Merrydown insured a member's grapes or wine against loss while it was at Horam, agreeing to compensate the grower at a rate of £336 a ton of fruit, a figure not expected to stay static. With the use of modern pressing equipment they estimated a maximum yield of 160 gallons of juice from a ton of fruit though the average was nearer 150 gallons. With the new excise duty and VAT at ten per cent, the cost of vinification for a ton of fruit was £252 and the value of the fruit, as seen, £336. This was forty-three per cent for processing and fifty-seven per cent for growing. On these percentages the 975 bottles of wine which they reckoned came from a ton of grapes were divided: 419 bottles to Merrydown and 556 to the grower.

The fact that from April 1 1973 the excise duty was lower meant that the grower received a larger share of bottled wine. But Merrydown got Customs and Excise to agree that the duty could be excluded from this calculation altogether, so long as the grower registered as a 'British Winemaker For Sale' and secured a licence which would cost him £5.25 a year. Payment of the duty was not to be excused of course, only deferred until each bottle was offered for sale; but its removal from Merrydown's calculation also reduced the VAT, and changed the vinification cost for a ton of fruit from £252 to £128, for the excise duty of 75p a gallon had amounted to £112. So now Merrydown took 273 bottles and the grower 702.

The lower excise duty was welcome but even more encouraging would have been no excise duty at all. The German and Italian governments saw no reason to impose an internal tax on German and Italian wine. Both of them regarded wine as fermented fruit juice which ranked as a genuine agricultural product. Cider with an alcohol content below fifteen degrees proof spirit was exempt in Britain, in spite of the fact that many such brands were stronger than draught beer which was not considered an 'agricultural crop' and paid duty calculated on its gravity.

How do grapes differ from apples, causing one fruit to become liable for duty and another not? asked Jack Ward in 1973. Perhaps Whitehall argued, he said, that cider and perry cease to be agricultural products when alcohol exceeds fifteen degrees proof spirit? Other fruit wines were liable to full excise duty whatever their strength.

> It is by no means certain that Whitehall will suffer a change of heart without our entry into Europe. For in spite of the fact that English vignerons will be asked to observe the multifarious regulations imposed by Brussels, the government of this country is permitted to dictate its own laws which, if imposed, could cause considerable marketing disadvantages to the producers of English wine. Some indication of the attitude likely to be taken by Her Majesty's Government can be seen in the following excerpt from an official Draft Directive referring to wine:

. . . it would therefore be unacceptable to take fiscal measures to encourage consumption in northern regions of a beverage which cannot be produced there, at the expense of the beer produced in these regions.

This clearly shows that Whitehall is either out of touch with reality, or is hoping that the present revival of English viticulture will grind to a halt.

'The future of the English vineyards' wrote Jack Ward in *About Wine*, February 1973,

must be the concern of the British Government if they are to survive. Events have shown that the present revival cannot be dismissed as a triviality. The movement shows signs of growth rather than decline. Quality wines can and will be produced in the United Kingdom in spite of the traditional hazards of climate and geographical position. Existing prejudice will be overcome, and with our entry into Europe fiscal and other inequalities should be eliminated. The cultivation of vines in Great Britain should be given the same facilities and opportunities as those which are available in France, Germany and Italy. If the English growers are compelled to observe the EEC regulations and restrictions, they must be permitted to benefit from the corresponding advantages. That is only fair.

Finally, the British Government must be persuaded to appreciate that wine, unlike beer and spirits, is a natural product of the land which cannot be divorced from the agricultural environment just because its contains alcohol.

But by my reading of the situation the determining factor is not that the fruit becomes alcohol but that it *becomes* anything—figs into that effective old-time laxative Syrup of Figs, blackcurrants into that child-builder 'Ribena'—instead of remaining itself and being taken in boxes, in the form it came off the tree and bush, to the wholesale fruit market. Horti-culture (a means) has ceased to be horticulture—when its end is not the one prescribed by government. A business is only a horticultural business if its horticulture ends up where government says it should.

The Government were equally intransigent in their attitude to grants. They still maintained the stand of the 1960 legislation. A viti-viniculture business was classified as non-horticulture on account of the final wine-making process. It was not therefore eligible for a grant under the Horti-cultural Capital Grant Scheme or the Farm Capital Grant Scheme. Jack Ward had been trying to get the Ministry to subsidise vine-growing in England and Wales, in the same way as it did hop-growing, ever since the EVA had been formed. He and others had a meeting, on January 11, 1972,

with James Prior, Minister of Agriculture to discuss this very question. 'Although the minister was unable to make specific promises', reported Jack Ward, 'it is to be hoped that our representations will be remembered when these matters come up for future consideration.'

As far as the Authorities were concerned, the re-introduction of English viticulture in the context of the twentieth century was not something that could be hurried.

1973 to 1977

EIGHT   The Explosion of Interest: Discipline from the EEC and Support from the Government

Bracknell, Long Ashton, East Malling Take an Interest

A large number of the people, now planting vineyards, or expanding existing ones, were not greatly worried by the lack of financial aid. Absence of a grant did not deter a man like Kenneth Macalpine from planning to extend the vineyard at Lamberhurst in 1974 from eight acres to thirty. In 1974 Basil Ambrose, a member of the Wine Society, had his first magnificent crop from the ten acres which he had planted a couple of years before at Nether Hall Manor, in the Suffolk village of Cavendish. For his 'Cavendish Manor' white wine, he claimed 'an enchanting freshness combined with a lingering, gentle bouquet'—as distinctly English as the Constable countryside in which the vineyard had its setting. Robert Capper planted what he considered to be the first vineyard in Worcestershire for four hundred years on his 200-acre farm at Suckley. He studied vinification in France and Germany, bought several thousand Mueller-Thurgau vines for 15p apiece, and planted them, 1,500 to the acre, at Stocks Farm where he hoped later to install a winery. By 1974 Peter Baillie-Grohman had 10,000 vines at Hascombe. Peter and Anne Latchford, who had planted two acres of Mueller-Thurgau at Boxmoor in Hertfordshire, had made 160 bottles of wine in 1973, and were proud to exhibit at the successful 1974 English Wine Fair at Beaulieu. In the Weald of Kent a small vineyard, planted in 1970 at Little Whatmans, Biddenden (where parish records show there had been one in earlier times), had grown to ten acres. It was run, as was now becoming the pattern, by a private limited company, formed for the purpose: Biddenden Vineyards Limited.

212

All these vignerons belonged to the English Vineyards Association, looked to it as their champion in the corridors of power and relied on it to relay the latest technical information from the world's research centres. As the lobby and political pressure group* of the revived English wine industry, the English Vineyards Association had won the greatest respect under the skilful guidance of Jack Ward and Irene Barrett. In August 1973, members and associate members numbered 330 with acreage under cultivation approaching the two hundred mark.

The Association held a two-day symposium in March at Horam and in London; an annual wine-tasting in London's Café Royal in September; it published a regular *Journal*. The support given by the Association to the suggestion, made in 1971, that Wye College should undertake a programme of viticultural research was rewarded when field trials began in 1973 after vines had been donated by viticultural research institutes from Germany, Switzerland and Austria.

Others now offered their services to help an enterprise which had demonstrated its potential. Joe Cochrane, of the Meteorological Office at Bracknell, in response to an increasing number of enquiries about areas suitable for commercial viticulture in England and Wales, made a limited study of climatic constraints on viticulture, including an analysis of meteorological data measured at Hambledon. Sir Guy was only able to make 1,000 bottles instead of his usual 8,000 in 1972. 'This drop in yield,' Cochrane observed,

> was probably largely due to the cool, dull and at times windy start to the season . . . The data for this single year at least suggests the probable effect on English viticulture of cooler summers and the economic dangers of trying to establish new vineyards in any but the most favourable sites.

The Long Ashton Research Station of Bristol University which had been started as a cider research institute, now turned its attention to the making of wine. Dr F. W. Beech, head of the Cider and Fruit Juices Section, gave authoritative details of *Harvesting and Wine Making Techniques*, from which many acquired their first knowledge of vinification. He warned that botrytis was becoming a major disease in English viticulture. In a comprehensive and authoritative leaflet, *Growing Vines in the Open in Great Britain* (1974), he recommended that all vineyards in England should be established on grafted stock resistant to the vine louse phylloxera. The material should be imported with health certificates from the country of origin and

---

* The £100 million a year British Wines Industry has its own body the National Association of British Wine Producers (secretary, Stanley Sleeman).

examined by a Plant Health Inspector of the Ministry of Agriculture. Three pages were devoted to the choice of varieties to grow. There were very few which had proved successful in all English vineyards, so there was a danger of there being very little variation in the flavour of English wine, most of which would eventually be made from Mueller-Thurgau and Seyve-Villard 5/276. Most other varieties which might be useful, because they ripened in September, were liable to be devastated by wasps and flies.

On April 17 1974, the EEC Commission published an official list of the varieties recommended and authorized for cultivation in the United Kingdom (Regulation no. 925/74). Vines omitted from the list were not banned; they could be planted, but for the time being were regarded as experimental. There were two categories:

Recommended	*Authorized*
Auxerrois	Bacchus
Mueller-Thurgau	Chardonnay
Wrotham Pinot (Pinot Meunier or Muellerrebe)	Ehrenfelser
	Faber
	Huxelrebe
	Kanzler
	Kerner
	Madeleine Angevine
	Madeleine Royale
	Madeleine Sylvaner
	Mariensteiner
	Ortega
	Perle
	Pinot Noir (Spatburgunder)
	Rulander (Pinot Gris)
	Seyval B (Seyve-Villard 5/276)
	Siegerrebe

In circulating this information the British Ministry of Agriculture added a list, compiled by the Merrydown Wine Company, of varieties not tested in the prevailing climatic conditions of the United Kingdom, but which were expected to perform equally as well, in the southern part of the country, as those in the EEC official list. There were eleven white varieties: Precoce de Malingre and Perle de Czaba (early); Reichensteiner, Alba Longa, Rabana, Regner, Septimer, Chasselas, Gutenborner, Wurzer (mid-season); and Schonburger (late). The two mid-season black varieties given were Blue Portuguese and Zweigeltrebe.

At a Christie's wine-tasting in 1975 connoisseurs could not tell the difference between German, French and English white wines of the same price in unlabelled bottles.

It is interesting to see how many varieties on this 1974 list were those tried and proved by Ray Barrington Brock at Oxted between 1947 and 1973.

C. D. Walker, National Fruit Adviser at the East Malling Research Station of the Ministry of Agriculture's Development and Advisory Service (ADAS), warned those who attended the Wine Production Conference at the Royal Show site at Stoneleigh in Warwickshire on February 26 1975 that viticulture could be a very expensive and capital intensive business. He suggested that, before the owner had his wine safely in bottles awaiting sale, it would be quite easy to spend £4,000 an acre on the establishment of a new vineyard, the subsequent wine-production and the paying of excise duty. He also said that there were serious problems due to disease and a grave risk of depredation by birds.

Viticulture is an enterprise which involves an above average risk of failure. It is therefore only prudent to think long and hard before making a final decision to go ahead and plant your vines. In ADAS we are only too well aware of the financial loss and disillusion that can occur when some in-dividual, who often has little or no practical experience in horticulture, sud-denly decides to go in for a speculative crop such as viticulture. It is all too

easy to be taken in by romantic ideas of sunny vineyards and ignore the many cultural problems that lie between planting the vines and selling your first bottle of wine.

As regards our ADAS involvement in viticulture, we treat it like any other fruit crop and if a client comes to us for advice we do our best to satisfy his needs. This may entail the solution of some minor cultural details but, particularly with prospective viticulturists, it does mean taking on the unpopular task of pointing out the limitations imposed by soil, site and climate on wine production in this country.

More English Wine than in the Middle Ages: but Not Enough

In the summer of 1974 an English Vineyard Census was held both by the Ministry of Agriculture and the English Vineyards Association. The list of English and Welsh Vineyards issued by the latter was headed with the following introductory remarks:

> The explosion of interest in the cultivation of outdoor grapes has captured the imagination of horticulturists and fruit farmers all over the country. Perhaps this is why the number of English vineyards now in existence and the acreage that is known to have been planted since the war more than outstrips the legendary sites of the Middle Ages.
>
> The sudden renaissance of English viticulture has enjoyed a generous measure of publicity but in spite of this few people are able to buy English wine from the shops. As a result the consumer is quite unaware of the recent developments which have done much to revive this ancient husbandry in our somewhat wayward climate. For such reasons the publication of this list may provide a service to the community.

There were 107 names on the EVA list. The area under vines was optimistically estimated at 380 acres. The largest acreage under one management was Suffolk Vineyards' five plots spreading over thirty-one acres at Cratfield, Halesworth; the second largest David Carr-Taylor's twenty-one-acre vineyard at Westfield near Hastings in Sussex; the third largest B. H. Theobald's at Westbury Farm near Reading in Berkshire of 14 acres; then Paget Brothers of Singleton near Chichester, 12½ acres; the Barretts at Felsted in Essex, 10½ acres; B. T. Ambrose in Cavendish in Suffolk, N. Poulter and R. Gibbons at Cranmore, Isle of Wight, and S. W. Greenwood at Purleigh in Essex, all 10 acres. Thirty-three were one acre and under.

Amateurs and enthusiasts, aided by men like Anton Massel and Ray Barrington Brock, had brought viticulture back into English life, and in the

process they had become the professionals. They had given English wine-making the scientific approach it had previously lacked. It was significant that the Government's recognition of viticulture had become official and its treatment of the issues involved serious.

It was now important that English wine became available nationally. The scale of the operations had to be increased, so that the making of English wine could properly be called an *industry*. If English viticulture was to fail now, the most likely cause would be lack of proper investment and financial aid. The Ministry of Agriculture was prepared to explore how best it could help; and, in March 1976, it seemed that the most likely way would be through the new Farm and Horticultural Development Scheme, which was designed to enable farmers and growers, whose incomes were below the average earnings in non-agricultural industry, to achieve a 'comparable income'. It offered a new kind of assistance to eligible farmers and growers to develop 'agricultural businesses', a term covering all normal types of agriculture and horticulture and freshwater fish farming. The scheme put into effect an EEC directive on Farm Modernization and was being partly financed by the Community's Agricultural Fund. Applicants for aid were invited to submit development plans (up to six years), and those whose plans were accepted received capital grants for the investment needed to carry through the plan, a grant towards the cost of keeping accounts, and guarantees for loans needed to carry out the plan.

In May the necessary amendments to the Farm and Horticulture Development Scheme were approved by Parliament and, for the first time, specific provision was made for viticulture in the schedule of items eligible for a grant: twenty-five per cent of the cost of providing, improving or replacing staking and wirework in *vineyards*. It must have been the first time the word had been seen in a statute since King Alfred's day.

Vine-growers would be eligible for the grant, so long as they satisfied the conditions of the scheme, whether their businesses were classified as 'agricultural' or 'horticultural'. In addition grant aid for other facilities listed in the scheme such as roads and drainage continued to be available.

There was a further concession: the government entitled a licensed producer of wine to set apart 120 gallons of the wine he made each year from his own grapes *for his own consumption* without paying duty on it: it could not be either sparkling or fortified; the bottles would have to carry a label marked 'Not For Sale', and VAT would still have to be paid. In addition ten per cent of all gallons over and above 120, up to a ceiling of 240, would be duty free.

However, the Government promptly increased the rate of excise duty to 41p a bottle to which eight per cent VAT had to be added. David Howell, MP for Guildford, took the matter up with the Treasury; but it was of little

avail to point to our Community partner Italy who had just agreed to give up to sixty per cent grants for the establishment of new vineyards and lend money at six per cent for the remaining costs.

The Treasury had no objection to expenditure on long term research, and, in April 1975, viticultural experiments were started at the Ministry of Agriculture's Experimental Horticulture Station at Efford near Lymington in Hampshire. A one-acre plantation was laid out for a variety of projects. These included a basic feasibility study, variety comparison, comparison of virus free and other stock, training methods, weed control and nutrition.

This work was complementary to the experiments which had been carried out, on behalf of the EVA and on limited funds, by the Hop Research Department at Wye College since 1973. In 1976, nineteen vine varieties were being grown on their one-acre plot at Ashford, and three systems of wire-work and pruning were being tested. This was also in the nature of a feasibility study and, in the spring of 1976, they had yet to harvest a crop. Some of the varieties were new to Britain and their potential was of great interest to English vine-growers. If they could show that grapes would grow and ripen in that part of Kent they hoped to expand the work to cover many practical aspects of vine-growing.

State Encouragement Shaped by EEC Experience

Government Departments now recognized English Viticulture as a serious, commercial activity which merited the expenditure of public money and civil servants' time. But there were no precedents on which the Ministry of Agriculture could draw. There had never been a Wine Production and Marketing Section of the Ministry whose files contained the minuted wisdom of the centuries. Because of this ignorance, and because of the small scale of English wine production, it is unlikely that the British Government would have given the activity more than token attention. But overnight, as it were, the Germans, the French and the Italians were at hand forcibly to lead the new European partner into ways of developing a wine industry which worked, and had a chance of continuing to work.

An indifferent Whitehall was galvanized into action. At the very outset the inclusion of viticulture in the Ministry of Agriculture's grant scheme was at the instance of an EEC directive. The diminutive scale of English viticulture was no longer a reason for excusing the government from participation. In November 1975 the Ministry's Statistics Division carried out a survey designed to establish the basic details of every known vineyard in the United Kingdom, and to provide a starting point for the

introduction of Community arrangements. In existing EEC States these entailed the keeping of a highly detailed record of the age and variety of the vines being grown in each vineyard—the Vineyard Register.

Without the statistical survey the Ministry reckoned, from press reports, that the 150 vineyards in England and Wales had a combined acreage of more than 200 hectares (500 acres); and growers were forecasting a record production of 170,000 bottles (1,250 hectolitres) in 1975.

Assuming that the 200 hectares in the UK were fully bearing by 1980, with a yield of 100 hectolitres per hectare—the present German average—UK production could amount to 20,000 hectolitres in 1980. This was 0.0001 per cent of current Community production and slightly less than one per cent of total wine consumption in the UK in 1974. Plans for planting over the next five years indicated prospects for rising production levels in the nineteen-eighties, but it was obviously going to be some time before the English wine industry achieved a significant output in comparison with that of other Member states. England's wine industry would not constitute serious competition, either by British consumption of English wine reducing British consumption of foreign wine, or by British export of English wine reducing domestic consumption of domestic wine.

As the drop is to the ocean so is English wine to the wine of the rest of Europe. In France the high-grade 'Appellation Contrôlée' wine alone amounts to 1,300 million bottles a year (made from the grapes of 300,000 individual vineyards) which is only *a sixth* of the total national production. In France one in six of the adult population earns a living directly from wine. And of course they *drink* so much more than we do; 135 bottles a head every year compared with seven* in Britain. France and Italy together account for eighty-five per cent of the Community's wine consumption.

Towards Formulating Common Techniques Best Suited to England

There is as yet no consensus of opinion among English and Welsh vignerons on how best to grow and ripen vines in the open-air. Everyone goes their

---

* The drinking of wine in Britain was stimulated by the clause in the Licensing Act 1961 which enabled off-licence shops to sell wine outside pub licensing hours. In 1975 Britain imported thirty-two million gallons of table wine; and it is reckoned that wine consumption in Britain trebled between 1967 and 1977 when spirits were heavily taxed. Britain's Wine Development Board calculate that the nation will be drinking twenty bottles of wine a head by 1985.

own way, each with a pet theory which often changes from year to year. Ian Paget, at Singleton in West Sussex, swears by 'foliar-feeding', which is giving the vine nourishment through its leaves; liquefied seaweed is mixed with fungicide to give iron and magnesium, and the whole two and a quarter hectares (thirteen acres) can be sprayed in five and a half hours. He insists that a touch of botrytis on his Mueller-Thurgau will improve the vintage and rhapsodizes over the benefits of the Noble Rot (la pourriture noble)—so long as it is not allowed to become the Grey Rot; Noble Rot, he says, extracts water and leaves a more sugary must. He keeps his vines low, no more than four feet, 'tucking in' to keep the tops regimented into a straight line. He has no time for netting but keeps the birds away by dawn patrols, walking round after early breakfast and again at lunch and dinner. He reckons he lost only two per cent of his crop in 1974 to birds—and to bad picking. Eighteen helpers cleared his grapes in eight days at three tons a day. He has six feet between his rows and wished he had given them six and a half. He has confined himself to three varieties.

Graham Barrett in Essex, however, has nine varieties each ripening at a different time so he can stagger the harvesting and keep the number of paid pickers small. It also spreads the risk of some ripening and some not. He sprays fourteen times a year but finds it cheaper and better to put manure in the soil. He nets his ten acres and grows his vines at least seven feet high, with the tops waving in the air and bushing out at the sides on the theory that the greater leaf area the greater sugar production: the Austrian way. His vines are close together and he would like them even closer, in the belief that each row shelters another and creates a highly beneficial micro-climate. He is concerned to devise systems which save labour.

In Hampshire, Sir Guy Salisbury-Jones treats his chalky soil with farmyard manure every other year and with fertilizer every year. Because of the chalk he follows the French system of narrow and low rows, four feet apart and three and a half feet high. The theory here is that low vines benefit from the heat of the earth, though it is not as beneficial to the backs of the pickers who have to stoop to the bunches. He nets the whole area in five days. In 1976 he was starting to replant the twenty-five-year-old vineyard with entirely new stock; the replanting would continue over a period of five years. This time Bill Carcary intended seeing that they were planted somewhat deeper than Ernie Blackman had thought necessary, with no danger of the tractor catching the roots as it passed along the rows.

In East Sussex at Horam, Merrydown hold to the more leaf area, more sugar theory—nine leaves above the bunch at least—and the branches wave high. For Jack Ward harvesting is a matter of leaving as long as you dare. The sugar content of the grape, which can be measured with something called a refractometer, is the determining factor, but it is a mistake to think

that it automatically increases as time goes on. Having reached a peak at the end of August it can *go down* if there is heavy rain, as there was in September 1975 following the heat of high summer. For him the choice of a site should be determined not by the hours of sunshine or latitude, but by the absence of humidity and wind.

Merrydown's Co-operative Scheme gave conformity to a large part of the English wine made at the beginning of the decade. In seven years the amount of fruit received for pressing from all over England rose from five to a hundred tons, an average annual increase of sixty-six per cent. The scheme succeeded mainly because it had set out to keep each wine separate and return to the grower what he could justifiably claim was the genuine product of his own vineyard. It was an exercise probably unparalleled in Europe. In 1975, wine was made from forty English vineyards. Financial re-structuring took place in 1976, since inflation had made nonsense of the charges to those who wished to take *all* of their wine instead of paying in kind. For those who participated fully in the co-operative scheme the calculation of how many bottles Merrydown was entitled to was made on an 'at cost' basis. From those who wanted all their fruit returned as wine, Merrydown derived a reasonable margin of profit. Of the 910 bottles which on average they now reckoned came from a ton of fruit, a grower not registered as a 'British Winemaker for Sale' (see page 209) received 346 and Merrydown took 564; one who was registered received 592 bottles and Merrydown took 318. Without the excise duty of £2.95 a gallon which added £413 to the cost of processing a ton of fruit, Merrydown calculated that it cost them £229, while the value of a ton of wine-grapes was £420. Those who wished to pay cash for the processing were charged £247 a ton if they were British Winemakers for Sale.

As more newcomers entered viticulture who concentrated in the first years, as others had before them, on vine-growing, and looked to Horam for vinification, Merrydown had to double their capacity. In 1976 they installed another eighteen 440-gallon fermentation tanks in their cool, half-underground winery where for the smaller amounts they had a number of wooden hogsheads and 'pipes'.

By 1976, however, there were many of the old guard like Graham Barrett and Ian Paget who decided that the moment had come to essay the ultimate satisfaction of turning their grapes into wine themselves. And with vinification, as with viticulture, there was no common *modus operandi*. Some followed Dr Beech, some Anton Massel, who offered a postal correspondence course, others Barrington Brock and the many treatises they found in public libraries. Some had a vertical press like Graham Barrett's manual, beechwood 'Mearelli' from Italy costing about £270; others a horizontal French, electrically driven machine like Sir Guy's 'Vaslin' which cost him

at least four times as much. Everyone had their own idea of how these foreign pieces of equipment should be modified. When I visited Graham Barrett at Felsted, he was busily replacing the mild steel screws with stainless steel and putting a fibreglass veneer over the mild steel base of his Mearelli.

He hoped to obtain a ton of juice every one and a half hours from his two and a half hectolitre press, which held eight hundredweight of crushed fruit. 'Milling' was a problem: he intended breaking down the grapes between plastic rollers to make a suitable mash for the press. He had acquired a number of old Marsala barrels with wax linings in which he planned temporarily to do the fermentation. He had devised his own bottling method, creating a sterile area by dropping a plastic canopy over it. He had received a Ministry grant for a new tractor shed, but had been refused one for a press-house, so he was converting an old barn, and replacing the concrete floor which grape juice easily penetrated. He had coped as well as he could with local bye-laws, building regulations, the excise man and the man from the Wine Standards Board, and in spite of it all visitors continued to tell him he looked as happy as Max Bygraves—whom he closely resembles.

Ian Paget was surrounded by the debris of making a winery and laboratory out of the old Singleton Station booking hall, where King Edward VII had so frequently alighted to attend the nearby Goodwood Races. Paget, in 1976, was preparing to receive the seven 4,000-litre tanks each eight feet high and the other equipment which the old booking hall would soon house, ready for the vendage of 1976. He hoped later to install an eighth tank to give him a storage capacity of 32,000 litres to take the wine from the juice of those four hundred rows of vines growing across a half mile front above the old railway line. That would be 40,000 bottles of 'Chilsdown'. His brother Andrew was taking Anton Massel's postal course to make sure they were all saleable.

No Concerted Promotion and Marketing of English Wine

And what could the English vigneron do about getting rid of this surge of English wine? How could he find his customers? Ian and Andrew Paget like Sir Guy, Brian Ambrose at Cavendish, C. L. B. Gillespie at North Wootton, Nigel Godden at Pilton, were making their vineyards tourist attractions, the takings from which—together with sales of wine and cuttings—also helped to keep down overheads, though English licensing laws forbade the sale of bottles of the vineyard's produce on the day when there were most visitors, namely Sunday.

The marketing of English wine, like its processing, was conducted in a variety of ways. There was no concerted effort to promote English wine commercially. A few wine merchants with national distribution facilities, such as Peter Dominic, were still handling some of the older brands, but most vignerons were content to rely on purely local outlets. It was a question of maintaining an eighteen-month cash flow and not thinking very much further ahead than that.

However there were many notable excursions into wider spheres. 'Adgestone' could be bought at Crockford's Club and Searcy's; 'Hambledon' at Ronnie Scott's restaurant; 'Pilton Manor', 'Adgestone', 'Hascombe' and 'Felstar' at Harrods. Gruff Reece received a £1,500 order for a hundred cases of his Gamlingay wine from Japan; Graham Barrett sold his twelve dozen bottles of Auslese at £4.10 each in two days; three thousand attended the first English Wine Exhibition at Michelham Priory in Sussex. Fortnum and Mason had a display of English wine in their Piccadilly window and put it on the wine list of their restaurant; further along Piccadilly Robert Jackson also had a display; British Transport Hotels chose a selection of six English wines at a tasting at the Charing Cross Hotel, and offered cases of five bottles at £23.64 to members of their 'Malmaison Wine Club'. The English Tourist Board were giving solid support to English wine: tourists would want to drink 'the wine of the country' but so far they had not been aware that England had any. At a Christie's wine-

Most English wine-makers market their wine locally; there is no central English wine marketing organization, but occasionally there is a get-together such as this English Wine Exhibition held at Michelham Priory in Sussex.

tasting connoisseurs could not tell the difference between six German, six French and six English white wines of the same price in unlabelled bottles.

The price level of the English product more than anything else determined its character in the scale of the world's wine, and also, of course, greatly affected the extent to which it was acceptable. Many had thought, up to 1975, that English wine was over-priced; the fact that 50p went on tax was irrelevant so far as the consumer was concerned, though he would feel the difference when the hoped-for equalization of EEC excise duties came in 1980. But no great profits were being made by the vignerons. Graham Barrett reckoned that with wine-grapes costing 25p a pound he made an average of 20p on a bottle of 'Felstar'.

In 1972 the most expensive English wine on sale in the Merrydown Wine Shop was Pilton Manor Riesling-Sylvaner at £1.47 and the least expensive Pinot St George for 70p. In 1976 New Hall Rosé at £2.30 and Pilton Manor Riesling-Sylvaner at £2.25 were the most expensive, and Anderida at £1.76 the cheapest. In May 1976, a wine store in London was offering Beaulieu Abbey 1969 Rosé at £1.40; and a Hastings wine merchant was offering a case of a dozen Pilton Manor Riesling Sylvaner at £18.75, or £1.56 a bottle. This wine merchant was also offering a Klusserather Bruderschaft Auslese 1971 at £20 a case; a Graacher Himmelreich Spatlese 1971 at £20.50 a case; and a Rudesheimer Rosengarten 1973, a German Nahe wine, for £13.50; Liebfraumilch 1973 at £13 a case; Geierslayer Sonnseite Kabinett 1971 at £18; and Piesporter Michelsberg 1973 at £14.50. White 'plonk' sold at Woolworths for 89p and at Marks and Spencers for £1.40, both were French. At any Yates's Wine Lodge a bottle of Australian White or Cape White, described as Dessert Wines, cost £1.49 or £1.40 respectively; and a bottle of Yates's Windott (extra strength vintage Australian wine with beef and malt extracts) cost £1.55.

Selling at prices between £1.50 and £2 a bottle, the small amount of English wine which was made each year in the nineteen-seventies found a ready market. The main concern was to make more of it. So it was no help to the English wine industry, suffering from under-production, to find itself bracketed with fellow Member States of the EEC in having to comply with measures to reduce the effects of their *over*-production.

In 1975 the Community had a 'structural surplus' of wine—the so-called Wine Lake. This was the result of a 1.7 per cent annual increase in wine production between 1964 and 1974, while consumption only rose 0.23 per cent. To adjust this situation the Brussels Commission proposed calling a halt to the planting of new vines in any EEC country until January 1, 1977.

Would the Minister of Agriculture take steps to protect the English wine industry in the light of EEC policy of restricting production? asked

Labour MP, Arthur Gould, in the House of Commons on July 31, 1975. George Strang, Parliamentary Secretary, told him he appreciated his concern, and agreed it would be inappropriate if the ban on planting were applied to the UK. 'We would not expect wine production to be restricted in this country if we can produce more efficiently than our counterparts in the Community.'

Fred Peart, who had followed James Prior as Agricultural Minister in the new Labour administration, tried to persuade the Commission in Brussels to have English vineyards exempted from the planting restriction. In September, a Commission spokesman in London said that, if the ban presented difficulties, Britain could be dealt with separately; and in the revised proposals there was provision to exempt producers with a 1974 output of less than 1,000 hectolitres (25,000 gallons), which gave Britain its release.

English wine was being given every chance to make the grade, and English vignerons knew that at last they were being taken seriously by both the British Government and the EEC.

English Commercial Vignerons Accept a Realistic Quality Standard

'The idea of being a wine-producer appeals to the romantic. It is suggestive of the warm south and of the patrician life. But since a business project must be judged by severe financial criteria, this conference will examine whether, and under what conditions, a vineyard can be a commercially viable enterprise.'

So ran the no-nonsense preface to the programme of the high level 'Wine Production in the United Kingdom' conference held in February 1975 at the National Agricultural Centre, Kenilworth, organized by the Royal Agricultural Society of England, the ADAS and the EVA. Papers were read by Jack Ward, C. D. Walker, Anthony Heath, Dr F. W. Beech, Nigel Godden and Robin Don on a variety of subjects ranging from Production Costs to Marketing.

If the Community wine regime had begun to pay proper respect to Britain's efforts to establish a wine industry, Europe's journalists were still highly amused. In France Britain's playing with viticulture had long been the subject of plaisanterie; but that had now given way to curiosité. Trying to explain to his readers in *La Journée Vinicole* the meaning of 'Grape Expectations'—the heading of an article in *The Guardian* by Diana Hanson—H. B. said it involved a subtlety untranslatable into French; but it derived from

BEAULIEU
Medium Dry White
English Table Wine

Produced from grapes grown
in the vineyards at
Beaulieu Abbey
United Kingdom
75cl

BOTTLED FOR LORD MONTAGU OF BEAULIEU
AT HORAM, SUSSEX

Felstar.
Madeleine Angevine
Dry
English White Table Wine

Produced from
SELECTED
Grapes Grown in Essex by
J. G. & I. M. BARRETT, *Wine-Growers*
THE VINEYARDS, CRICK'S GREEN,
FELSTED, ESSEX, ENGLAND.

Produce of England
Bottled in the Country of Origin

Frogmore
English Table Wine

Produced by Brian Hole
FROGMORE FARM · BRADFIELD · BERKSHIRE
BOTTLED BY MERRYDOWN WINE COMPANY · HORAM · SUSSEX
Produce of the United Kingdom

Chilsdown
1975
English White Table Wine

Made from Müller-Thurgau &
Reichensteiner Grapes grown on Chilts Down
in the County of Sussex.
72 cl.

Grown and Bottled by Paget Brothers

BAGET BROTHERS, THE OLD STATION HOUSE, SINGLETON, CHICHESTER.

LANGHAM
MÜLLER THURGAU
White Table Wine

Grown by
LANGHAM FRUIT FARMS LTD
Langham, Colchester, Essex

Produce of England   Vol 70cl

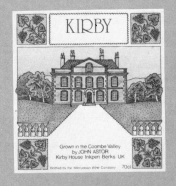

KIRBY

Grown in the Coombe Valley
by JOHN ASTOR
Kirby House Inkpen Berks UK

Bottled for the Merrydown Wine Company   70cl

"The Island of Vines"

U.K.
TABLE WINE
70cl

St Etheldreda
English
White Wine

PRODUCED FROM GRAPES GROWN AT THE ISLE OF ELY VINEYARD, WILBURTON, CAMBRIDGESHIRE
BOTTLED AT HORAM IN SUSSEX

ENGLISH TABLE WINE

from the vines of the Suffolk vineyard at

KELSALE

Müller-Thurgau and Seyve Villard vines
made and bottled for J.T.Edgerley, Kelsale.
70cl

NEW HALL

Pinot Selection
**ENGLISH WHITE
TABLE WINE**
PRODUCED FROM GRAPES GROWN BY
S. W. GREENWOOD, NEW HALL, PURLEIGH, ESSEX

1976
FLEXERNE
English White Table Wine

Produced from grapes grown on Müller-Thurgau vines by
Flexerns Fruit Farm Ltd at Newick in Sussex

Bottled by
THE MERRYDOWN WINE COMPANY LIMITED, HORAM MANOR, HORAM, SUSSEX

70 cl.   PRODUCE OF THE UNITED KINGDOM

Harcombe Manor
Dry
White Table Wine

Harcombe Estate
Ropley   Produce of
Hampshire England   United Kingdom

Frithsden
English White Table Wine

MEDIUM - DRY

Produced from grapes grown in Hertfordshire

P and A Latchford · Frithsden · Hemel Hempstead · Herts

OLD SHIELDS
MÜLLER
THURGAU
Table wine

OLD SHIELDS VINEYARD, ARDLEIGH, ESSEX
PRODUCE OF THE UNITED KINGDOM

70CL.

Genesis.

Creation of human work and the vine.

ENGLISH TABLE WINE
MEDIUM DRY

Estate grown by Fuller Roope Partnership
Genesis Green Vineyards, Wickhambrook, Suffolk, England.

HASCOMBE

SURREY'S
FIRST
WINE

1976

ENGLISH TABLE WINE

PRODUCE OF THE UNITED KINGDOM

70 cl

HORAM MANOR

Estate Bottled
Table Wine
70cl.

Merrydown Wine Co. Ltd. Horam Heathfield, East Sussex.
Produce of the United Kingdom

1975
Cavendish Manor
English White Wine

PRODUCED IN A STOUR VALLEY VINEYARD
FROM SELECTED MUELLER THURGAU GRAPES
GROWN BY B. T. AMBROSE,
NETHER HALL, CAVENDISH, SUFFOLK, ENGLAND.

Bottled in Country of Origin
70 c l Medium Dry Riesling Sylvaner Type Table Wine

hendred

medium dry white wine

A MEDIUM DRY WHITE TABLE WINE PRODUCED FROM
REICHENSTEINER GRAPES IN THE VALE OF THE WHITE HORSE

PRODUCED, BOTTLED & DISTRIBUTED BY HENDRED VINEYARD, EAST HENDRED, OXFORDSHIRE
CONTENTS 70Cl   PRODUCE OF ENGLAND

RAKE
MANOR

Mueller Thurgau

TABLE WINE
70cl   70cl

P.J.Gomme, Rake Manor, Milford, Surrey
Bottled by Merrydown Wine Co.Ltd. Horam Manor,Horam,Heathfield, Sussex
Made in United Kingdom

Bowden
ENGLISH WHITE WINE

ANDERIDA
ENGLISH TABLE WINE
prepared exclusively from grapes grown in Britain
1975

Bottled by the Merrydown Wine Co Ltd Horam Manor Heathfield Sussex
70 cl

English White Table Wine

Wenden

Made from Mueller Thurgau grapes grown at Wenden Vineyard.
Nr. Saffron Walden, Essex, England.

70cl

LITTLEFIELD

FROGGATT

ENGLISH WHITE TABLE WINE

Produced from grapes grown by
R. D. & J. C. Cooper
Oak Cottage
West Peckham
Kent   0.70 litres

Bottled by
Merrydown Wine Co. Ltd.,
Horam Manor
Horam
Sussex

the hope which succoured 'les rares mais vaillants viticulteurs d'outre-Manche', hope of their ability over the coming years to reap harvests less and less modest in volume and above all of a quality 'sans cesse affirmée'.

There is no doubt that Britain's membership of the EEC was responsible for the government taking a strict stand on the maintenance of wine quality: 'at a stroke' a Wine Standards Board came into being as part of the Ministry of Agriculture, with inspectors recruited through the Vintners Company. Since Britain had become part of the EEC an English wine-maker had to decide into which of the EEC categories his wine would fall, and to make it strictly according to the specification of that category, which he declared to the consumer on the label in letters twice as large as any other information.

No English wine-maker had ever conceived English wine as 'plonk', and equally no one aspired to match the classic *appellation contrôlée* (a.c.) wine of France. It was the eventual aim of English wine-makers to achieve the status of what the French called *vins de qualité produits dans regions délimitées* (V.Q.P.R.D.), the Germans *qualitätswein* and the English 'quality wines produced in specific regions', or simply 'quality wine'. At first it was up to each Member State to fix the minimum *natural* alcoholometric strength of what it designated 'quality wine', (without chaptalization, the adding of sugar) and the UK put it at not less than six per cent by volume. Later Brussels fixed it at 6½ per cent for all Member States, but in 1977 the Commission had yet to make up its mind whether this was required information for printing on the label.

To qualify for a 'quality wine' rating an English vigneron had to be prepared to limit the quantity of grapes harvested from an acre of vines. If a French vigneron, accustomed to producing *appellation contrôlée* wine, grew more vines per hectare than the French Government permitted for that rating, he was liable to forfeit the right to call his wine a.c. The principle was that in order to produce a small number of grapes rich in sugar content rather than a large number weak in sugar, the root of a vine plant required a specified area of earth in which it could grow: roots with plenty of room produced grapes with plenty of sugar—and vice versa. Vines should be spaced so that they yielded no more than a specified weight of grapes per hectare per season. The object was to encourage quality and not quantity.

In 1976 English wine-makers had to be content with having their wine rated as 'table wine', the *tafelwein* of Germany and the *vin de table* of France. It was, however, proposed that most English wine could be regarded as 'regional wine', known in France as *vin de pays*, in Germany as *Landwein* and in Italy as *vino tipico*.

French *vin de pays* carried with it restrictions regarding demarcation.

Previous page: twenty-three labels for bottles of English wine. English vignerons have to adhere strictly to the regulations of the EEC Wine Regime regarding labelling and how they describe the wine in the bottle.

228

Britain had so far imposed no controls on the use of geographical descriptions for English wine, but the EEC was anxious to introduce mandatory conditions as soon as possible: they would not be embodied in UK legislation, but form part of a 'Code of Practice'. One of the requirements was that the name of the Member State of Origin should be printed on the label, and, as far as the Community was concerned, that was 'United Kingdom' and not 'England'; but the label of an 'Article 30-type table wine' had also to show the Region of Origin, and for the UK 'regional' was English, Welsh and Channel Islands.

The EEC labelling regulation eventually came into effect on September 1, 1976 (though UK vignerons were given a year's grace to use up their old labels). It was a sensible piece of consumer protection and very much in the interests of the vigneron concerned with the long-term reputation of the UK wine industry. Other regulations on a variety of other aspects of viticulture were 'pending'.

So 'English Wine' was not to disappear after all. The ideal, it seems to me, would be to produce a wine known to the world as 'English Wine' with a character as distinctive as 'Burgundy', 'Claret', 'Hock', 'Moselle', or 'Chianti'. Of this regional type there would then be, of course, as many 'brands' as there are of claret or hock.

1976: the Tonnage of English Wine-Grapes is Trebled

The phenomenally hot summers of 1975 and 1976 gave England and Wales and the Channel Islands continental timing and a vintage which promised to equal the quantity of Germany, but owing to the September rain, not the quality.

The August sun of 1975 ripened the wood very well indeed and increased the potential for the following season which began with fat fruit buds. Though there was a site in Hertfordshire which lost eighty per cent of its crop from spring frost, the majority of vineyards in England, Wales, Ireland and the Channel Islands were little troubled. The critical June flowering period which can make or mar a crop took place two weeks earlier than usual in some of the hottest days of the summer, and was over before normally it started. On June 26 the temperature rose to 95°F in London, the capital's hottest day since the Weather Centre's records began in 1940. In most vineyards harvesting, which takes place about a hundred days after the end of flowering, took place three weeks earlier.

As a result, on the same area of ground and from the same number of vines, the tonnage of wine-grapes gathered from English vineyards in

1976, compared with 1975, trebled. News of bumper crops came from all over England; but the most astonishing increase came from the Chills Down Vineyard. Ian and Andrew Paget found that they had completely under-estimated their 13-acre vineyard's capabilities. In 1975 they sent twenty tons of grapes to Merrydown for processing, but in 1976 they harvested seventy tons. Their new winery was designed to handle forty tons only, so they sold as much of the surplus fruit as they could to amateur wine-makers.

In 1976, in spite of no longer having to process grapes from the Pagets, their biggest customer, Merrydown, which had estimated an increase from the 100 tons of grapes processed in 1975 to 120 tons, found themselves handling 188 tons of fruit (171,080 bottles of wine). In 1975 Merrydown were making slightly more than half of England's wine; in 1976 just less than half the total of 400,000 bottles. The vignerons of England were steadily moving away from mere vine-growing to wine-making: a trend that could not but accelerate.

Richard Capper had had 1,200 bottles of 'Stocks Riesling-Sylvaner' from his five acres at Suckley near Bromyard in Worcestershire, and in 1976 expected 5,000 bottles of what he would have to sell with another name; for the EEC banned the use of 'Riesling-Sylvaner' in wine titles on the grounds that it was too vague. Jack Ward re-named the wine he made in 1976 from the twelve tons of grapes from his Sussex vineyard, 'Horam Manor'. In 1975 he harvested only three and a half tons from the same plot of ground for the white wine he called 'Merrydown Riesling Sylvaner'. The familiar 'hock' bottle was also on its way out. The EEC Wine Regime have ostracized the slim necked 70 Centilitre Bottle as non-standard.

Many English vignerons, new to the game, feared that the drought of the 1976 summer—the worst for 250 years—would affect the growth of their vines. But vines are seldom affected by lack of water. The only green patches to be seen by anyone flying over the southern counties of England in July and August 1976 were the vineyards. The extreme warmth may have delayed the swelling of the fruit, but the principal loss came not from sun but from rain.

Some 6.3 inches of rain fell over Britain in September, 110 per cent more than normal. The plants greedily drank up the water; sap rushed into the fruit, made more juice at a time when the grapes already contained their optimum, and diluted the sugar content. Thus an extra quantity of grape juice was created which never had time to strengthen. The rain not only continued but intensified. Another 5.7 inches fell in October. The two months together were the rainiest since 1903. As the picking took place in rain which got progressively more heavy, the sugar content of grapes picked at the end of harvesting was thinner than that of the fruit which went into the first baskets. This declining sugar content was very noticeable

in the loads delivered to Merrydown over a four week period. Grapes which came from the west country, however, where the rain had been less, were demonstrably 'stronger'.

The biggest crop of wine-grapes per acre England had ever seen would in any event have meant low sugar readings: the more bunches, and the bigger bunches per vine, means that less sugar goes into each grape; but the timing of the rain was unfortunate in reducing it even further. If the rain had come two weeks later, the 1976 vintage would have been not just very good but superb. For apart from its effect on the roots and the sap, the damp conditions encouraged botrytis.

France and Austria had a fine crop in 1976, but there were mixed prospects for the wines of other European countries. Germany produced less wine-grapes in 1976, and so did the more southerly, traditionally sunny countries of Italy, Spain and Portugal. In Italy (which produces seven million bottles of wine a year) the crop sagged five and a half per cent below 1975. There was heavy rain in Italy in August as well as September, and the vineyards of Puglia, Piedmont and the Chianti region were battered by hail as well. Wine production in Spain went down by eleven per cent in 1976; mildew dampened hopes around Valencia, and La Mancha wine was expected to be of much lower quality. In Portugal rain fell in August too, creating grape fungus, and the crop was only thirty per cent of the 1974 harvest.

The trebling of output from England's vineyards in 1976 was fortuitous because, at this stage in the revival of English viticulture, increasing the quantity is more important than raising the quality. In 1977 there is just not enough English wine about to make impact: on the shelves and in the windows of wine merchants up and down the country, in the restaurants, bistros and hotels of Britain. Few people in Britain are aware that such a drink as English wine exists; even less do they suppose that spending £2 on a bottle of English wine will give as much satisfaction as a 'safe' bottle of German hock or moselle with which they have been assured they 'can't go wrong'. Skilful promotion has made the Blue Nun a universal attraction. It has been the theme of this book that it is not England's climate which has kept England from having more vineyards but the ignorance of her viticulturists. England is nowhere near in top gear yet. In the first decade of the twentieth century, Europe increased her average output of wine-grapes per acre from two tons to five and a half tons. The latest EEC report shows that in France and Italy the yield is three and a half tons an acre; on average Germany produces six tons an acre; Luxembourg, eight tons. On the continent the Mueller-Thurgau vine—fifty-six per cent of all vines planted in England are of this variety—has an average yield of nine hundred to thirteen hundred gallons of juice an acre which signifies a harvest of up

to eight tons an acre.

Yet in England there are vignerons who do not produce two tons of grapes an acre. If Luxembourg can raise eight tons, England should at least be able to grow four. It is a question of getting the viticulture right and of applying the techniques which are known to produce results: proven methods of pruning, spraying, fertilizing, netting and the rest; carrying them out methodically, meticulously and, above all, *professionally*.

Many have learnt their lesson and operate in the knowledge that there are no short cuts. Nigel Godden *does* get five tons of grapes an acre from his Pilton Manor four and a half-acre vineyard; and if he can, so can everyone else. Godden not only gets the quantity but the quality too. He has twice won the Robert Gore-Browne Trophy for the best English 'Wine of the Year', chosen by a panel of experts from some sixty varieties. There are others who get yields as big as Nigel Godden's, but the majority do not. One newcomer is so far only producing one ton of grapes from five acres.

Britain has been exempted by the EEC Commission from measures which it is taking to further reduce the Wine Lake: no new vineyards are to be planted in Europe until the beginning of 1978. This exemption highlights the inadequacy of the whole English viticultural exercise. For in the eyes of the EEC a Member State is not in the big league (and thus a competitor of other continental wine-producers and a contributor to the Wine Lake) until it produces at least 110,000 gallons of wine a year. Britain's priority should be to raise its current production of 60,000 gallons (400 tons of grapes) to this minimum requirement.

Unfortunately for English vignerons, it seems that they cannot expect a lowering of the excise duty on English wine for some time to come. Up to the mini-Budget of November 1976 the UK excise duty was 45p a bottle (£2.95 a gallon), and by use of the 'ten per cent regulator' in that month rose to 50p a bottle (£3.25 a gallon). With VAT, the total proportion going to the government averaged 60p.

By now Customs and Excise have accepted that 'British Wines' and 'English Wine' are different, but their thinking has led them to tax 'made-wine' *less* than 'wine'. The relationship between import duty on imported wine and internal duty on English wine is regulated by the Treaty of Rome which brought the EEC into existence. When, in the British House of Commons on November 18, 1976, Stephen Ross MP asked the Chancellor of the Exchequer if he would give wine-producers in the UK greater encouragement by a reduction in excise duty, he was told that the UK had an obligation under Article 95 of the treaty to charge the same rate of excise duty on wine produced in the UK as on imported wine. 'I do not believe' stated Robert Sheldon, the junior minister at the Treasury in answering the parliamentary question 'that a reduction in the level of excise duty on

all wine would be an appropriate way to encourage UK wine producers.'

English vignerons' belief that they are being unfairly treated may be enhanced by the fact that the governments of Germany, Italy and Luxembourg have chosen not to impose excise duty of any kind on wine produced in their countries; that Australian wine has recently become exempt, and that the French government sees fit only to impose a tiny tax. All such considerations are put to the Government by the English Vineyards Association on the frequent occasions when they press the various departments concerned to take heed of English viticulture's special problems in these important, early years of its revival.

On the question of the price they should ask for their wine, English wine-makers differ. Gruff Reece who made a loss of £5,000 in 1975 says he could make a profit if he charged £2.20 a bottle for his Gamlingay wine, but in fact is sticking to £1.50. Bruce Hole sells his 'Frogmore Wine' at £1.30 a bottle so long as it is bought by the case. Sir Guy Salisbury-Jones on the other hand has no hesitation in charging £2.30 a bottle for 'Hambledon'; and Bernard Theobald prices his Berkshire wine between £2.50 and £3. In 1977 Justerini & Brooks were offering for sale *The English Wine Case* (three bottles each of Adgestone, Genesis, Lamberhurst Priory and New Hall) for £30.00; and Jacksons of Piccadilly an *English Wine Jubilee Selection* (Cavendish Manor, Elmham Manor, Frogmore, Hascombe, New Hall Pinot Noir and Flexherne)—six bottles for £12.25.

In the event, in spite of the rain and the botrytis, the 1976 vintage has turned out 'very well', if reports from the Merrydown Co-operative are any guide. There is nothing tragic about having missed a superlative vintage at this stage. As Jack Ward has wisely observed, it is more important now to produce three bottles of good, but not brilliant, wine than one bottle of brilliant wine which has to be offered at a high price.

Two hot years in succession at a time when viticulture was being considered as a potential activity by so many farmers, fruit-growers and others with money and energy to invest were providential. Large numbers of them were young people prepared to devote the rest of their working lives to English Wine and hand the enterprise on to their children. A series of bad summers and bad crops would have deterred many would-be venturers, and would have given them reason to join the ranks of the 'unsuitable climate' theorists; but the tide was running in viticulture's favour and many were persuaded by the good weather to go with it. A tradition, hitherto jerky and diffident, was being re-born in the hands of a new section of the community who looked for assurance that it was something they could stay with.

It would seem that the 485 acres (196 hectares), recorded by the British Ministry of Agriculture Survey of November 1976 as being 'down to vines' in England and Wales, will now rapidly expand. They have multiplied more than nine times in the five years since 1971, when there were fifty-three (21.5 hectares). Up to December 1975 there were 140 known vineyards being run wholly or partially commercially; and a further thirteen acres of vines were being grown privately. Eighty-five per cent of England's vineyards were in East and South-east England—as reflected in the enormous interest shown in the Third Festival of English Grape Wines and Vineyards which Christopher Ann of Drusillas organized at Seaford in September 1977.

The absence of English wine in quantity in the past is related to behaviour and fashion, not to an 'unsuitable' climate. In May 1976, Professor Hubert Lamb, who is now director of the Climatology Research Unit of the University of East Anglia at Norwich, forecast that Britain could expect persistently drier weather for many years to come. However, though the English sky is likely to remain as blue as ever and the English fields as green, it would be as well for the would-be viticulturist to keep his feet on the ground and take the advice of Harry Baker, the RHS Fruit Officer at Wisley. 'Be careful' he said in 1976,

Opposite: Mr and Mrs Nigel Godden bought Pilton Manor in the Mendips in 1964 and replanted the land with vines.

Seventeen tenants of Glastonbury Abbey were tilling this land in 1189; and in 1235 William Aurifaber is recorded as looking after all the Abbey vineyards, which will have included the one at Pilton. There are few better illustrations of the long history of the English Wine Tradition than the vineyard at Pilton Manor, and few finer examples of contemporary English wine-making than Nigel Godden's.

not to be tempted to plant a vast vineyard, and not spend a lot of money, perhaps with the roseate vision of buxom maidens treading tons of grapes in the future. Do not expect a vintage year after year, as with our climate, birds and wasps, there can be almost as many bad years as good. For example 1972 was a disaster; 1974 was not much better, though 1973 and 1975 were very good ones. We are, in effect, a marginal area as far as grape growing is concerned. Start with a few vines at first and see how they fare; there is time to extend the planting once you have had experience of the cultivars and the effect of our variable English climate upon them.

Any aspiring vigneron should follow Harry Baker's advice; for inspiration he should read Norman Sneesby's *A Vineyard In England* (1977); he should also obtain all the information available through the English Vineyards Association; he can buy vines from the nurseries advertised in its journal and elsewhere; and he can obtain technical information and equipment for wine-making from Anton Massel, Barrett Soldani and others. If, having first secured a south-facing plot of land, he plants his first vineyard, he will do so in the knowledge that he is following in the footsteps of those who, having proved the irrelevance of 'unsuitable' climate and soil and discounted the superiority of foreign vintages, have built up a Tradition of English Wine—the pace-setters of the English Viticultural Revival, which, in 1978, is only just beginning to gather momentum.

Bibliography

GENERAL

H. H. Lamb, 'Britain's Changing Climate', *Geographical Journal*, 133, 1967

A. L. Simon, *English Wines and Cordials,* London: Gramol Publications, 1946

Edward Hyams, *The Grape Vine in England*, London: Bodley Head, 1949

—— (ed.) *Vineyards in England*, London: Faber & Faber, 1953

George Ordish, *Wine Growing in England*, London: Rupert Hart-Davies, 1953

H. M. Tod, *Vine-Growing in England*, London: Chatto & Windus, 1911

Notes and Queries, July 13, 1946, p. 19 'Outdoor Vine Culture in England'
(W. W. Porteous, H. A., H. C. Andrews, C. A. Knapp, D. H. Allport)

Miller Christy, 'Essex as a wine-producing county', *The Essex Naturalist,*
vol. 11, 1899, pp. 34–8

Horace J. Round, 'Vines in Essex', *Essex Archaeological Society Transactions,*
vol. 7, pp. 249–51

Rev. Canon Henry E. Ellacombe, 'The Vineyards of Somerset and
Gloucestershire', *Bath Field Club Proceedings,* January 15, 1890

—— *The Plant-Lore and Garden-Craft of Shakespeare,* Exeter: The Author, 1878

Dorothy Vinter, 'The Ancient Vineyards of the West Country', *Gloucestershire
Life*, vol. 17, 1966–7

Tunstall's *Rambles About Bath*, Bath: 1876

Victoria County Histories, Hampshire, vol. 4, pp. 160–5; Somerset, vol. 2,
pp. 269, 405; Dorset, vol. 3, p. 23; Bedfordshire, p. 203; Surrey, vol. 3,
pp. 144, 328, 469, 538, vol. 4, p. 230; Essex, vol. 1, p. 382; Bucks, vol. 3,
p. 80, vol. 4, p. 88; Berks, vol. 2, pp. 168, 171, vol. 3, pp. 145n, 302, 434,
436, vol. 4, p. 436; Gloucestershire, pp. 16, 43, 125, 138, 142, 257; Sussex,
vol. 2, p. 285; Kent, vol. 3, p. 422; Cambridgeshire, vol. 2, pp. 203, 308,
vol. 4, pp. 37, 38, 39, 44, 48, 70.

E. J. Willson, 'The Records of Nurserymen', *Archives*, vol. 12, no. 55,
Spring 1976 (British Records Association)

William J. Pinks, *The History of Clerkenwell* (E. J. Wood, ed.), pp. 188–9,
London, 1881

Thomas Faulkner, *History and Antiquities of Kensington*, p. 23, London: 1820

ROMAN OCCUPATION, DARK AGES, MIDDLE AGES

Archaeologia or Miscellaneous Tracts relating to Antiquity (Society of Antiquities
of London), vol. 28, p. 413; vol. 57, p. 252; vol. 58, p. 427; vol. 60, p. 216

Sir H. Godwin, *The History of the British Flora*, p. 290, Cambridge University
Press, 1956

D. & H. Webster and D. F. Petch, 'A possible vineyard of the Romano-British period at North Thoresby, Lincolnshire', *Lincolnshire History and Archaeology*, vol. 2, pp. 55–61, 1967

A. R. Bramston and A. C. Leroy, *Historic Winchester*, p. 137, London: Longmans, 1882

Chaloner W. Chute, *A History of 'The Vyne' in Hampshire*, Winchester, 1888

Giraldus Cambrensis, *The itinerary through Wales*, p. 85, London: Dent, 1908

Somerset Record Society, vol. 5 (Glastonbury); vol. 7 (Timberscombe)

James Bentham, *History . . . of the Cathedral Church of Ely*, 1812

The Registrum Antiquissimum of the Cathedral Church of Lincoln, vol. 1, Lincoln Record Society, vol. 27, 1931

C. J. Bond, 'The Estates of Evesham Abbey; a Preliminary Survey of Their Mediaeval Topography', *The Vale of Evesham Historical Society Research Papers*, vol. 4, 1973

J. M. Lappenburg, *A History of England Under the Anglo-Saxon Kings,* translated from the German by Benjamin Thorpe, vol. 2, p. 359, London: John Murray, 1845

Sir John Dunlop, *The Pleasant Town of Sevenoaks; a History*, pp. 60, 68, Sevenoaks, 1964

Sussex Archaeological Transactions: vol. 3, 1850, p. 179, E. Turner 'On the military earthworks of the South Downs' (Cissbury); vol. 11, p. 103; vol. 12, 1857, p. 13, E. Turner, 'Uckfield Past and Present'; vol. 17, 1865, p. 32, E. Turner, 'Battle Abbey'

Archaeologia Cantiana: vol. 1, 1856, p. 232; vol. 2, 1859, p. 225 'Notes of Vineyards'; vol. 6, p. 327; vol. 10, 1876, p. 110 'Faversham Accounts'; vol. 13, 1880, p. 294; vol. 15, p. 356; vol. 16, p. 12; vol. 18, 1889, p. 347–8, 'The Vineyards of Northfleet & Teynham in the 13th century' by Dorothy Sutcliffe; vol. 29, 1911, p. 115; vol. 40, 1934, p. 148

Notes and Queries, November 27, 1869 (Bury St Edmunds)

Sir Henry Ellis, *A General Introduction to Domesday Book,* vol. 1, pp. 116, 117, 118, 120, 121, London: Commissary of the Public Records, 1833

H. C. Darby & I. B. Terrett, *Domesday Geography of Western England*, Cambridge University Press, 1971: Gloucestershire, Worcestershire

H. C. Darby & R. Welldon Finn, *Domesday Geography of South-West England*, Cambridge University Press, 1967: Wiltshire, Dorset, Somerset

H. C. Darby, *Domesday Geography of Eastern England*, Cambridge University Press, 1971: Suffolk, Essex

H. C. Darby & Eila M. J. Campbell, *Domesday Geography of South-East England*, Cambridge University Press, 1962: Beds, Herts, Middlesex, Bucks, Berks, Hants, Surrey, Kent

Bridgemaster's Account Rolls 1381–89, Translation, Corporation of London Record Office

Robert Richard Tighe & James Edward Davis, *Annals of Windsor*, vol. 1, London: Longmans, 1858

F. M. Underhill, 'Vineyard at Windsor', Notes and Queries *Berkshire Mercury*, December 5, 1974

K. C. Newton, *Thaxted in the 14th century*, Essex Record Office Publications, no. 33, p. 9

FOURTEENTH TO NINETEENTH CENTURIES

Bridge House Rental 1460–1484, Translation and Transcript, Bridge House Estates, 1461/2, Corporation of London Record Office

William Camden, *Britannia or a Chorographical Description of Great Britain and Ireland*, vol. 1, 1586 in Latin; English translation by P. Holland as 'Britain', 1610, with revisions by Edmund Gibson, DD, Bishop of Lincoln, 1722

William Lambarde of Lincolnes Inn, Gent, *A Perambulation of Kent,* written in the year 1570, p. 319, Chatham, 1826

John Stow, *A Survey of London* written the year 1598 (ed. H. Morley), p. 238, London: Routledge, 1893

Fynes Morison, *Itinerary*, 1617

Sir Thomas Hanmer, *The Garden Book*, 1633

John Parkinson Apothecarye of London and King's Herbalist, *Theatrum Botanicum, The Theater of Plantes or An Universall and Complete Herball,* Tribe 16, Chap. 104, para 1555 '*Vitis the Vine*', London, 1640

William Somner, *The Antiquities of Canterbury*, 1640

Samuel Hartlib, *The Compleat Husband-man; or, a Discourse of the whole art of Husbandry both Forraign and Domestick Wherein many rare and most hidden secrets, and experiments are laid open to the view of all, for the enriching of these nations,* London, 1659

Samuel Pepys, *Diaries* (ed. H. B. Wheatley) London: G. Bell, 1924, vol. 2, p. 68, July 22, 1661 (Hatfield); vol. 4, p. 405, May 1, 1665 (Blackheath), London: F. Warne, 1889, p. 416, July 17, 1667 (Walthamstow)

John Evelyn, *Diaries* 1643 (Hatfield and Much Hadham); 1655 (Blackheath)

John Rose, *The English Vineyard Vindicated,* London, 1666

William Hughes, *The Compleat Vineyard*, London, 1670

Sir Hugh Plat, *The Garden of Eden, or an Accurate Description of all Flowers and Fruits now growing in England*, London, 1675

Dr R. Plot, *Natural History of Oxfordshire,* 1677

—— *Natural History of Staffordshire*, 1686

Archaeologia, vol. 12, p. 181, 'A Short Account of Several Gardens near London . . . upon a view of them in December 1691', communicated to the Society of Antiquities of London by Rev. Dr Hamilton from an original manuscript in his possession, July 3, 1794

Archaeologia, vol. 1, pp. 332, 334, 357 (Arundel)

Gladys Taylor, *Old London Gardens*, p. 110, London: Batsford, 1953

E. J. Willson, *James Lee and the Vineyard Nursery, Hammersmith*, London: Hammersmith Local History Group, 1961

Thomas Fairchild, Gardener of Hoxton, *The City Gardener*, pp. 17, 35, London, 1722

Richard Bradley, *The Vineyard*, London, 1724

S. J., *The Vineyard, being a Treatise . . . being the Observations made by a Gentleman on his Travels*, London, 1727

Dr Hales of Teddington, *Compleat Treatise on Practical Husbandry*, London, 1727

Stephen Switzer, *Ichnographia Rustica*, London, 1742

Dr Richard Pococke, *Travels Through England* . . . during 1750, 1751 and later
years (James Noel Cartwright, ed.), vol. 2, Camden Society 1889
(Painshill and Westbrook)

Claude Martin, 'David Geneste—a Huguenot Vine Grower at Cobham' *The
Surrey Archaeological Collections*, vol. 68, 1971 (Painshill)

Phillip Miller, *The Gardeners Dictionary*, London, 1759

Thomas Mortimer, *Whole Art of Husbandry*, London, 1761

Sir Robert Atkyns, *The Ancient and Present State of Gloucestershire*, p. 17,
London, 1768

Rev Samuel Pegge versus Hon Daines Barrington Controversy: *Archaeologia*,
vol. 3, 1771, pp. 53 to 95

Richard Gough, (R.G.), 'Wine antiently made in England, contended for',
Gentleman's Magazine, 1775, p. 513

Sir Edward Barry, *Observations Historical, Critical and Medical on the Wines of
the Ancients and the Analogy between them and MODERN WINES*
(Includes Charles Hamilton's own account of Painshill), London, 1775

T. Nash, *History and Antiquities of Worcestershire*, p. 307, 446, Worcester, 1781

F. X. Vispré, *A Dissertation on the Growth of Wine in England; to serve as an
Introduction to a Treatise on the Method of Cultivating Vineyards in a Country
from which they seem at present entirely eradicated; and making from them
GOOD SUBSTANTIAL WINE*, Bath, 1786

—— *Le Vin du Pays, A Letter on the Culture of the Vine in England* (in French),
Londres, 1787

William Speechley, *A Treatise on the Culture of the Vine . . . together with New
Hints on the Formation of Vineyards in England*, Welbeck, 1789

Edward Hasted, *The History and Topographical Survey of the County of Kent*,
London, 1797: vol. 3, p. 386; vol. 5, pp. 164, 196, 353, 480; vol. 7, pp.
303, 416, 498; vol. 9, pp. 102, 148, 225; vol. 10, p. 302; vol. 11, pp. 204,
330, 350, 535, 536

Charles Softley (1829–1915), 'Godalming and Its Neighbourhood', *Notebooks*
(Stanley C. Dedman, ed.), Godalming Public Library, 1968 (Westbrook)

Dr Richard Worthington, *An Invitation to the Inhabitants of England to the
Manufacture of Wines from the Fruits of their own Country*, Worcester, 1812

William Cobbett (1763–1835), *The English Gardener*, p. 285 (Painshill),
London, 1829

J. C. Loudon, *Encyclopaedia of Gardening*, vol. 2, para. 5216 (Painshill),
London, 1834

William Hone, *The Every-Day Book and Table Book, or Everlasting Calendar*,
vol. 3, p. 623 (Holwood, Keston), London, 1841

Anon, 'Home-Grown Wine', *The Floral World and Garden Guide*, vol. 8,
p. 33, London, 1865

A. Pettigrew, 'The Vineyard at Castle Coch', *Transactions, Cardiff Naturalists
Society*, 16, pp. 6–11, Cardiff, 1884

A. A. Pettigrew, 'Welsh Vineyards', *Transactions, Cardiff Naturalists Society*,
59, pp. 25–34, Cardiff, 1926

TWENTIETH CENTURY

R. Barrington Brock, *Outdoor Grapes in Cold Climates*, Report no. 1, Viticultural Research Station Oxted, Tonbridge, 1949
—— *More Outdoor Grapes*, Report no. 2, 1950
—— *Progress With Vines and Wines*, Report no. 3, 1961
—— *Starting A Vineyard*, Report no. 4, 1964
S. M. Tritton, *Grape-Growing and Wine-Making from Grapes and other fruits*, Aldmondsbury: The Grey Owl Research Laboratories, 1951
Margaret Gore-Brown, *Let's Plant A Vineyard*, London: Mills & Boon, 1967
Gillian Pearkes, *Growing Grapes in Britain*, London: Amateur Winemaker, 1969
Alan Rook, *The Diary of an English Vineyard*, London: Wine & Spirit Publications, 1969
Sir G. Salisbury-Jones, 'Wine growing in Great Britain', *Journal of Royal Society of Arts*, pp. 455–65, 1973
J. Cochrane, 'Meteorological Observations in Hambledon Vineyard in 1972', *Weather*, vol. 29, no. 4, April 1974
William Younger, *God's Men and Wine* (for the Wine & Food Society)
Norman Sneesby, *A Vineyard in England*, London: Robert Hale, 1977
Anthony Hogg, *Guide to Visiting Vineyards*, London: Michael Joseph, 1977

GROWING WINE-GRAPE VINES

A. F. Barron, *Vines and Vine Culture*, 1883
W. B. N. Poulter, *Growing Vines*, London: Amateur Winemaker, 1972
A. Massel, *Basic Viticulture*, London: Heidelberg Publishers, 1971
—— *Viticulture in Britain*, lecture to Nuffield Scholars Association, December 6, 1971
F. W. Beech, E. Catlow, E. G. Gilbert, *Growing Vines in the Open in Great Britain*, Long Ashton Research Station, Bristol, 1974

WINE-MAKING

William Graham of Ware, *The Art of Making Wines from fruits, flowers and herbs, all the native growth of Great Britain*, London, 1780
Philip Pery Carwell, *A Treatise on family wine making*, London: Sherwood, 1814
Henry Seymour Mathews, 'On Making Wine from the leaves of the Claret Grape', read March 1, 1814, *Transactions of the Horticultural Society of London*, vol. 2, 1827
James Robinson, *The whole art of making British wines*, London: Longmans, 1848
W. B. N. Poulter, *Wines From Your Vines*, London: Amateur Winemaker, 1972
F. W. Beech & A. Pollard, *Wines and Juices*, London: Hutchinson
—— *Wine Making and Brewing*, London: Amateur Winemaker

A. Massel, *Applied Wine Chemistry and Technology*, Pt 1 Viticulture, Pt 2
    Vinification, London: Heidelberg Publishers, 1969
—— *Basic Oenology*, London: Heidelberg Publishers, 1972
L. Frumkin, *The Science and Technique of Wine*, London: H. C. Lea, 1974
F. W. Beech, 'Harvesting and Wine Making Techniques' *Journal*, no. 9, June
    1975, p. 57, English Vineyards Association, Horam
Bravery & Turner, *Home wine-making and vine growing*, London: Macdonald,
    1973
Ben Turner, *Growing Your Own Wine*, London: Pelham, 1977

English Vineyards in 1977

Not less than one acre in size

AVON
Cambarn, Dunkerton, Bath (C. H. H. Roughton)
Thornbury Castle, Thornbury, Bristol (F. G. Bell)

BEDFORDSHIRE
Gamlingay, Sandy (G. P. Reece)

BERKSHIRE
Bowden, Pangbourne (Mrs Cardy)
Frogmore, Bradfield (G. B. Hole)
Kirby, Inkpen (Hon J. Astor)
Warren Lodge, Wokingham
   (I. Vaughan-Morgan)
Westbury, Reading (B. H. Theobald)
Winterbourne Manor, Newbury (D. R. Baylis
   & L. Potter)

CAMBRIDGESHIRE
Chilford Hall, Linton (S. Alper)
Isle of Ely (St Etheldreda), Wilberton
   (N. Sneesby)
Manor Farm, Bury (L. A. Mason)

CHANNEL ISLANDS
La Mare, St Mary, Jersey (R. H. Blayney)

CORNWALL
Polmassick, St Austell (P. J. Crowe)

DERBYSHIRE
Renishaw, Renishaw (R. Sitwell)

DEVONSHIRE
Clyston, Crediton (A. E. Forbes)
Hatswell, Tiverton (N. MacDonald)
Whitstone, Bovey Tracey (G. C. Barclay)
Yearlstone, Bickleigh (G. Pearkes)

DYFED
Werndog, Wanarth (G. I. Thomas)

DORSET
Blackwater Farm, Wimbourne (K. Waters)

ESSEX
Boyton, Halsted (M. W. Crisp)
Crow Lane, Ardleigh, Colchester (C. E. George)
Felstar, Felsted (J. G. Barrett)*
Fyfield Hall, Fyfield (D. M. Gilberston)
Heath Lodge, Colchester (W. A. Williams)
Henny, Sudbury (S. R. Copley)
Langham, Colchester (R. Leslie)
Newards, Boxted, Colchester (R. E. Barrett)*
New Hall, Purleigh (S. W. Greenwood)
Old Shields, Ardleigh, Colchester (A. E. Marshall)
Saffron Walden, Saffron Walden (B. J. Hoar)
Wenden, Saffron Walden (R. V. E. Jeffries)

GLAMORGAN
Croffta, Pontyclun (J. C. M. Bevan)

GLOUCESTERSHIRE
Rhyle, Newent (A. McKechnie)

HAMPSHIRE
Beaulieu, Beaulieu (Montagu Ventures Ltd)*
Drews Farm, Rowlands Castle (C. D. Suter)
Efford, Lymington (Ministry of Agriculture)
Frensham Manor, Fareham (G. Jackson)
Gorley, Fordingbridge (R. O. Kinnison)
Hambledon, Hambledon (Sir G. Salisbury-Jones)*
Harcombe Manor, Ropley (Sir D. Vestey Bt. &
    P. E. Vestey)
Poulner, Ringwood (H. I. Bird)

HEREFORD & WORCESTER
Broadfield, Bodenham (K. R. H. James)
Clyro Court, Clyro (C. Posswit)
Kinver, Stourbridge (E. I. Garratt)
Shelsley Beauchamp, Shelsley Beauchamp
    (J. Wilkinson)
Stocks, Suckley (R. M. O. Capper)

HERTFORDSHIRE
Frithsden, Hemel Hempstead (P. G. Latchford)

ISLE OF WIGHT
Adgestone, Sandown (K. C. Barlow)*
Barton Manor, Cowes (A. H. Goddard)
Cranmore, Yarmouth (W. G. N. Poulter &
    R. H. Gibbons)

KENT
Biddenden, Ashford (R. A. Barnes)*
Cherry Hill ('Kentish Sovereign') Nettlestead
    (T. Bates)*
Cryals Court, Matfield, Tonbridge (C. Tunney)
Ightham, Sevenoaks (J. M. B. Corfe)
Knowle Hill, Maidstone (I. A. Grant)
Lamberhurst Priory, Tunbridge Wells
    (K. McAlpine)*
Littlefield, Maidstone (R. D. Cooper)
Marriage Hill, Wye, Ashford (M. Waterfield)
Paynetts Oast Farm, Goudhurst (J. A. Cave)
Staple, Canterbury (W. T. Ash)
The Grove, Penshurst (W. H. Westphal)

LEICESTERSHIRE
Cheval House, South Kilworth, Lutterworth
    (J. H. Daltrey)

LINCOLNSHIRE
City of Lincoln Vineyard, Lincoln (Lincoln City
    Council)
Stragglethorpe Hall ('Lincoln Imperial'), Lincoln
    (A. Rook)

NORFOLK
Aspen Hall, Hepworth, Diss (P. J. Simms)
Bunwell, Bunwell (J. A. Goodman)
Chickering, Hoxne, Diss (P. H. Day)
Eastfield House, East Harling (J. Milkovitch)
Elmham, Dereham (R. S. Don)
Heywood, Diss (R. C. Aikman)
Lexham Hall, Kings Lynn (N. W. D. Foster)
Silver Green, Hempnall, Norwich (W. S. C.
    Gurney)
Wood Farm, Fressingfield, Diss (Mr & Mrs. D.
    Shepherd)

NOTTINGHAMSHIRE
Costock, Ruddington (A. Skuriat)

OXFORDSHIRE
Newington Grounds, Banbury (W. B. Stapleton)
Shipton, Shipton-under-Wychwood (M. Grundy)

SOMERSET
Axbridge, Cheddar (J. Lukins)
Brympton d'Evercy, Yeovil (C. E. B. Clive-
    Ponsonby-Fane)
Pilton Manor, Shepton Mallet (N. de Marsac
    Godden)*
Virgins Farm, Taunton (R. G. Jenkins)
Whittington, Churchill (R. D. White)
Wootton, Shepton Mallet (C. L. B. Gillespie)*
Wraxall, Shepton Mallet (A. S. Holmes)

STAFFORDSHIRE
Martlet, Stretton (S. Monckton)

SUFFOLK
Anglia, Framlingham (I. H. Berwick)
Barningham Hall, Bury St Edmunds (M. R. Hope)

Cavendish Manor, Sudbury (B. T. Ambrose)*
Cratfield, Halesworth (Suffolk Vineyards Ltd)
Finn Valley, Otley, Ipswich (C. Clark)*
Genesis Green, Newmarket (M. Y. Fuller)
Highwaymen's, Bury St Edmunds (M. MacRae)
Kelsale, Saxmundham (J. T. Edgerley)
Peasenhall, Saxmundham (I. W. MacFarlane)
The Wetheringsett, Stowmarket
    (K. E. R. Bolton)

SURREY
Hascombe, Godalming (T. P. Baillie-Grohman)
Rake Manor, Milford (P. Gommes)
The Little Priory, Nutfield (K. H. Cornwell)
Tilgate, Bletchingley (T. Ridley)

SUSSEX
Birchen Wood, Ticehurst (A. P. Moray)
Bookers, Bolney (J. M. & R. U. Pratt)
Breaky Bottom, Lewes (P. A. I. Hall)
Broad Oak, Brede (D. Thorley)
Castlehouse, Lewes (J. C. Crossland-Hinchliffe)
Chilsdown, Chichester (I. R. Paget)*
Downers, Henfield (E. G. Downer)

Flexerne, Newick (P. A. Smith)*
Herrings Farm, Heathfield (H. Royce)
Horam Manor, Horam, Heathfield (Merrydown
    Wine Co)*
Little Pook Hill, Burwash Weald
    (D. H. Simmons)
Nash, Brighton (T. B. C. Parker)
Rock Lodge, Haywards Heath (N. C. Cowderoy)
Uckfield, Uckfield (N. Tollemache)
Valley Wines, Alfriston (C. M. D. Ann)*
Vine Cottage, Arundel (H. B. Evans)
Westfield, Hastings (D. Carr-Taylor)*

WILTSHIRE
Aeshton Manor, Cricklade (C. Stuart)
Bradford, Bradford-on-Avon (A. R. Shaw)
Church Farm, Swindon (A. K. Bowley)
Jesses, Dinton, Salisbury (R: Beck)
Southcott, Pewsey (H. H. Crabb)
Tytherley, West Tytherley, Salisbury
    (J. R. M. Donald)

IRISH REPUBLIC
Brittas Bay, Dublin (K. W. B. Thomson)

* denotes vineyard open to the public, who should however give advance notice.

Vineyard Sites from the Roman Occupation to 1920

AVON
Bath, 18th C.
Claverton, Bath, 18th C.
Cold Ashton, 11th C.
Henbury, Bristol, 11th C.
Tortworth (Cromhall), 18th C
    & 19th C.

BEDFORDSHIRE
Astwick, Biggleswade, 15th C.
Dunstable, 12th C.
Eaton Socon, 11th C.
    (Domesday)

BERKSHIRE
Abingdon, 13th C.
Bisham, 11th C. (Domesday)
Reading Abbey, 12th C.

Reading Abbey, 13th C.
Tidmarsh, 13th C.
Wallingford, 13th C.
Whitley Abbey, 12th C.
Windsor Castle, 12th C.

BUCKINGHAMSHIRE
Iver, 11th C. (Domesday)

CAMBRIDGESHIRE
Croyland, 13th C?
Denney Abbey, 13th C?
Ely, 11th C.
Ramsey Abbey, 12th C.
Thorney, 10th C.
Trumpington, 13th C.

CORNWALL
Gear, 13th C.
Halnoweth, 13th C.
St Gluvias, Penryn, 16th C. &
    18th C.
Truro, 18th C.

DERBYSHIRE
Darley Abbey, 16th C.
Winfield, 16th C.
Wingerworth, 16th C.

DEVONSHIRE
Lundy Island, 14th C.
Northleigh, 14th C.

DORSET
Durweston, 11th C.

243

(Domesday)
Sherborne Castle, *12th C.*
Wootton, *11th C.* (Domesday)

DURHAM
Durham City, *12th C.*

DYFED
Maenor Byr (Manorbier
    Castle), *12th C.*

EAST SUSSEX
Battle (Santlac), *11th C.*
Battle, *16th C.*
Buston, *13th C.*
Ewhurst, *13th C.*

ESSEX
Ashdon, *11th C.* (Domesday)
Belchamp, *11th C.* (Domesday)
Castle Hedingham, *11th C.*
    (Domesday)
Colchester, *13th C.*
Copford, *15th C.*
Debden, *11th C.* (Domesday)
Fobbing, *16th C.*
Gidea Hall, *19th C.*
Great Baddow, *15th C.*
Great Coggeshall, *13th C.*
Great Hallingbury, *13th C.*
Great Horkseley, *13th C.*
Great Waltham, *11th C.*
Havering, *13th C.*
Maldon, *13th C.*
Mundon, *11th C.*
North Ockendon, *13th C.*
Rayleigh, *11th C.* (Domesday)
Roydon, *13th C.*
Saffron Walden, *13th C.*
Saffron Walden, *17th C.*
Stambourne, *11th C.*
    (Domesday)
Stapleford Abbots, *13th C.*
Stebbing, *11th C.* (Domesday)
Tendring, *13th C.*
Thaxted, *14th C.*
Tilty Abbey, *16th C.*
Toppesfield, *11th C.* (Domesday)

244

Waltham, *11th C.* (Domesday)
West Thurrock, *16th C.*

GLOUCESTERSHIRE
Badgeworth, *11th C.*
Batheaston, *14th C.*
Berkeley, *19th C.*
Churchdown, *11th C.*
Deerhurst, *15th C.*
Forest of Dean
    Mangotsfield, *18th C.*
    Matson, *18th C.*
Gloucester (Rom.)
Gloucester, North Hamlets,
    10th C.
Over, *11th C.*
Stonehouse, *11th C.*
    (Domesday)
Tewkesbury, *12th C.*
            14th C.
            16th C.
Thornbury, *11th C.*
Upton St Leonards, *11th C.*
Winchcombe Abbey, *11th C.*

HAMPSHIRE
Lomer ? *11th C.* (Domesday)
Sherborne St John (Rom.)
Southampton, *19th C.*
Winchester, *12th C.*

HEREFORD &
    WORCESTER
Allesborough Hill, *12th C.*
Brushley, *12th C.*
Chaddesley Manor, *12th C.*
Cotteridge, *12th C.*
Droitwich, *13th C.*
Elmley Castle, *18th C.*
Fladbury, *13th C.*
Grimley, *13th C.*
Hampton-by-Evesham, *11th C.*
Hereford, *13th C.*
Ledbury, *18th C.*
Leigh, *18th C.*
Leigh Abberton, *12th C.*
Pershore, *16th C.*
Pershore Abbey, *12th C.*

Ripple, *18th C.*
Sedgebarrow, *18th C.*
Severn Stoke, *12th C.*
Upton-on-Severn, *19th C.*

HERTFORDSHIRE
Benges, *18th C.*
Berkhamsted, *11th C.*
    (Domesday)
Hatfield, *17th C.*
Much Hadham, *17th C.*
Rickmansworth, *20th C.*
St Albans, *13th C.* (?)
Standon, *11th C.* (Domesday)
Thorley, *13th C.*
Ware, *11th C.* (Domesday)

KENT
Barming, *18th C.*
Berton, *13th C.*
Birchington, *17th C.*
Boughton Malherbe, *16th C.*
Brook, *13th C.*
Canterbury, *13th C.*
Chart Sutton, *11th C.*
    (Domesday)
Chislet, *11th C.* (Domesday)
Colton, *13th C.*
Coningbrook Sellinge, *14th C.*
Egerton, *16th C.*
Faversham, *14th C.*
Fishpoole Littlebourne, *14th C.*
Folkestone, *15th C.*
Godinton, *17th C.*
Great Charte, *17th C.*
Halling, *13th C.*
Harrietsham, *16th C.*
Hawkhurst, *14th C.*
Hollingbourn, *13th C.*
Ightham (Rom.)
Keston (Holwood), *19th C.*
Langley, *14th C.*
Leeds Castle, *11th C.*
    (Domesday)
Malling, *14th C.*
Northfleet, *13th C.*
Northolme, *14th C.*
Rochester (Bishop), *14th C.*

Rochester (St Andrews Priory),
 14th C.
Sevenoaks, *14th C.*
Snodland, *13th C.*
St Martins Chartham, *13th C.*
Sutton Valence, *13th C.* (?)
Teynham, *13th C.*
Tonbridge, *14th C.*
Tonbridge Castle, *18th C.*
Tong, *15th C.*
Wengeham (Wingham),
 (Rom.)
Westwell Priory, *16th C.*

LINCOLNSHIRE
Lincoln, *12th C.*
North Thoresby (Rom.)

LONDON
Barnes, *13th C.*
Bermondsey (Rom.)
Blackheath, Writtlemarsh,
 17th C.
Brompton, *18th C.*
Camberwell, *18th C.*
Chenetone, *19th C., 11th C.*
 (Domesday)
Clerkenwell, *13th C.*
Clerkenwell, *18th C.*
Coldbath Fields, *18th C.*
Colham, *11th C.* (Domesday)
Drury Lane, *18th C.*
Feltham, *13th C.*
Hammersmith, *18th C.*
Hampton Court, *18th C.*
Harmonsworth, *11th C.*
 (Domesday)
Hendon, *13th C.*
Holborn, *11th C.* (Domesday)
 13th C.
Houndsditch, *13th C.*
Hoxton, *18th C.*
Kempton, *11th C.* (Domesday)
Kensington (Ball), *18th C.*
Kensington (Shaw), *18th C.*
Lambeth, *18th C.*
Leicester Fields, *18th C.*
Londinium (Rom.)

Middle Temple, *13th C.*
Minories, *13th C.*
Parsons Green, *18th C.*
Rotherhithe, *18th C.*
Smithfield, *10th C.*
Southwark (Rom.)
Southwark (Bridge House
 Garden), *13th C.*
Staines, *11th C.* (Domesday)
St Giles in the Fields, *13th C.*
St James's Palace, *17th C.*
Vine Street, Piccadilly, *18th C.*
Waltham Green, *18th C.*
Waltham Green, *18th C.*
Watford (?), *17th C.*
Westminster Palace, *13th C.*
Wimbledon, *13th C.*
 17th C.

NORTHAMPTONSHIRE
Brackley, *20th C.*
Rockingham, *12th C.*

NOTTINGHAMSHIRE
Welbeck, *18th C.*

OXFORDSHIRE
North Leigh (Rom.)
Oxford, *17th C.*

SCOTLAND
Edinburgh, *12th C.*

SHROPSHIRE
Cravenleigh's Estate, *18th C.*

SOMERSET
Dunster, *14th C.*
Glastonbury, *10th C.*
 11th C.
 (Domesday)
Meare, *11th C.* (Domesday)
Michelney, *11th C.* (Domesday)
Michelney, *11th C.* (Domesday)
Minehead, *14th C.*
North Curry, *11th C.*
 (Domesday)
Pamborough, *11th C.*

 (Domesday)
Pilton, Shepton Mallet, *13th C.*
Timberscombe (Dunster),
 13th C.
Thorney, *11th C.* (Domesday)
Watchet (Wecet), *10th C.*
Wells (including Winesham),
 12th C.
Wells, *13th C.*
 14th C.

SOUTH GLAMORGAN
Cardiff (Castell Coch and
 Swanbridge), *19th C.*

STAFFORDSHIRE
Over-Arley, *17th C.*

SUFFOLK
Barking, *11th C.* (Domesday)
Bury St Edmunds, *13th C.*
Clare, *11th C.* (Domesday)
Ixmouth, *11th C.* (Domesday)
Lavenham, *11th C.* (Domesday)
Wherstead, *13th C.*

SURREY
Boxmoor (Rom.)
Charte Park, Dorking, *17th C.*
Cobham (Painshill), *18th C.*
Godalming (Westbrook),
 18th C.
Great Bookham (Aylynchagh),
 14th C.
Oatlands, *17th C.*
Oxted, *20th C.*
Purley, *12th C.*
Richmond, *13th C.*
Sheen, *17th C.*
Wandsworth (?), *11th C.*
 (Domesday)

WEST GLAMORGAN
Margam, *12th C.*

WEST SUSSEX
Arundel, *18th C.*
Buxted, *13th C.*

Cissbury (Rom.)
East Dean (Rom.)
Three Bridges, *13th* C.

WILTSHIRE
Bradford-on-Avon, *11th* C.
    (Domesday)
Lacock, *11th* C. (Domesday)

Tollard Royal, *11th* C.
    (Domesday)
Wilcot. *11th* C. (Domesday)

Index

Figures in italics refer to illustrations